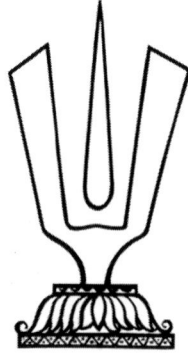

Vedartha Sangraha of Ramanuja

A Collective Essence of the Vedas & Upanishads in Vishishta Advaita Vedanta

Shraddhesh Chaturvedi

First Printing, 2024

Vedic Scriptures Publishing
Gomti Nagar, Lucknow
Uttar Pradesh, India 226010

Cover Background – Designed by "freepik/Freepik"

तस्मै रामानुजार्याय नमः परमयोगिने ।
यः श्रुतिस्मृतिसूत्राणामन्तर्ज्वरमशीशमत् ॥

I bow to great Ramanuja, the supreme Yogi, who has removed the internal fever (inconsistency) among the texts such as the Upanishads, Smritis, Sutras, etc.

Contents

Preface

After bowing to the great Ramanuja, we will discuss the meaning of the terms used in the title and subtitle of this text. 'The Veda' is the repository of spiritual knowledge since the beginning of the time. The term 'Veda' means to know. Since it is a vast collection of text, it is difficult to understand it in its entirety. Therefore, Rananuja has described its essential meaning or 'artha' in this text. As it is a collective essence, he terms it 'sangraha' or collection.

The primary focus of the Upanishads, which come at the end of the Veda, is to attain liberation. Liberation means to realize our intrinsic reality. Since Upanishads are the primary source of self-knowledge to attain liberation, in them, our knowledge attains its culmination. Interchanging use of Veda and Upanishads is quite common in Vedic literature. Upanishads are the end part of the Veda, they are also known as Vedanta ('anta' means end).

There are various philosophical viewpoints that take Upanishads as their basis, and describe our intrinsic reality. Ramanuja accepts an omniscient and all-powerful reality or Supreme Being above all. It controls and regulates two other types of entities, viz. living beings (sentients) and non-living beings (insentients). Supreme Being pervades all sentient and insentient entities as their innermost soul and they are like his body. Just as the sky, though it pervades everything, does not get dirty by the presence of dust, etc. likewise Supreme Being does not get affected by the defects of living and non-living beings and retains its blissful characteristics at all times. In this way, Supreme is special or distinguished (Vishishta) from the other two types of entities. Moreover, the Supreme Being is unique or non-dual (Advaita) with respect to its magnificent qualities; none is its equal or superior. Hence, Ramanuja's view of reality is referred to as Vishishta Advaita or distinguished non-duality. Some others call it by the name 'qualified monism'.

How does Ramanuja form his viewpoint? Ramanuja derives the basic tenets of his philosophy from various scriptures such as Veda, Upanishads, Itihas, Purana, Smriti, etc. in conjunction with his experience of reality. In doing so, he has established the central goal of all texts to attain the Supreme Being. He has also resolved the apparent conflicts among various texts systematically. He assigns an order of priority among the texts that is unanimously accepted. Vedas and Upanishads, which are heard in a sublime state of reality, are simply irrefutable and have the highest priority. There is no internal inconsistency among them. The next priority is Itihasa (it means that is how it occurred) or history texts. We have two historical texts – Ramayana and Mahabharata. Thereafter, he accepts the authority of Puranas. There are 18 of them and 18 sub-Puranas, which discuss incarnations, the dynasties of kings, creation, dissolution, etc. Finally, he accepts the authority of Smriti or memory-based texts. The sages write these texts after going through a spiritual experience and recollect it again later for everyone's benefit.

The writing of this text has an interesting story associated with it. Once Ramanuja addressed an assembly at the temple of Tirupati Balaji, situated on Venkata Mountain, for an hour and a half. This address enthralled the audience and had a profound effect on their thinking about reality. They wished it to be recorded for everyone's benefit. Later, this lecture was compiled into this text as 'Vedartha Sangraha'.

To resolve a contentious matter in spiritual talks, there are three ways in which wise interact – Jalpa, Vitanda, and Vada. Jalpa is a one-sided discussion, in which a person defends his view only. Vitanda is another extreme, in which a person only refutes the claims of the opponent. Vada is the most righteous form of discussion, in which a person not only defends his view but also refutes the opposing claims by pointing out their inadequacies or errors. When you are refuting someone's claim, you have to point out the errors in their thinking and show why those errors do not exist in your viewpoint. Whatever logic is given in doing this should be based on the scriptures, which are accepted by all the parties in discussion. It is this unbiased form of discussion or thinking that leads us to the truth. Lord Krishna says in Gita –

अध्यात्मविद्या विद्यानां वादः प्रवदतामहम् ॥ (गीता१०/३२)

Among all types of knowledge, I am the knowledge of the Self; among all debates, I am the righteous discussion (Vada). (Gita 10/32)

Vedartha Sangraha is also a Vada text. Ramanuja describes his viewpoint in the light of other authoritative scriptures. He shows how using this viewpoint, one can achieve coherence and alignment among various texts without any internal inconsistency. The opposing philosophies, which he refutes here, are of Shankara, Bhaskara, and Yadava Prakasha.

To make the discussions in the text more understandable, let us summarize the basic tenets of the Vishishta Advaita philosophy of Ramanuja. We will see in the text later how they are derived from the scriptures.

1. The Supreme Lord has infinite auspicious qualities. He is untouched by any evils. He is not attributeless as Advaita (non-dualist) philosophers claim. At the same time, he is also devoid of any imperfections or defects. His auspicious qualities are omniscience, omnipotence, omnipresence, ever-blissful, eternality, etc.

2. Narayana is the Supreme Lord of the universe. He is called by various names such as Vishnu, Hari, Rama, Krishna, supreme reality, Brahman, truth, etc. The Supreme Being is the only cause of this world; he is its creator, sustainer, and dissolver.

The term 'GOD' in English also refers to one who is the Generator of the universe (G), Operator (sustainer) of it (O), and its Destroyer (D).

3. There are three types of fundamental realities - Supreme Being, individual souls (living beings), and nature (non-living beings). Supreme Being pervades the individual souls and nature. He is also their controller. Though the Supreme Being pervades it all, he is unaffected by their defects.

4. Suppose a potter makes a pot from clay using some tools, then we say that clay is the material cause of the pot, the potter is the efficient cause of the pot, and the tools are the instrumental cause of it. Since the Supreme Being is the material, efficient, and instrumental cause of the world, by knowing him one can know it all.

5. If a spider can create its web from within, without undergoing any change, then, an almighty God can possess a similar type of capability. When we mix different color threads such as white, black, and red to make a multi-color cloth, they appear as mixed in the cloth. However, there is no mixing in the colors of different threads themselves. Similarly, when the Supreme Being creates the insentient nature and individual souls from himself, where souls are enjoyers, nature is to be enjoyed and the Supreme Being is their controller, it appears that the Supreme Being has changed. However, there is no actual mixing among them. The changes in the (gross) effect cannot cause a change in its (subtle) cause. We can understand this by the example of clay (subtle cause) and pots (gross effects).

6. The Supreme Being is the innermost soul of all sentient and insentient entities; alternatively, we can say that all individual souls and non-living entities are the body of the Supreme Being or his attributes. He is also the protector and well-wisher of all.

7. Individual souls are countless in number and infinitesimal in size. They are of three types – eternally free, free, and bound.

The eternally free souls are the associates of the Supreme Being; they are always free and have never come under bondage. Goddess Shri and Lakshmi his consorts, Shesha, the serpent on which Lord Vishnu resides, golden eagle or Garuda, his vehicle, enlightened sages (Suris) who serve him at all times, etc. are all in this category. Free souls are those souls that were earlier bound, and later attained enlightenment by serving the Supreme Being.

8. The insentient matter or nature is devoid of knowledge and tends to change. The Supreme Being creates the changing world, including our bodies, senses, minds, etc. through twenty-four elements of nature.

9. An individual soul is like a tiny spec of conscious light. Its conscious light has an intrinsic ability to know anything without any hindrance. However, when an individual soul comes in contact with this insentient matter, its capability becomes limited due to the influence of its previous actions by the Supreme Being's inconceivable wish. It is the bound state of an individual soul.

10. An individual soul is the doer of its action and it is also the reaper of their results just as a farmer enjoys his crop. However, the worldly doership of a soul is due to its association with nature. Its real doership is spiritual or non-worldly, which it realizes after liberation.

11. Ramanuja discards the Mimansaka view that actions can themselves give their results independently. He shows that the Supreme Being is the ultimate provider of the results of our actions. The scriptures also support this view.

12. The doership of an individual soul is limited by the Supreme Being's will. Based on its efforts Supreme Being motivates it to progress further. In modern terms, we can say that there is no free will for a bound individual soul.

13. When an individual soul liberates, its intrinsic knowledge becomes all-pervading like the light of the sun and its association with nature breaks down. Just as light makes it possible for us to distinguish various objects, likewise knowledge also makes it possible to recognize between right and wrong. Due to this similarity, knowledge is said to have an illuminating power like light.

14. How does an individual soul liberate? When one worships and serves the Supreme Lord through all his actions single-mindedly, he receives His grace; this releases a soul from its bondage permanently. Devotion or surrender to the Supreme Lord is the way to liberation.

15. I also want to share a startling fact of Ramanuja's philosophy here - all words ultimately refer to the Supreme Being. If two things do not separate, we can refer to them by a common word in a normal usage, e.g. we use body and soul interchangeably in the common language. The word 'I' can refer to our body, mind, or soul. Its correct intention is known by the context in which one uses it. However, the primary meaning of 'I' is for our soul. Similarly, scriptures sometimes refer to the individual soul and supreme soul by the same word 'soul' since an individual soul is like the body of a supreme soul, and both are, therefore, inseparable. The correct meaning is decided by the context in such a way that any contradiction does not arise from this interpretation.

As in previous books, I have kept my explanations within square brackets to separate them from the translated text. Though I took utmost care in writing this book, some errors might remain. To enhance the quality of this feel free to give your feedback and valuable reviews. I will be highly grateful.

Auspicious Invocations

[Ramanuja begins this text by bowing to his beloved Lord. In Vedic literature, it is customary to invoke the Supreme Being before doing anything significant. Not only is it auspicious, it removes obstacles from our path.]

अशेषचिदचिद्वस्तुविशेषिणे शेषशायिने ।
निर्मलानन्तकल्याणनिधये विष्णवे नमः ॥

I bow to Lord Vishnu who is the ocean of infinite auspicious qualities and is devoid of any imperfections. He is the basis of all sentient (living) as well as nonsentient (non-living) entities. He rests on the serpent Shesha.

[This verse highlights the essence of Ramanuja philosophy. Let us list them here as they define what Ramanuja is going to discuss and deduce later on the basis of various Vedic texts.

1. There are three types of entities – a) Living beings like us, animals, trees, etc. b) Non-living beings like stones, rocks, etc., and c) the Supreme Being, who controls them all.

2. The connection of numerous living and non-living beings with the Supreme Being is like that of a body and the soul. Sometimes, we refer to our bodies and souls interchangeably, though they are different. When someone says 'I', it actually (and ultimately) refers to his soul but loosely it is used for the body. In a similar sense, Vedic texts also refer to an individual soul as the Supreme Lord. However, it is important to understand their differences carefully.

3. The Supreme Being has a definite divine form and he rests on the serpent Shesha, we call him Vishnu because he is all-pervading. Just as an individual soul pervades a single body, likewise the Supreme Soul Vishnu pervades the entire world, which consists of living and non-living beings, as its soul.

4. Reference to the serpent Shesha shows that there are other eternally free souls that always accompany and serve the Supreme Being. It also indirectly shows one can attain his true form by serving the Supreme Lord.

5. Lord Vishnu is the abode of infinite auspicious qualities like knowledge, truth, love, bliss, etc. At the same time, he is devoid of all imperfections like death, old age, hunger, bondage, etc.]

[In the second verse, Ramanuja bows to his guru Yamunacharya. He also mentions the opposing views which he is going to refute in this text with the grace of his guru (preceptor).]

परं ब्रह्मैवाज्ञं भ्रमपरिगतं संसरति तत्परोपाध्यालीढं विवशमशुभस्यास्पदमिति ।
श्रुतिन्यायापेतं जगति विततं मोहनमिदं तमो येनापास्तं स हि विजयते यामुनमुनिः ॥

Victory to the sage Yamuna, who has dispelled the darkness of delusion of false ideologies, spread out in this world, by the authority of the scriptures and his reasoning. Those false ideologies are (1) the Supreme Reality (Supreme Being) itself, under the influence of ignorance, falls into the bondage of births and deaths, (2) the Supreme Reality becomes helpless owing to its connection with adjuncts (wrappers) other than itself and (3) the Supreme Reality undergoes various changes (imperfections) due to its association with the sentient and the non-sentient entities.

[After bowing to his guru, Ramanuja says that whatever he is going to discard is solely based on the authority of the scriptures, which is backed by reasoning. He refers to three philosophies (views) here as an introduction, along with the inconsistencies they will lead us to. Later, he will discuss them in detail.

Non-dual (Advaita) philosophy of Shankara assumes that there is no difference between an individual soul and a Supreme Soul or there is just one soul. According to Ramanuja, it would imply that the

Supreme Being, being the only soul, itself goes into bondage like an ignorant person. This is not a desirable trait in the Supreme Being.

Bhaskar's philosophy assumes the existence of a wrapper (ignorance) on the Supreme Being due to which it comes under bondage. For them, the non-difference between the Supreme Being and individual souls is natural; however, the difference between them appears due to ignorance. For non-living entities, their difference as well as non-difference from the Supreme Being is both natural. According to Ramanuja, they accept the existence of ignorance and also say it to be false which is self-contradictory. For them also, the Supreme Being itself comes under bondage as they effectively say its non-difference with individual souls.

Yadava Prakash's philosophy says that for both living and non-living beings, non-difference and difference from the Supreme Being is natural. Ramanuja discards this view because if we accept non-difference between non-living entities and the Supreme Being as natural, the Supreme Being will acquire the tendency to change like insentient things, which is a defect.]

Essential Introduction of Vishishta Advaita

[Now, Ramanuja describes his philosophical view concisely and how it has been formed.]

अशेषजगद्धितानुशासनश्रुतिनिकरशिरसि समधिगतोऽयमर्थः - जीवपरमात्मयाथात्म्यज्ञानपूर्वक वर्णाश्रमधर्मेतिकर्तव्यताकपरमपुरुषचरणयुगलध्यानार्चनप्रणामादिरत्यर्थप्रियस्तत्राप्तिफलः ॥

The essential meaning of the Upanishads, which is the most important part (crown) of the Vedas, and engaged in the benefit of the whole world is to impart the distinctive knowledge of the true nature of the individual living being and the Supreme Being. Thereby, follow the duties of one's caste and stage of life, which culminates into the meditation, worship, bowing, etc., of the holy feet of the Supreme Being. When this devotion is done with intense love, it results in his attainment. It is the liberation of an individual soul.

[By knowing the real difference between an individual soul and the Supreme Soul, one attains liberation. One knows this difference by following his duties and through intense and single-minded love (devotion) towards the Supreme Lord.]

[What are those statements of the Upanishads which support his views?]

अस्य जीवात्मनोऽनाद्यविद्यासंचितपुण्यपापरूपकर्मप्रवाहहेतुकब्रह्मादिसुरनरतिर्यक्स्थावरात्मक चतुर्विधदेहप्रवेशकृत-तत्तदभिमानजनितावर्जनीयभवभयविध्वंसनाय, देहातिरिक्तात्मस्वरूपत त्स्वभावतदन्तर्यामिपरमात्मस्वरूपतत्स्वभाव तदुपासनतत्फलभूतात्मस्वरूपाविर्भावपूर्वकानव -धिकातिशयानन्दब्रह्मानुभवज्ञापने प्रवृत्तं हि वेदान्तवाक्यजातम्, 'तत्त्वमसि' (छा० उ० ६/९/४), 'अयमात्मा ब्रह्म' (बृ० उ० ६/४/५), 'य आत्मनि तिष्ठन्नात्मनोऽन्तरो यमात्मा न वेद यस्यात्मा शरीरं य आत्मानमन्तरो यमयति स त आत्मान्तर्याम्यमृतः' (बृ० उ० ५/७/२६), 'एष सर्वभूतान्तरात्मापहतपाप्मा दिव्यो देव एको नारायणः' (सु० उ० ७), 'तमेतं वेदानुवचनेन

ब्राह्मणा विविदिषन्ति यज्ञेन दानेन तपसानाशकेन' (बृ॰ उ॰ ६/४/२२), 'ब्रह्मविदाप्नोति परम्' (तै॰ उ॰ २/१), 'तमेवं विद्वानमृत इह भवति । नान्यः पन्था अयनाय विद्यते' (पु॰ सू॰ ७, तै॰ आर॰ ३/१२/१७) इत्यादिकम् ॥

Under the influence of beginningless ignorance (of its true nature), an individual soul performs endless actions, virtuous and sinful. The accumulation of such actions is the cause of its various births (and deaths). An individual soul can enter into four kinds of bodies – heavenly deities like the creator Brahma, etc., human, animal, and plant. When an individual soul enters a body, it is deluded of its identity and considers itself as this body. This delusion inevitably brings about all the fears inherent in the state of worldly existence. The various statements of the Vedanta aim to destroy these fears in their entirety. They describe the essential nature of the individual self as different from the body, its attributes, the real nature of the Supreme Being, who is the individual soul's innermost reality, and the attributes of the Supreme Being. By the worship of the Supreme Being, an individual soul first realizes its intrinsic nature, and then later, it knows the Supreme Being, which is of the nature of infinite and perfect bliss. The statements which convey these meanings are the following:

You are that (reality). - Chhandogya Upanishad 6/9/4;

This self is the Supreme Being (reality). – Brihad Aranyaka Upanishad 6/4/5;

He, who dwells in the self, who is more intrinsic than the self, whom the self does not know, whose body this self is, who rules this self from within, that one is your self, the inner Ruler, the Immortal. - Brihad Aranyaka Upanishad 5/7/26;

He is the inner self of all creatures, free from all imperfections, the divine, the sole God Narayana. - Subala Upanishad 7;

The seekers desire to know him (Supreme Being), through the study of the Vedas, through fire-worship, charity, austerities, and fasting. -Brihad Aranyaka Upanishad 6/4/22;

The knower of the Supreme Being attains the supreme. - Taittiriya Upanishad 2/1;

He, who knows him (Supreme Being) thus, attains immortality here. There is no other way to attain immortality. - Purush Sukta 7 (Taittiriya Aranyaka 3/12/17)

Moreover, there are many more statements like these.

[Here, Ramanuja tells how an individual soul gets bound by his actions and identifies itself with a body. This worldly experience invokes fear in him in many ways, e.g. diseases, old age, death, etc. Then, when one follows his duties and learns (hears) Vedanta, he knows the essential nature and attributes of his soul which differs from the body. He also becomes aware of the essential nature of the Supreme Soul as the innermost controller of the individual soul and how His worship destroys all types of fears and gives liberation. Then, he decides to worship the Supreme Lord and engages in it, he knows his essential nature first, after his sins are washed away. This knowledge motivates him further to experience (and know) the Supreme Being, who is the infinite ocean of bliss. When one knows him, all his purposes are fulfilled. Except for intense worship, there is no other way to attain him.]

[What is the essential nature of an individual soul? The essential nature implies those properties of the soul that do not change.]

जीवात्मनः स्वरूपं देवमनुष्यादिप्रकृतिपरिणामविशेषरूपनानाविधभेदरहितं ज्ञानानन्दैकगुणं । तस्यैतस्य कर्मकृतदेवादिभेदेऽपध्वस्ते स्वरूपभेदो वाचामगोचरः स्वसंवेद्यः, 'ज्ञानस्वरूपम्' इत्येतावदेव निर्देश्यम् । तच्च सर्वेषामात्मनां समानम् ॥

The essential nature of an individual soul (jiva, embodied soul) does not undergo any changes when it accepts various types of bodies, such as demigods, humans, etc. The soul has blissful knowledge alone as its attribute. When the differences arising between the bodies of god, humans, etc., due to its actions are destroyed, the difference between a soul to another one, can be experienced (known) by the souls themselves but it is not expressible through words. Only this much can be said of the soul, that it is of the nature of knowledge or consciousness. This essential nature of the soul is the same for all individual souls.

[When one enters a dark room, he cannot distinctly see or know the objects present in it; however, if a lamp is lit over there, he can clearly observe the presence of various objects. So, in essence, the light reveals the presence of various objects. Similarly, the light or consciousness of our soul makes us aware of various objects and their underlying differences. Hence, we say that the nature of the soul is like a light or pure consciousness. Since there is nothing else in this world that we can compare with a soul, hence it is like itself; through it, we know other things. There are many types of living beings due to their different body forms but their underlying souls are all of the same type. If we cover a lamp with a thin veil, the intensity of its light or its capacity to distinguish various objects decreases. The thicker the veil, the lesser will be this distinguishing ability of the covered lamp. Likewise, in the case of our souls, according to the thickness of our ignorance, our capabilities or understanding vary.]

[What is the essential nature of the Supreme Being?]

एवंविधचिदचिदात्मकप्रपञ्चस्योद्भवस्थितिप्रलयसंसारनिर्वर्तनैकहेतुभूतः, समस्तहेयप्रत्यनीका-
नन्तकल्याणतया च स्वेतरसमस्तवस्तुविलक्षणस्वरूपः, अनवधिकातिशयासंख्येयकल्याणगुण-
गणः सर्वात्म-परब्रह्म-परज्योतिः-परतत्त्व-परमात्म-सदादिशब्दभेदैर्निखिलवेदान्तवेद्यो भगवा-

न्नारायणः पुरुषोत्तम इत्यन्तर्यामिस्वरूपम् । अस्य च वैभवप्रतिपादनपराः श्रुतयः स्वेतरसमस्त-
चिदचिद्वस्तुजातान्तरात्मतया निखिलनियमनं, तच्छक्ति-तदंश-तद्विभूति-तद्रूप-तच्छरीर-
तत्तनुप्रभृतिभिः शब्दैस्तत्सामानाधिकरण्येन च प्रतिपादयन्ति ॥

The Supreme Being is the sole cause of the origin, continuance, and dissolution of this world, which consists of living and non-living beings; he is also the cause of the liberation (release) of other souls from this world. He is devoid of all defects and consists of infinite blissful qualities. Thus, his essential nature is different from all other beings as he possesses unbounded, infinite, and countless auspicious qualities. He is referred to in all the Upanishads by varied terms like the Universal Soul, the Supreme Being, the Supreme Light, the Supreme Truth, the Supreme Soul, and Reality. He is to be known by the Upanishads as God Narayna or the highest soul (Purushottama). This is the essential nature of the Supreme Being, the inner ruler of all.

The Upanishads (Vedantic texts) are devoted to describing His greatness. They refer to Him as the soul of all other living and non-living beings, who controls them by His power. All other living and non-living beings are referred to in various ways as his parts, his special power, his form, his body, and his expanse, etc. However, all such varying descriptions refer to the same underlying Supreme Being as their basis (or soul).

[Ramanuja describes Narayana, who has a sublime divine form, as the Supreme Being. He consists of infinitely many auspicious qualities. He is also devoid of any evil properties. In his all-pervading form, he is the innermost soul of all living and non-living beings. He, alone, is the creator, preserver, and destroyer of the universe. By taking his refuge, any bound soul can attain liberation. Using the above-mentioned qualities of the Supreme Being and the individual souls, Ramanuja will resolve all apparent inconsistencies in Upanishad statements; he will also refute other viewpoints using these properties.]

Description of Opposing Philosophies

[Now, Ramanuja describes the basic tenets of the non-dual (Advaita) philosophy of Shankara. He also points out the inconsistencies that will occur if one accepts it.]

तस्य वैभवप्रतिपादनपराणामेषां सामानाधिकरण्यादीनां विवरणे प्रवृत्ताः केचन "निर्विशेषज्ञान-मात्रमेव ब्रह्म, तच्च नित्यमुक्तस्वप्रकाशस्वभावमपि तत्त्वमस्यादिसामानाधिकरण्यावगतजीवै-क्यं, ब्रह्मैवाज्ञं, बध्यते, मुच्यते च, निर्विशेषचिन्मात्रातिरेकेश्वरेशितव्याद्यनन्तविकल्परूपं कृत्स्नं जगन्मिथ्या, कश्चिद्बद्धः, कश्चिन्मुक्त इत्ययमवस्था न विद्यते । इतः पूर्वं केचन मुक्ता इत्ययमर्थो मिथ्या । एकमेव शरीरं जीववन्निर्जीवानीतराणि, तच्छरीरं किमिति न व्यवस्थितम्; आचार्यो ज्ञानस्योपदेष्टा मिथ्या, शास्त्रं च मिथ्या, शास्त्रप्रमाता च मिथ्या, शास्त्रजन्यं ज्ञानं च मिथ्या, एतत्सर्वं मिथ्याभूतेनैव शास्त्रेणावगम्यत" इति वर्णयन्ति ॥

In their attempt to explain the glory of the Supreme Being mentioned in these statements, some say that the Supreme Being is without any attribute and is pure knowledge (or consciousness) alone. Though he is eternally liberated and self-luminous, the statements like "You are that (reality)", "All is Supreme Being." etc. imply that it is identical to the individual self (bound soul). Hence, the Supreme Being itself undergoes bondage owing to ignorance and later liberates. Since the Supreme Being is just the attribute-less consciousness, the whole world with its endless differences like its controller (Lord) and controlled sentient (living) beings and non-sentient (non-living) entities, which are other than Him, is illusory. Hence the distinction that one soul is bound and that another is free has no basis; it is also illusory to think that some souls have attained salvation from bondage before. Since only one body is animated by the soul (or self), the other bodies are soulless; it is impossible to state which that one body is. The preceptor who reveals divine knowledge is illusory; scripture is illusory too; the one who understands the scripture is illusory and likewise the knowledge arising from the scripture; and all this is understood only from this illusory scripture.

[Shankara accepts a single or non-dual soul to explain statements like 'You are that'; it is attributeless and has the form of knowledge or consciousness alone. For him, there is no difference between an individual soul and the Supreme soul in liberation and so whatever difference we experience in the worldly state is illusory.

Ramanuja says that if there is just one soul without any attribute or specialty, this supreme soul will itself have to undergo bondage and experience the troubles of the world. Moreover, using one soul, Shankara cannot explain the presence of those individual souls that are already liberated. Or, one has to consider their liberation as virtual or unreal. As Shankara does not accept the existence of this world as real, in his view, knowledge, scriptures, and their knowers are all unreal. How can a false scripture or knowledge result in liberation? Therefore, this point of view cannot be correct. We will come back to this refutation in greater detail shortly.]

[The second viewpoint, which Ramanuja contends, is the 'difference and non-difference' (Bhedabheda) philosophy of Bhaskara. We can also call it 'dual and non-dual' (Dvaitadvaita) philosophy.]

अपरे तु "अपहतपाप्मत्वादिसमस्तकल्याणगुणोपेतमपि ब्रह्म, तेनैवैक्यावबोधेन, केनचिदुपाधि-विशेषेण संबद्धं, बध्यते मुच्यते च, नानाविधमलरूपपरिणामास्पदं च" इति व्यवस्थिताः ॥

Others maintain that the Supreme Being, though it possesses all auspicious qualities like freedom from sins, etc. undergoes bondage and release owing to its association with some limiting adjunct (wrapper, obstruction, Upadhi) and that it is also subject to various modifications of an impure nature. This we know in the light of the texts declaring identity (between the Supreme Being and the world and between the Supreme Being and the individual self).

[To explain statements like 'You are that', Bhaskara says that non-difference between the Supreme Being and individual souls is natural (innate) and their difference appears due to the presence of an obstruction. This is similar to the division of the space, say, due to the presence of a container, its internal space, and the vast external space. Thus, one can explain the presence of various bound and liberated souls on the basis of this obstruction.]

[Yadavaprakasa accepts a special type of 'difference and non-difference' (Bhedabheda) philosophy.]

अन्ये पुनरैक्यावबोधयाथात्म्यं वर्णयन्तः "स्वाभाविकनिरतिशयापरिमितोदारगुणसागरं ब्रह्मैव सुर-नर-तिर्यक्स्थावर-नारकि-स्वर्ग्यपवर्गि-चेतनेषु स्वभावतो विलक्षणमविलक्षणं च वियदादि-नानाविधमलरूपपरिणामास्पदं च" इति प्रत्यवतिष्ठन्ते ॥

Others still, in explaining the truth of the text teaching identity hold that Supreme Being is the sea of unsurpassed and boundless qualities inherently. However, he himself becomes gods, men, animals, dwellers in hell and in heaven, and souls that have attained release. By nature, He is different as well as not different from these souls. Moreover, he is subject to various modifications of an impure nature when he takes the various insentient forms such as sky, etc.

[To explain the identity in the statement 'You are that', Yadavaprakash maintains that the difference, as well as the non-difference between the individual soul and the Supreme Being, are natural. Moreover, the Supreme Being itself changes into various non-sentient beings like sky, air, water, etc.]

Criticism of Shankara's Advaita

[In this section, Ramanuja refutes the tenets of the non-dual philosophy of Shankara on the basis of various scriptures and reasoning. At the same time, he also resolves those apparent inconsistencies using his viewpoint of distinguished reality (Vishishta Advaita).]

तत्र प्रथमपक्षस्य श्रुत्यर्थपर्यालोचनपरा दुष्परिहारान् दोषानुदाहरन्ति । तथा हि - प्रकृतपरामर्शितच्छब्दावगत स्वसंकल्पकृतजगदुदयविभवविलयादयः 'तद् ऐक्षत बहुस्यां प्रजायेय' (छा० उ० ६/२/३) इत्यारभ्य 'सन्मूलाः सोम्येमाः सर्वाः प्रजाः सदायतनाः सत्प्रतिष्ठा' (छा० उ० ६/८/४) इत्यादिभिः पदैः प्रतिपादितास्तत्संबन्धितया प्रकरणान्तरनिर्दिष्टाः सर्वज्ञता-सर्वशक्तित्व-सर्वेश्वरत्व-सर्वप्रकारत्व-समाभ्यधिकनिवृत्ति-सत्यकामत्व-सत्यसंकल्पत्व-सर्वावभासकत्वाद्यनवधिकातिशयासंख्येयकल्याणगुणगणा 'अपहतपाप्मा' (छा० उ० ८/७/१) इत्याद्यनेकवाक्यावगत निरस्तनिखिलदोषता च सर्वे तस्मिन् पक्षे विहन्यन्ते ॥

Those, who have comprehensively studied the meaning of the Vedas, point out various fallacies against the first view (Shankara's Advaita), which cannot be countered.

For instance, the word 'That' (in "You are that") refers to the Supreme Being in the context of the creation of the world. The origin, sustenance, and dissolution of the world occur from its will. This is described in the statement that begins with "It willed to become many" (Chhandogya Upanishad 6/2/3) and ends with "The world with all the souls in it, my child, has its origin in Reality (Sat or Supreme Being), its support and sustenance in Reality and its dissolution in Reality" (Chhandogya Upanishad 6/8/4). In other contexts related to the Supreme Being, it is said to have boundless, unsurpassed, and innumerable auspicious attributes like omniscience, omnipotence, the lordship of all, having all things as its modes (types), having neither equals nor superiors, the power of truthful desires and resolutions, the power to illuminate all other entities. At the same time, he is free from any form of imperfections. This we know from the various statements such as "he is untouched by sin" (Chhandogya Upanishad 6/7/1) etc. All these attributes of the Supreme Being are compromised in this view (Advaita), as it holds that the Supreme Being is without any particularity or attribute.

[To explain identity in the statement 'you are that', non-dualists say that the Supreme Reality is attributeless, similarly individual soul is also without attributes in its pure state, hence they can be the same as a tiny and vast part of space. However, Ramanuja discards this this on the basis of other statements in the same and related sections of the Chhandogya Upanishad which say that Supreme Reality consists of innumerable auspicious attributes like omniscience, omnipotence, the lordship of all, etc. If we accept Supreme Reality as attributeless, these later statements of the Upanishad in the same section and other related sections will become inconsistent. Hence, the assumption of attributeless Supreme Reality is not correct.]

[The non-dualists offer a further explanation for their assumption of attributeless reality.]

अथ स्यात् उपक्रमेऽप्येकविज्ञानेन सर्वविज्ञानमुखेन कारणस्यैव सत्यतां प्रतिज्ञाय तस्य कारणभूतस्यैव ब्रह्मणः सत्यतां विकारजातस्यासत्यतां मृद्दृष्टान्तेन दर्शयित्वा सत्यभूतस्यैव ब्रह्मणः 'सदेव सोम्येदमग्र आसीदेकमेवाद्वितीयम्' (छा० उ० ६/२/१) इति सजातीय-विजातीयनिखिलभेदनिरसनेन निर्विशेषतैव प्रतिपादिता । एतच्छोधकानि प्रकरणान्तरगत-वाक्यान्यपि 'सत्यं ज्ञानमनन्तं ब्रह्म' (तै० २/१), 'निष्कलं निष्क्रियं', 'निर्गुणं', 'विज्ञानम्', 'आनन्दम्' इत्यादीनि सर्वविशेषप्रत्यनीकैककारतां बोधयन्ति । न चैककारताबोधने पदानां पर्ययिता । एकत्वेऽपि वस्तुनः सर्वविशेषप्रत्यनीकतोपस्थापनेन सर्वपदानामर्थवत्त्वादिति ॥

To counter this, the non-dualists (followers of Advaita) might say, "At the beginning of that section (in Chhandogya Upanishad), it is declared that, "by knowing the One, all things are known". This implies that only the ultimate cause is true. The Upanishad then gives an example of clay to illustrate how the cause alone is true and how all its effects are false. Then, it says that "Sat (Reality or Supreme Being) alone, my child, existed in the beginning (of the universe), One and without a second" (Chhandogya Upanishad 6/2/1). Hence, it discards the existence of all types of differences – differences among like things and differences among unlike things. The statements in different contexts of other texts also clarify that the Supreme Being is without any difference, particularity, or attribute and is uniformly non-dual. These sentences are: 'Supreme Being is truth (eternal), knowledge, and infinite.' (Taittiriya Upanishad 2/1); (Supreme Being) is without parts, without action, and without attributes. (Supreme Being) is of the nature of consciousness and bliss and the like. It is wrong to say that, many synonymous words are used to signify the same object (as in truth, knowledge, and infinite). Though the object signified is only one, the use of all these words is meaningful as they establish the Supreme Being free of all differences or particularities.

[The non-dualists say that the section starts with the assertion that by knowing the reality all else becomes known. It also says that in the beginning, only this reality was present. Then, the example of clay was given to show how this reality appears to be many. As clay (as a cause) alone is real and its transformation (effect) in various containers is false or is for namesake, similarly, this world is unreal (or for namesake) and only its underlying non-dual cause is real. Since this reality was devoid of any differences in the beginning, we can say that it is attributeless. We also see similar statements in other Upanishads which support that Supreme Reality is without any attributes.]

[Ramanuja again contradicts this explanation of non-dualists.]

नैतदेवम् । एकविज्ञानेन सर्वविज्ञानं सर्वस्य मिथ्यात्वे सर्वस्य ज्ञातव्यस्याभावान्न सेत्स्यति । सत्यत्वमिथ्यात्वयोरेकताप्रसक्तिर्वा । अपि त्वेकविज्ञानेन सर्वविज्ञानं सर्वस्य तदात्मकत्वेनैव सत्यत्वे सिध्यति ॥

This interpretation is not correct as it cannot stand the vow that all things are known by knowledge of the One. In this view (Advaita), since everything is illusory, there is nothing else to know. If they say by knowing the Supreme Being, one knows everything else which is illusory; it will cause a mixing of the real (Supreme Being) with the unreal. Rather, knowledge of One Supreme Being can lead to knowing of all things in a right manner only when the Supreme Being is the (innermost) soul of all.

[Ramanuja says that in the view of non-dualists, everything other than Supreme Reality is unreal, so there is nothing else to know. Hence, the assertion to know everything by knowing one does not hold. Moreover, the Supreme Being is alone real, and other entities are unreal, how can then one know unreal entities by knowing a real entity? In the example of clay and the pots made from it, there is a cause-and-effect relationship between the two. However, in the non-dualist view, this cause-and-effect relation does not exist. Only if the Supreme Being is the inner soul of everything else, its knowledge can lead to knowledge of everything else.]

[Now, Ramanuja explains the meaning of the passage according to his view of distinguished non-duality. Just as clay is the material cause of the pots made from it, the Supreme Being is also the material cause of the world which consists of living and non-living entities. In the case of pots, their efficient cause is a potter which is different from their material cause clay. However, the Supreme Being alone is the material and efficient cause of this world.]

अयमर्थः - श्वेतकेतुं प्रत्याह - 'स्तब्धोऽस्युत तमादेशमप्राक्ष्य' (छा० उ० ६/१/३) इति, परिपूर्ण
इव लक्ष्यसे तानाचार्यान् प्रति तमप्यादेशं पृष्टवानसीति । आदिश्यतेऽनेनेत्यादेशः । आदेशः
प्रशासनम् । 'एतस्य वा अक्षरस्य गार्गि सूर्याचन्द्रमसौ विधृतौ तिष्ठत' (बृ० उ० ५/८/९)
इत्यादिभिरैकार्थ्यात् । तथा च मानवं वचः - 'प्रशासितारं सर्वेषाम्' (म० स्मृ० १२/१२२)
इत्यादि । अत्राप्येकमेवेति जगदुपादानतां प्रतिपाद्याद्वितीयपदेनाधिष्ठातरनिवारणादस्यैवाधिष्ठा-
तृत्वमपि प्रतिपाद्यते । अतस्तं प्रशासितारं जगदुपादानभूतमपि पृष्टवानसि, येन श्रुतेन मतेन
विज्ञातेनाश्रुतममतमविज्ञानं श्रुतं मतं विज्ञातं भवतीत्युक्तं स्यात् ॥

This is the meaning (of the previous statement): The father asks
Shvetaketu, "You appear as if you know everything. Did you ask
about that instruction from your guru?" By instruction of whom
everything functions? The instruction means rule here. It is used in
the same sense here - "O Gargi, the sun and the moon continue to
perform their functions under the rulership of this indestructible
reality." (Br. Up. 5/8/9) Manu also uses the word in the same sense:
"Supreme Being is the ruler of all." (Manu Smriti 12/122) Here, too,
after declaring that there is just one material cause of the world, it
denies the existence of any other ruler by using the word "without a
second". So, the Supreme Being alone is the ruler of the world. So, it
means: Did you ask about the One who rules the Universe and who
is also its material cause? It is by hearing of Him, by thinking of
Him, by knowing Him, (all other things) that have not been heard of,
thought of, or known, become heard of, thought of and known."

[If the material and efficient causes of this world are one, only then
their knowledge can result in the knowledge of the world. So if we
can show that the Supreme Being is the material as well as an
efficient cause of this world, it would mean that knowing the
Supreme Being is sufficient to know it all.]

[In the beginning, before the creation of the universe, there was
nothing that was visible as everything was in its subtle (invisible)
state. Later, it expanded to form this world. It is necessary to

assume the existence of everything during creation; otherwise, it would mean existence (reality) comes out from non-existence (unreality). Or, we can say, without a cause, there can be no effect. Hence, everything existed during creation as well but in a subtle form.]

निखिलजगदुदयविभवविलयादिकारणभूतं सर्वज्ञत्व-सत्यकामत्व-सत्यसंकल्पत्वाद्यपरिमितो-दारगुणगणसागरं किं ब्रह्मापि त्वया श्रुतमिति हार्दो भावः । तस्य निखिलकारणतया कारणमेव नानासंस्थानविशेषसंस्थितं कार्यमित्युच्यत इति कारणभूतसूक्ष्मचिदचिद्वस्तुशरीरकब्रह्मविज्ञाने-न कार्यभूतमखिलं जगद्विज्ञातं भवतीति हृदि निधाय 'येनाश्रुतं श्रुतं भवत्यमतं मतमविज्ञातं विज्ञातं' स्यात्' (छा० उ० ६/१/३) इति पुत्रं प्रति पृष्टवान् पिता । तदेतत्सकलस्य वस्तुजातस्यै-ककारणत्वं पितृहृदि निहितमजानन् पुत्रः परस्परविलक्षणेषु वस्तुष्वन्यस्य ज्ञानेन तदन्यविज्ञान-स्या घटमानतां बुद्ध्वा परिचोदयति 'कथं नु भगवः स आदेशः' (छा० उ० ६/१/३) इति ॥

The idea in the mind (of the father) is this: "Have you learned (from your teachers) about the Supreme Being who is the ultimate cause of the origin, the welfare, and the dissolution of the whole world, who is also omniscient, with truthful desires and resolves, and who is the limitless ocean of infinite noble attributes?"

Since the Supreme Being is the only cause of all the varied configurations situated in distinct forms within this world, he himself is present in these effects. Therefore, if one knows the Supreme Being, having subtle sentient and insentient entities as its body as the cause, the whole world, which is its (visible or manifested) effect, becomes known. Having this (truth) in mind, the father asks his son, "Did you ask about that reality by hearing of which everything is heard of, by thinking of which everything is thought of, and by knowing which everything is known?"

The son does not understand the underlying meaning of his father's question that all entities have the same non-dual originating cause. He thinks that when two things are different from each other, it is not possible to know one of them by knowing the other. So he asks, "Of what nature, revered sir, is that instruction?"

[If one knows the cause, he can know its various effects. Having this in mind, the father says if you know the Supreme Being, which is the cause of everything else, you can know it all. Before creation, this world exists in a subtle form, with the Supreme Being as its soul. Then, during creation, it expands to take this visible form.]

[However, the son does not understand what his father meant so he asks his doubt again.]

परिचोदितः पुनस्तदेव हृदि निहितं ज्ञानानन्दामलत्वैकस्वरूपमपरिच्छेद्यमाहात्म्यं सत्यसंकल्पत्व-मिश्रैरनवधिकातिशयासंख्येयकल्याणगुणगणैर्जुष्टमविकारस्वरूपं परं ब्रह्मैव, नामरूपविभागा-नर्हसूक्ष्मचिदचिद्वस्तुशरीरं स्वलीलायै स्वसंकल्पेनानन्तविचित्रस्थिरत्रसस्वरूपजगत्संस्थानं स्वांशेनावस्थितमिति ॥

When the father is urged again to explain the idea of his mind, he states it as follows. The essential nature of the Supreme Being is consciousness, bliss, and free from all imperfections. Its magnificence is infinite; it possesses infinite, unsurpassed, and innumerable collections of auspicious attributes including omnipotence. Supreme Being is ever the same without any change or modification. In the causal state, sentient and non-sentient entities remain as his body, undifferentiated in name and form. Through his sportive activity and by His will, he, in a part or portion of Himself, assumes the configuration of the world with its countless varied forms consisting of moving and non-moving objects.

[Supreme Being is the material cause of everything, living and non-living because before creation everything exists as his body in a subtle form, which we cannot classify on the basis of name and form. From this subtle state, this world has emerged, which we can classify on the basis of name and form. Moreover, the Supreme Being is also the efficient cause because due to His will, this expansion has taken place.]

[To explain this identity of cause and its effect, Upanishad cites the example of clay and pots.]

तज्ज्ञानेनास्य निखिलस्य ज्ञाततां ब्रुवंल्लोकदृष्टं कार्यकारणयोरनन्यत्वं दर्शयितुं दृष्टान्तमाह – 'यथा सोम्यैकेन मृत्पिण्डेन सर्वं मृन्मयं विज्ञातं स्याद्वाचारम्भणं विकारो नामधेयं मृत्तिकेत्येव सत्यम्' (छा० उ० ६/१/४) इति । एकमेव मृद्द्रव्यं, स्वैकदेशेन, नानाव्यवहारास्पदत्वाय घटशरावादिनानासंस्थानावस्थारूपविकारापन्नं नानानामधेयमपि, मृत्तिकासंस्थानविशेषत्वान्मृ-द्द्रव्यमेवेत्थमवस्थितं न वस्त्वन्तरमिति । यथा मृत्पिण्डविज्ञानेन तत्संस्थानविशेषरूपं घटशरावादि सर्वं ज्ञातमेव भवतीत्यर्थः ॥

By knowing Him, everything is known. To show that the effect is identical to its cause, he explains it with an example, seen in the world of everyday life. "O dear, after knowing a single lump of clay, one knows all pots made from clay. We refer to the various pots (forms) of clay by different names in our speech for practical convenience. However, in essence, they are all just clay. The meaning is this: The clay, initially situated in a place as a lump, attains varied configurations, such as pots, pans, dishes, etc. due to modifications in its state. However, all these forms are not different from the clay as it is present in them; hence they just denote its various states and not any other substance. Just as by knowing a lump of clay, its modifications like pots, dishes, etc. become known, in the same way, knowing of the Supreme Being leads to the knowledge of all.

[We can compare the causal state of the world with the lump form of the clay. Just as a lump transforms into distinct pots of various shapes and sizes, the causal state of the world transforms into distinct species, both living and non-living, of various shapes and sizes. If one knows clay, he can know its distinct transformations.

Similarly, if one knows the causal state of the world, he can know it all.]

[A potter is different from the clay and the pots he makes. Knowing clay or pots is not sufficient to know the potter. How can then knowing the Supreme Being results in knowledge of all?]

ततः कृत्स्नस्य जगतो ब्रह्मैककारणतामजानन् पुत्रः पृच्छति 'भगवांस्त्वेव मे तद्ब्रवीतु' (छा० उ० ६/१/७) इति । ततः सर्वज्ञं सर्वशक्ति ब्रह्मैव सर्वकारणमित्युपदिशन् स होवाच 'सदेव सोम्येदमग्र आसीदेकमेवाद्वितीयम्' (छा० उ० ६/२/१) इति । अत्रेदमिति जगन्निर्दिष्टम् । अग्र इति च सृष्टेः पूर्वकालः । तस्मिन् काले जगतः सदात्मकतां सदेवेति प्रतिपाद्य, तत्सृष्टिकाले-ऽप्यविशिष्टमिति कृत्वैकमेवेति सदापन्नस्य जगतस्तदानीमविभक्तनामरूपतां प्रतिपाद्य तत्प्रति-पादनेनैव सतो जगदुपादानत्वं प्रतिपादितमिति स्वव्यतिरिक्तनिमित्तकारणमद्वितीयपदेन प्रतिषिद्धमिति । 'तमादेशं प्राक्ष्यो येनाश्रुतं श्रुतं भवति' (छा० उ० ६/१/३) इत्यादावेव प्रशास्तितैव जगदुपादानमिति हृदि निहितमिदानीमभिव्यक्तम् ॥

Thereafter, the son, who does not know the Supreme Being is the sole cause of the whole world, asks, "Revered Sir, kindly explain this to me." (Chhandogya Upanishad 6/1/7) In order to show that Supreme Being, who is omniscient and omnipotent, is the sole cause of all, he says, "O dear, the reality (Supreme Being) alone was present at first before this, without a second." (Chhandogya Upanishad 6/2/1)

In this statement, "this" refers to the world. "At first" means "the time before creation". During that time the world was present as reality is shown by the use of the words 'the reality alone was present'. It means during that time the world was present without any distinction of names or forms, merged in reality. From this explanation itself, it is clear that reality is the material cause of the world. The word without a second explains how the Supreme Being alone is the instrumental cause and denies the existence of any other cause other than it. The thought in his mind that the one who governs (or controls) the world is also its material cause, is clearly expressed here through the question put at the very beginning, "Did you ask about that instruction by hearing of which everything else that is unheard of becomes heard of?" (Chhandogya Upanishad 6/1/3).

[Since in the beginning, there was nothing but Supreme Reality, it alone has to be the material as well as instrument (efficient) cause of everything, which we see after creation. Since Supreme Reality alone has become everything, knowing it would mean one knows it all.]

[Now, the next section of the Upanishad explains how the Supreme Being, as the material as well as the instrumental cause of the world, transforms this world as its innermost soul.]

एतदेवोपपादयति - स्वयमेव जगदुपादानं जगन्निमित्तं च सत् 'तदैक्षत बहुस्यां प्रजायेय' (छा० उ० ६/२/३) इति । तदेतच्छब्दवाच्यं परं ब्रह्म सर्वज्ञं सर्वशक्तिसत्यसङ्कल्पमवाप्तसमस्त - काममपि लीलार्थं विचित्रानन्तचिदचिन्मिश्रजगद्रूपेणाहमेव बहुस्यां तदर्थं प्रजायेयेति स्वयमेव संकल्प्य स्वांशैकदेशादेव वियदादिभूतानि सृष्ट्वा, पुनरपि सैव सच्छब्दाभिहिता परा देवतैवमैक्षत, 'हन्ताहमिमास्तिस्रो देवता अनेन जीवेनात्मनानुप्रविश्य नामरूपे व्याकरवाणि' (छा० उ० ६/३/२) इति । अनेन जीवेनात्मनेति जीवस्य ब्रह्मात्मकत्वं प्रतिपाद्य, ब्रह्मात्मजीवानुप्रवेशादेव कृत्स्नस्याचिद्वस्तुनः पदार्थत्वमेवंभूतस्यैव सर्वस्य वस्तुनो नामभाक्त्वमिति च दर्शयति ॥

The following statement shows that the Supreme Being itself is the material and the instrumental cause of the world – That reality willed, let me be many or I will be born (as many). Chhandogya Upanishad 6/2/3

The reality is referred to as the Supreme Being, who is omniscient, omnipotent, and has fulfilled desires and resolutions. Still, as if it is his divine sport, he willed to become the world with all its diverse and countless beings, sentient and non-sentient. He resolves to become this world from a fraction of His, in a specific part and creates the elements beginning with sky (space), etc. Again the same Supreme Deity denoted by the word truth (Sat) willed: "Let me enter into these three deities as their (innermost) 'self' and endow them with names and forms." (Chhandogya Upanishad 6/3/2) The term, "as the self of the embodied being" shows that the innermost self (soul) of the individual (embodied) being is Supreme Being. After showing that the Supreme Being is the soul of individual sentient beings, it further shows that all non-sentient things become entities only owing to the entrance of the Supreme Being into them as their individual self. Thus, it shows that all things, whether sentient or insentient, acquire names and forms due to the presence of the Supreme Being.

[Having entered everything as their soul, the Supreme Being, alone, has created various names and forms in this world. Due to His wish, this world has transformed into its visible state from its initial invisible (subtle) state. Just as clay is present in all the pots made from it, the Supreme Being is also present in every name and form it creates.]

[Another Upanishad clarifies the body and soul relationship between the Supreme Soul and an individual soul.]

एतदुक्तं भवति - जीवात्मा तु ब्रह्मणः शरीरतया प्रकारत्वाद्ब्रह्मात्मकः । 'यस्यात्मा शरीरम्' (बृ० उ० ५/७/२६) इति श्रुत्यन्तरात् । एवंभूतस्य जीवस्य शरीरतया प्रकारभूतानि देवमनुष्या-दिसंस्थानानि वस्तूनीति ब्रह्मात्मकानि तानि सर्वाणि । अतो देवो मनुष्यो राक्षसः पशुमृगः पक्षी वृक्षो लता काष्ठं शिला तृणं घटः पट इत्यादयः सर्वे प्रकृतिप्रत्यययोगेनाभिधायकतया प्रसिद्धाः शब्दा लोके तत्तद्वाच्यतया प्रतीयमानतत्तत्संस्थानवस्तुमुखेन तदभिमानिजीवतदन्तर्यामिपरमा-त्मपर्यन्तसंघातस्यैव वाचका इति ॥

What has been said so far means this: The individual self is the body of the Supreme Being; it is an attribute or mode of His. In this way, it has the Supreme Being as its soul. Another Vedic statement declares this relationship: "He, whose body is the individual self." (Brihat Aranyaka Upanishad 5/7/26) Thus, in this way various types of bodies of living beings, whether gods, men, and the like, all have the Supreme Being as their souls. Therefore, all common words like god, man, Yaksha, demon, cow, deer, bird, tree, creeper, wood, stone, grass, pot, cloth, etc., which are formed by the combination of a root and suffix, used in the world to denote the respective entities with similar configurations as well as the underlying individual self, and culminate into the inner dweller of all, the Supreme Being.

[Just as we can call all pots of clay as clay, likewise we can call all living and non-living beings as the Supreme Being. This is a startling fact. When we refer to a person by a name, the name interchangeably refers to the body as well as the soul of that person. All living and non-living entities are the body of the Supreme Soul, or he is the soul of all other souls so we can refer to a soul and Supreme Soul interchangeably by a single word. Hence, the ultimate meaning of a word, which expresses a living or non-living entity, refers to the Supreme Being. We will discuss more on it, in a short while, again.]

[The section related to the interpretation of the statement 'you are that' concludes with the following statements.]

एवं समस्तचिदचिदात्मकप्रपञ्चस्य सदुपादानता-सन्निमित्तता-सदाधारता-सन्नियम्यता-सच्छेषतादि सर्वं च 'सन्मूलाः सोम्येमाः सर्वाः प्रजाः सदायतनाः सत्प्रतिष्ठा' (छा० उ० ६/८/४) इत्यादिना विस्तरेण प्रतिपाद्य, कार्यकारणभावादिमुखेन 'एतदात्म्यमिदं सर्वं तत्सत्यम्' (छा० उ० ६/८/६) इति कृत्स्नस्य जगतो ब्रह्मात्मकत्वमेव सत्यमिति प्रतिपाद्य, कृत्स्नस्य जगतः स एवात्मा, कृत्स्नं जगत्तस्य शरीरं । तस्मात्त्वंशब्दवाच्यमपि जीवप्रकारं ब्रह्मैवेति सर्वस्य ब्रह्मात्मकत्वं प्रतिज्ञातं 'तत्त्वमसि' (छा० उ० ६/९/४) इति जीवविशेषे उपसंहृतम् ॥

Thus, the Upanishad shows the Supreme Being as the material and instrument cause of the world which consists of all the sentient and non-sentient entities. Likewise, the Supreme Being is also the support (basis) of the world, and this world is governed by it. This world is a part of the Supreme Being. All of this is explained at length in the Upanishad through the statement - "O dear, all these beings (sentient and non-sentient) have their origin in Supreme Being; they abide in him, their sustenance is due to him." (Chhandogya Upanishad 6/8/4)

Having established this, the Upanishad shows the relationship between the Supreme Being and the world as between cause and its effect. "This entire world has this (Supreme Being) as its soul and that he is real." (Chhandogya Upanishad 6/8/6) Thus, it points out that the whole world exists (as real) because the Supreme Being is its soul. Having declared that He alone is the soul of the whole world and that the whole world is His body, the individual being, which is referred to as 'You' is also a type of Supreme Being. Since the Supreme Being is the soul of everything, the Upanishad concludes the discussion after applying this universal truth in the case of a particular individual self (namely, Shvetaketu) by saying "You are that". Therefore, 'you' or individual self signifies Supreme Being in this statement."

[This section of Upanishad clearly shows that the Supreme Being as cause and the entire world as its effect are both real whereas non-dualists consider this world as unreal. Since the Supreme Being is the soul of this world, everything is a type of Him; the same is true for Shvetaketu, the questioner. So, we can refer to him as a type of Supreme Being.]

[When we say a pot is nothing but clay or an individual soul is a type of Supreme Being, what does it imply? Are the cause and effect identical or is one a type (body) of another? Let us analyze it closely on the basis of Upanishad statements. We have to interpret it in such a way so that it does not contradict any Upanishad statement.]

एतदुक्तं भवति – 'ऐतदात्म्यमिदं सर्वं' (छा० उ० ६/२/३) इति चेतनाचेतनप्रपञ्चमिदं सर्वमिति निर्दिश्य तस्य प्रपञ्चस्यैष आत्मेति प्रतिपादितः, प्रपञ्चोद्देशेन ब्रह्मात्मकत्वं प्रतिपादितमि-त्यर्थः । तदिदं ब्रह्मात्मकत्वं किमात्मशरीरभावेन उत स्वरूपेणेति विवेचनीयम् । स्वरूपेण चेद्ब्रह्मणः सत्यसङ्कल्पाद्याः 'तदैक्षत बहु स्यां प्रजायेय' (छा० उ० ६/२/३) इत्युपक्रमावगता बाधिता भवन्ति । शरीरात्मभावेन च तदात्मकत्वं श्रुत्यन्तराद्विशेषतोऽवगतम् 'अन्तःप्रविष्टः शास्ता जनानां सर्वात्मा' (तै० आ० ३/११/३) इति प्रशासितृत्वरूपात्मत्वेन सर्वेषां जनानामन्तःप्रविष्टोऽतः सर्वात्मा सर्वेषां जनानामात्मा सर्वं चास्य शरीरमिति विशेषतो ज्ञायते ब्रह्मात्मकत्वम् । 'य आत्मनि तिष्ठन्नात्मनोऽन्तरो यमात्मा न वेद यस्यात्मा शरीरं य आत्मानमन्तरो यमयति स त आत्मान्तर्याम्यमृतः' (बृ० उ० ५/७/२६) इति च । अत्राप्यनेन जीवेनात्मनेतीदमेव ज्ञायत इति पूर्वमेवोक्तम् । अतः सर्वस्य चिदचिद्वस्तुनो ब्रह्मशरीरत्वात्सर्व-प्रकारं सर्वशब्दैर्ब्रह्मैवाभिधीयत इति तत्त्वमिति सामानाधिकरण्येन जीवशरीरतया जीवप्रकारं ब्रह्मैवाभिहितम् ॥

What has been said is this: In the phrase "All this has Supreme Being as its soul" (Chhandogya Upanishad 6/2/3), 'all this,' means the world consisting of sentient and non-sentient entities. So, the Upanishad declares the Supreme Being as the soul of this world. In this way, the world is not different from the Supreme Being.

We should now analyze what exactly it means to have the Supreme Being as its soul. "Is their relationship like that exists between soul and body or is it identity of their nature? If we assume the identity of the world and Supreme Being, the qualities of the Supreme Being indicated at the beginning, such as his desires and wills are ever fulfilled, etc. which we know from the text, "He will to be many and was born as many." (Chhandogya Upanishad 6/2/3) would become contradicted. The relationship between the world and the Supreme Being is like that of body and soul is understood specifically from another statement of the Upanishad, viz., "Having entered within all as the ruler, He is the soul of all." (Taittiriya Aranyaka 3/11/3) From this, it is specifically understood that the Supreme Being is the soul or self of all, that He is the soul of all persons, and that everything is His body. (Further), there is another statement in the Upanishad that says: "He who sits within the (individual) soul and is internal to the (individual) soul, of whom the (individual) soul is not aware, to whom the (individual) soul is the body and who controls the (individual) soul, He is your (Supreme) soul, the Inner Ruler, who is immortal." (Brihat Aranyaka Upanishad 5/7/26)

Here also, by the phrase "by means of the individual self who is my body", the same is meant as we have already stated. Therefore, all sentient and non-sentient things are the body of the Supreme Being. Since the Supreme Being has everything as His body and everything is His mode (type), all words signify Him also. In the phrase "You are that", the word 'you' signifies the Supreme Being since the individual self is its body or a mode.

[If we assume the identity between an individual and the Supreme soul, it will contradict the statements like 'let me be many'. Hence, such an interpretation is not possible. Other Upanishads also depict the Supreme Being as the ruler and the individual soul as the ruled. Then, it is also said Supreme Being controls the individual soul from within. This shows that the Supreme Being is the innermost soul of an individual soul. Or, we can say that all living and non-living entities are the body of the Supreme Being.]

[After establishing the relationship between the Supreme and individual soul, Ramanuja now proceeds to interpret the statement 'you are that'.]

एवमभिहिते सत्ययमर्थो ज्ञायते - त्वमिति यः पूर्वं देहस्याधिष्ठातृतया प्रतीतः स परमात्मशरीरतया परमात्मप्रकारभूतः परमात्मपर्यन्तः । अतस्त्वमिति शब्दस्त्वत्प्रकारविशिष्टं त्वदन्तर्यामिणमेवाचष्ट इति । 'अनेन जीवेनात्मनानुप्रविश्य नामरूपे व्याकरवाणि' (छा॰ उ॰ ६/३/२) इति ब्रह्मात्मकतयैव जीवस्य शरीरिणः स्वनामभाक्त्वात्तत्त्वमिति सामानाधिकरण्य-प्रवृत्तयोर्द्वयोरपि पदयोर्ब्रह्मैव वाच्यम् । तत्र च तत्पदं जगत्कारणभूतं सकलकल्याणगुणगणा-

करं निरवद्यं निर्विकारमाचष्टे । त्वमिति च तदेव ब्रह्म जीवान्तर्यामिरूपेण सशरीरप्रकारविशिष्ट-
माचष्टे । तदेवं प्रवृत्तिनिमित्तभेदेनैकस्मिन् ब्रह्मण्येव तत्त्वमिति द्वयोः पदयोर्वृत्तिरुक्ता । ब्रह्मणो
निरवद्यं निर्विकारं सकलकल्याणगुणगणाकरत्वं जगत्कारणत्वं चाबाधितम् ॥

When it is stated in this manner, it means that the word 'you'
initially appears to be used for the individual self, who is the
presiding authority of the body. Since this individual self is himself
the body of the Supreme Self and is a mode (or type) of it, this word
ultimately refers to the Supreme Self. Hence, the word 'you'
signifies the inner dweller of the individual self who has the
individual self as His mode.

According to the Upanishad's statement "I will enter into the
individual self, and differentiate everything into names and forms."
(Chhandogya Upanishad 6/3/2), the individual self, who has a body
of his own, acquires his name only by being the body of Supreme
Being. Hence, both the words 'that' and 'you' refer to the Supreme
Being as it is their common basis.

Of the two, the word 'that' signifies the Supreme Being, the ultimate
cause of the world, the abode of all auspicious qualities, free from
all imperfections and changeless. The word 'you' refers to the same
Supreme Being, the inner controller of all individual selves,
distinguished from the individual self, which is His body. Thus, the
two words 'that' and 'you' refer to the same Supreme Being, albeit
with a difference in the way, we arrive at their meanings. Moreover,
in this interpretation, no contradiction arises if the Supreme Being
is simultaneously free from imperfection and changes, the abode of
all auspicious qualities, and the cause of the world.

[In the statement 'you are that', 'you' refers to the innermost soul of
an individual soul, and 'that' refers to the creator of the world. Both
of them refer to the same Supreme Being. Whether we look for
Supreme Reality outside ourselves or within, we arrive at the same
reality. Just as we see changes in our bodies without any change in

our souls, likewise, the innermost soul of all does not change if its body changes i.e. there are changes in this world or the bound souls.]

[Now, Ramanuja explains how all words ultimately refer to Supreme Being.]

अश्रुतवेदान्ताः पुरुषाः पदार्थाः सर्वे जीवात्मनश्च ब्रह्मात्मका इति न पश्यन्ति । सर्वशब्दानां च केवलेषु तत्तत्पदार्थेषु वाच्यैकदेशेषु वाच्यपर्यवसानं मन्यन्ते । इदानीं वेदान्तवाक्यश्रवणेन ब्रह्मकार्यतया तदन्तर्यामितया च सर्वस्य ब्रह्मात्मकत्वं सर्वशब्दानां तत्तत्प्रकारसंस्थितब्रह्म-वाचित्वं च जानन्ति ॥

Those persons, who have not studied Vedanta, do not realize that all non-sentient things and all individual selves have the Supreme Being as their soul. They think that the significance of all words is confined only to the respective objects they refer to. However, it is only a portion of what is expressible by them. Those who have studied Vedanta are aware that all things are created out of the Supreme Being and have the Supreme Being as their Inner Ruler. Since they have the Supreme Being as their soul and hence all words that are used to refer to them also signify the Supreme Being, who has all things as His modes or attributes.

[According to Ramanuja, the common meaning of a word used in our day-to-day activities is only its limited expression. Since the soul of everything is the Supreme Being; all words ultimately refer to him.]

[One can say that if a common word like 'cow' refers to the Supreme Being, it might affect our daily understanding adversely.]

नन्वेवं गवादिशब्दानां तत्तत्पदार्थवाचितया व्युत्पत्तिर्बाधिता स्यात् । नैवं सर्वे शब्दा अचिज्जीव-विशिष्टस्य परमात्मनो वाचका इत्युक्तम् । नामरूपे व्याकरवाणि' (छा॰ उ॰ ६/३/२) इत्यत्र ।

तत्र लौकिकाः पुरुषाः शब्दं व्याहरन्तः शब्दवाच्ये प्रधानांशस्य परमात्मनः प्रत्यक्षाद्यपरिच्छेद्य-त्वाद्वाच्यैकदेशभूते वाच्यसमाप्तिं मन्यन्ते । वेदान्तश्रवणेन च व्युत्पत्तिः पूर्यते ॥

You might ask, "Well, if it is so, the significance of words like 'cow' as denoting the respective object (as commonly understood in ordinary life) will be affected adversely." We say it is not so. It is said that all words also signify the Supreme Being, who is distinguished from the sentient and insentient entities. It is stated, "I will endow them with names and forms." (Chhandogya Upanishad 6/3/2)

When worldly persons use a word, they assume its significance ends in a visible and finite part of space. Since the unbounded Supreme Being, who is the primary part of the significance of a word, is not understood by direct perception. By the study of Vedanta, one knows the significance of a word in its entirety.

[Supreme Being has classified all living and non-living by entering inside them. Without him, nothing is distinctly known. Since normal persons do not perceive his presence, they think a word denotes whatever is visible to them. Those, who have studied Upanishads and realized the truth, perceive him directly as the soul of all.]

[Now, Ramanuja shows the evidence for this interpretation in various other texts.]

एवमेव वैदिकाः सर्वे शब्दाः परमात्मपर्यन्तान् स्वार्थान् बोधयन्ति । वैदिका एव सर्वे शब्दा वेदादेवोद्धृत्योद्धृत्य परेणैव ब्रह्मणा सर्वपदार्थान् पूर्ववत्सृष्ट्वा तेषु परमात्मपर्यन्तेषु पूर्ववन्नामतया प्रयुक्ताः । तदाह मनुः – 'सर्वेषां तु नामानि कर्माणि च पृथक्पृथक् । वेदशब्देभ्य एवादौ पृथक्संस्थाश्च निर्ममे ॥' (म० स्मृ० १/२१) इति । संस्थाः संस्थानानि रूपाणीति यावत् । आह च भगवान् पराशरः – 'नाम रूपं भूतानां कृत्यानां प्रपञ्चनम् । वेदशब्देभ्य एवादौ दैवादीनां चकार सः ॥' (वि० पु० १/५/६३) इति । श्रुतिश्च – 'सूर्याचन्द्रमसौ धाता यथापूर्वमक-ल्पयत्' (तै० आ० १/४४) इति । सूर्यादीन् पूर्ववत्परिकल्प्य नामानि च पूर्ववच्चकार इत्यर्थः ॥

Thus, all words used in the Veda point to their respective meanings and their significance ends in referring to the Supreme Being. All words have their origin in the Vedas; the Supreme Being took the same words again and again from the Vedas to denote the same things. He creates the world the same way as in previous creations. All words signify the Supreme Being as their ultimate meaning (soul) viz., the Supreme Being. So says Manu: "He (the Supreme Being) created the names of all things, their varied activities, and also their specific forms from the words in the Veda". (Manu Smriti 1/21)

The word forms in the verse mean various configurations. Likewise, Lord Parashara says: "At the beginning, he (the Supreme Being) fixed the names and forms of all beings such as gods and their activities only from the words in the Vedas." (Vishnu Purana 1/5/63)

So says the Upanishad: "The Supreme Being created the sun and the moon as before." (Taittiriya Aranyaka 1/44) This means that he created the sun, etc. as before, and also gave them the names as before.

[Just as a potter gives the clay various shapes, the Supreme Being constructs this world and distinctly classifies all living and non-living beings in it. So it is the efficient cause of this world also. However, as a potter is distinct (or separate) from its creations, the Supreme Being is not separate from its creations, rather it is their innermost reality or soul.]

[Until here, we have shown that the Supreme Being is the material as well as the efficient cause of the world. So, if a person knows the Supreme Being, what will happen?]

एवं जगद्ब्रह्मणोरनन्यत्वं प्रपञ्चितम् । तेनैकेन ज्ञातेन सर्वस्य ज्ञाततोऽपपादिता भवति । सर्वस्य ब्रह्मकार्यत्वप्रतिपादनेन तदात्मकतयैव सत्यत्वं नान्यथेति तत्सत्यमित्युक्तम् । यथा दृष्टान्ते सर्वस्य मृद्विकारस्य मृदात्मनैव सत्यत्वम् ॥

Thus, we have explained that the world is not different from the Supreme Being. This proves that by knowing one Supreme Being, all things become known. Since all things are the effects of the Supreme Being, and it is their soul, due to the reality of the Supreme Being, they are also real. There is no other way, through which they can described as real. The same thing is said in the example, all modifications of clay are intrinsically the same as clay, and similarly this world is also real as its intrinsic Supreme Being is.

[Thus, we know this world, which consists of living and non-living beings, is intrinsically real as the Supreme Being is its innermost soul. If we know such a reality, we know it all. This is explained by the example of clay and pots in the Upanishad. Ramanuja has meticulously shown his interpretation in accordance with the context of Chhandogya Upanishad and it does not contradict other Upanishads in any way. The non-dualist interpretation of calling the world unreal like the confusion of a snake for a rope does not adhere to the context of the Chhandogya Upanishad.]

[There are some statements in the Upanishads that explain the intrinsic properties of the Supreme Being clearly; we can call them clarifying statements. Such statements also do not depict the Supreme Being as attributeless as claimed by non-dualists.]

शोधकवाक्यान्यपि निरवद्यं सर्वकल्याणगुणाकरं परं ब्रह्म बोधयन्ति । सर्वप्रत्यनीकाकारता-बोधनेऽपि तत्तत्प्रत्यनीकाकारतायां भेदस्यावर्जनीयत्वान्न निर्विशेषवस्तुसिद्धिः ॥

The statements, which clarify the essential nature of the Supreme Being, also show him to be free from all imperfections and an abode of all good qualities. Even if someone describes the Supreme Being as a negation of all attributes and forms, he cannot avoid the presence of their opposite attributes and forms, thus the difference would arise. Hence, one cannot show the existence of an attributeless entity.

[For example, if someone negates the presence of whiteness in an object, it can still be of black or some other color. If he further says that the object is colorless, it can have still some other quality. If he says it does not have any quality whatsoever, then it would be impossible to perceive such an object.]

[Now, non-dualists put forward their arguments in support of an attributeless reality.]

ननु च ज्ञानमात्रं ब्रह्मेति प्रतिपादिते निर्विशेषज्ञानमात्रं ब्रह्मेति निश्चीयते । नैवम् । स्वरूपनिरू-
पणधर्मशब्दा हि धर्ममुखेन स्वरूपमपि प्रतिपादयन्ति । गवादिशब्दवत् । तदाह सूत्रकारः -
'तद्गुणसारत्वात्तद्व्यपदेशः प्राज्ञवत्' (ब्र॰ सू॰ २/३/२९), 'यावदात्मभावितत्वाच्च न दोष'
(ब्र॰ सू॰ २/३/३०) इति । ज्ञानेन धर्मेण स्वरूपमपि निरूपितं न ज्ञानमात्रं ब्रह्मेति । कथमिद-
मवगम्यत इति चेत्, 'यः सर्वज्ञः सर्ववित्' (मु॰ उ॰ २/३/७) इत्यादिज्ञातृत्वश्रुतेः । 'परास्य
शक्तिर्विविधैव श्रूयते स्वाभाविकी ज्ञानबलक्रिया च ।' (श्वे॰ उ॰ ६/८), 'विज्ञातारमरे केन
विजानीयात्' (बृ॰ उ॰ ४/४/१४) इत्यादिश्रुतिशतसमधिगतमिदम् । ज्ञानस्य धर्ममात्रत्वाद्धर्म-
मात्रस्यैकस्य वस्तुत्वप्रतिपादनानुपपत्तेश्च । अतः सत्यज्ञानादिपदानि स्वार्थभूतज्ञानादिविशिष्ट-
मेव ब्रह्म प्रतिपादयन्ति ॥

If a non-dualist says that the Supreme Being is declared to be pure knowledge (or consciousness), hence it must be attributeless (or undifferentiated) knowledge itself is the Supreme Being (i.e. knowledge is not an attribute of the Supreme Being).

We say it is not so. The words denoting the intrinsic attributes of an object also signify the object through those attributes, as is seen in words like 'cow'. (It denotes an object cow as well as a specific object in the mind with its intrinsic qualities. We can call it cognition of the cowness in the mind. Using this mental picture, one can recognize a cow. Hence, the word cow denotes a cow and cowness both.) So, the author of the Brahma Sutra, Vyasa says: "Since knowledge is the essential quality of the soul, the soul is (sometimes) referred to as knowledge (instead of knower) as in the reference of the Supreme Being as a distinguished knower (Prajna)." (Brahma Sutra 2/3/29) Vyasa further says, "This is not improper to address the soul as knowledge because (the quality) lasts as long as the soul exists." (Brahma Sutra 2/3/30) Hence, by the attribute 'knowledge', the nature of the Supreme Being is also indicated. It does not mean that the Supreme Being is mere knowledge (without any knower).

If a non-dualist asks, "How do you know that it is so?" The answer is that it is described in hundreds of Vedic texts like the following: "He who knows all and sees whatever is in all" (Mundaka Upanishad 2/3/7) indicates that the Supreme Being is the knower. Other such statements are - "The divine power of the Supreme Being is declared to be supreme and varied. His knowledge, strength, and action are natural to him." (Shvetashvatara Upanishad 6/8) "By what means can one know the knower?" (Brihat Aranyaka Upanishad 4/4/14)

Since knowledge is only an attribute, it cannot be proved to exist as an (independent) entity. Therefore, the words truth, knowledge, and infiniteness denote a distinguished Supreme Being who possesses these attributes like knowledge, etc. signified by these words.

[Supreme Being is referred to as "Truth, knowledge and infiniteness" because these are His essential qualities. Moreover, other Upanishads also refer to him as a knower so he cannot be mere knowledge. The only way to settle (reconcile) the difference in two descriptions of the Supreme Being (as knower and knowledge) is to accept him as a knower and knowledge as his essential or intrinsic characteristics.]

[Now, Ramanuja shows that acceptance of the attributeless Supreme Being results in improper interpretation of the sentences like 'you are that'. When a direct interpretation is possible, the non-dualists unnecessarily resort to an indirect interpretation.]

तत्त्वमिति द्वयोरपि पदयोः स्वार्थप्रहाणेन निर्विशेषवस्तुस्वरूपोपस्थापनपरत्वे मुख्यार्थपरित्याग-श्च । नन्वैक्ये तात्पर्यनिश्चयान्न लक्षणादोषः । सोऽयं देवदत्त इतिवत् । यथा सोऽयमित्यत्र स इति शब्देन देशान्तरकालान्तरसंबन्धी पुरुषः प्रतीयत अयमिति च संनिहितदेशवर्तमानकाल-संबन्धी, तयोः सामानाधिकरण्येनैक्यं प्रतीयते । तत्रैकस्य युगपद्विरुद्धदेशकालसंबन्धितया प्रतीतिर्न घटत इति द्वयोर्पदयोः स्वरूपमात्रोपस्थापनपरत्वं स्वरूपस्य चैक्यं प्रतिपाद्यते इति चेन्नैतदेवम् । सोऽयं देवदत्त इत्यत्रापि लक्षणागन्धो न विद्यते । विरोधाभावात् । एकस्य भूत-वर्तमानक्रियाद्वयसंबंधो न विरुद्धः । देशान्तरस्थितिभूत्वा संनिहितदेशस्थितिर्वर्तते । अतो भूतवर्तमानक्रियाद्वयसंबन्धितया ऐक्यप्रतिपादनमविरुद्धम् । देशद्वयविरोधश्च कालभेदेन परिहृतः । लक्षणायामपि न द्वयोरपि पदयोर्लक्षणासमाश्रयणम् । एतेनैव लक्षितेन विरोधपरि-हारात् । लक्षणाभाव एवोक्तः । देशान्तरसंबन्धितया भूतस्यैवान्यदेशसंबन्धितया वर्तमानत्वा-विरोधात् ॥

If you say, in "You are that", the two words, 'that' and 'you' lose their primary meaning and declare only the attributeless object, it will incur the error of ignoring the primary (or direct) meaning of these words.

The non-dualist might further say, 'Since the aim of the sentence is to show that the two are one, the indirect (implied) interpretation of the words incurs no fault. For example, in the statement "This is that Devadatta" the word "that" denotes Devadatta related to a particular place and a particular time, and the word 'this' Devadatta related to a place close by and the present time; the unity or oneness of Devadatta is thereby indicated. Here, it is impossible for the same (person) to simultaneously appear at two different places and times. Therefore the two words establish only the mere object "Devadatta" and its oneness.

We say that it is not to. In the statement, "This is that Davadatta", there is no trace of indirect (implied) interpretation, as no inconsistency arises if we take the (primary and) direct meaning of the words. There is no inconsistency if a person is related to two activities, one in the past and another in the present. One can remain in a distant place in the past and live in a nearby place in the present. Therefore, there is no contradiction in declaring an object to be one based on its relation to two different positions in the past and present. The difference between the past and the present locations is removed by the difference in time.

Even if we accept indirect (implied) interpretation to exist, the inconsistency is removed if we take the implied meaning of just one word (i.e. it is not required for both words). But, we maintain that there is no need to take indirect or implied meaning at all (in it), since what was connected with one place in the past may, without any contradiction, be connected with a different place at present.

[Here, Ramanuja interprets the statement 'This is that Devadatta' without any indirection. He says it is very much possible for a person to exist in two different places at different times. There is no need to interpret 'This' and 'that Devadatta' after discarding the attributes like space and time and then show their equality.]

[In a similar way, one can interpret the statement 'you are that' without discarding any attributes of an individual and Supreme soul. It denotes the equality of individual and cosmic reality directly.]

एवमत्रापि जगत्कारणभूतस्यैव परस्य ब्रह्मणो जीवान्तर्यामितया जीवात्मत्वमविरुद्धमिति प्रतिपादितम् । यथा भूतयोरेव हि द्वयोरैक्यं सामानाधिकरण्येन प्रतीयते । तत्परित्यागेन

स्वरूपमात्रैक्यं न सामानाधिकरण्यार्थः । भिन्नप्रवृत्तिनिमित्तानां शब्दानामेकस्मिन्नर्थे वृत्तिः
सामानाधिकरण्यमिति हि तद्विदः । तथाभूतयोरैक्यमुपपादितमस्माभिः । उपक्रमविरोध्युप-
संहारपदेन वाक्यतात्पर्यनिश्चयश्च न घटते । उपक्रमे हि तदैक्षत बहु स्यामित्यादिना
सत्यसंकल्पत्वं जगदेककारणत्वमप्युक्तम् । तद्विरोधि चाविद्याश्रयत्वादि ब्रह्मणः ॥

In the same way here, it is shown that there is no inconsistency in
the Supreme Being, who is the cause of the world, being also the
soul of the individual self as his inner controller. The identity of two
things can be shown by the common reference (samanadhikarana)
of their respective attributes on one basis. By ignoring their
attributes, the intrinsic identity between them as they are cannot
be arrived at. Those who understand the meaning of common
reference declare that it exists when words expressive of different
meanings (or attributes) apply to the same object. It is this kind of
identity that is proved by us.

Further, it is not proper to determine the meaning of a sentence
occurring at the end (of a context) in a manner different from what
is said at the beginning. The section begins with the statement,
"Supreme Being willed to become many", and it also says that the
will of the Supreme Being is always true and he is the sole cause of
the world. The non-dualist philosophy assumes the Supreme Being
as the seat of ignorance. This is opposed to what we have started
with.

[It is possible for the Supreme Being to coexist as the innermost
reality of an individual soul as well as the grandest cosmic reality. It
is two different aspects of the same reality. To a single flower, one
can refer to a red flower and another person as a beautiful flower.
When we say it is a beautiful red flower, we assign a single basis
(flower) to different attributes (aspects) and settle the difference in
two interpretations. This assignment of a common reference is
called 'samana-adhikarana'. The non-dualists show the identity of
two interpretations by dropping the attributes 'red' and 'beautiful'

and then they say the remaining entity is the same in two cases. This does not bring out the true essence of the reality.

Ramanuja further points out that the interpretation of the non-dualists contradicts the introductory context of the Upanishad which says the Supreme Being desired to be many and all his desires are truthful and ever-fulfilled. For, non-dualists assume that all individual souls are unreal (virtual) like a dream. This shows that the desire of the Supreme Being is false. Moreover, they accept just one soul; it implies that the Supreme Being itself comes under bondage. Hence, their interpretation is totally inconsistent.]

[Now, Ramanuja shows that the words cannot signify an attributeless entity.]

अपि चार्थभेदतत्संसर्गविशेषबोधनकृतपदवाक्यस्य स्वरूपतालब्धप्रमाणभावस्य शब्दस्य निर्विशेषवस्तुबोधनासामर्थान्न निर्विशेषवस्तुनि शब्दः प्रमाणम् । निर्विशेष इत्यादिशब्दास्तु केनचिद्विशेषेण विशिष्टतयावगतस्य वस्तुनो वस्त्वन्तरगतविशेषनिषेधपरतया बोधकाः । इतरथा तेषमप्यनववबोधकत्वमेव । प्रकृतिप्रत्ययरूपेण पदस्यैवानेकविशेषगर्भत्वादनेकपदार्थसंसर्ग-बोधकत्वाच्च वाक्यस्य ॥

Moreover, the words convey their meaning by a combination of their root part and suffix, by a combination of various words in a sentence, and in the presence of an existing entity with some attributes. Therefore words (Upanishads) do not have the capability to signify an attributeless object. So, we cannot accept the authority of the words for the existence of an object without attributes (particularities). Words like attributeless etc. can be understood only after knowing an object with some attribute and then negating the existence of that attribute in some other object. Otherwise, such words cannot signify anything. Words that are constituted of various roots and suffixes imply through them many special attributes and this is also true in the case of sentences, as they signify the connection among more than one word.

[Words themselves consist of many attributes and rules; they can only denote the objects which have some qualities. Since the Upanishads are also a collection of words, they cannot denote an attributeless reality. Words create a mental picture of an object with some attributes. However, if we say an object is devoid of any attribute, it does not create any cognition. Saying something as attributeless is as useless as someone saying my mother is a barren lady. This statement does not mean anything due to its inherent inconsistency.]

[Non-dualists further argue that since self-evident attributeless reality already exists, it does not require the support of words for its existence.]

अथ स्यात् नास्माभिर्निर्विशेषे स्वयंप्रकाशे वस्तुनि शब्दः प्रमाणमित्युच्यते । स्वतःसिद्धस्य प्रमाणानपेक्षत्वात् । सर्वैः शब्दैस्तदुपरागविशेषा ज्ञातृत्वादयः सर्वे निरस्यन्ते । सर्वेषु विशेषेषु निवृत्तेषु वस्तुमात्रमनवच्छिन्नं स्वयंप्रकाशं स्वत एवावतिष्ठत इति । नैतदेवम् । केन शब्देन तद्वस्तु निर्दिश्य तद्गतविशेषा निरस्यन्ते । ज्ञप्तिमात्रशब्देनेति चेन्न । सोऽपि सविशेषमेव वस्त्ववलम्बते । प्रकृतिप्रत्ययरूपेण विशेषगर्भत्वात् । 'ज्ञा' अवबोधन इति सकर्मकः सकर्तृकः क्रियाविशेषः क्रियान्तरव्यावर्तकस्वभावविशेषश्च प्रकृत्यावगम्यते । प्रत्ययेन च लिङ्गसंख्यादयः । स्वतःसिद्धावप्येतत्स्वभावविशेषविरहे सिद्धिरेव न स्यात् । अन्यसाधनस्वभावतया हि ज्ञप्तेः स्वतःसिद्धिरुच्यते ॥

Non-dualists might say "We do not say that the words are the authority for the existence of a self-luminous entity which is attributeless since a self-evident entity does not require any other proof for its existence. All words, the attributes denoted by them, and the act of being a knower, etc. are all denied (in an attributeless entity). When all particularities disappear, the self-luminous entity,

Supreme Being (reality), unrelated to any attribute, stands by (reveals) itself."

We say it cannot be like this. By what word is the Supreme Being indicated when its attributes are negated? If you say that the word knowledge signifies it, we say it does not stand to reason. That word (knowledge), too, relates to an entity with attributes since all words reveal their meaning through their root and suffixes. Its root word means "to know". It implies an object (that is known) and a subject or agent (that knows) and denotes also a special kind of action that distinguishes it from other actions. The suffix indicates the gender, the number (singular, dual, or plural), etc. In the absence of these particularities given above, the existence of the self-luminous nature of the Supreme Being cannot be proved. The self-luminosity of the Supreme Being can only be established by its power to illuminate other objects.

[Ramanuja says that as per rules of word formation, any word, including knowledge, cannot be used to denote an attributeless reality because all words reveal their meaning through a particularity. So it is not possible in case of an attributeless reality which does not have any particularity whatsoever.]

[Non-dualists say that attributeless reality is hidden from us due to our ignorance. This confusion is akin to the confusion of a snake in a rope. Ramanuja refutes this explanation for justifying the existence of self-luminous reality.]

ब्रह्मस्वरूपं कृत्स्नं सर्वदा स्वयमेव प्रकाशते चेन्न तस्मिन्नन्यधर्माध्यासः संभवति । न हि रज्जुस्वरूपेऽवभासमाने सर्पत्वादिरध्यस्यते । अत एव हि भवद्भिराच्छादिकाविद्याभ्युपगम्यते । ततश्च शास्त्रीयनिवर्तकज्ञानस्य ब्रह्मणि तिरोहितांशो विषयः । अन्यथा तस्य निवर्तकत्वं च न स्यात् । अधिष्ठानातिरेकिरज्जुत्वप्रकाशनेन हि सर्पत्वं बाध्यते । एकश्रेद्धिशेषो ज्ञानमात्रे वस्तुनि शब्देनाभिधीयते स च ब्रह्मविशेषणं भवतीति सर्वश्रुतिप्रतिपादितसर्वविशेषणविशिष्टं ब्रह्म भवति । अतः प्रामाणिकानां न केनापि प्रमाणेन निर्विशेषवस्तुसिद्धिः ॥

Moreover, if the whole of the Supreme Being shines by itself forever, it is not possible to superimpose the properties of anything else (ignorance) on it. When the nature of the rope shines as it is, the illusory attributes of a snake, etc. cannot be superimposed on it. That is why you have to postulate ignorance (nescience) to conceal the Supreme Being. Hence, only that part of the Supreme Being, obscured by ignorance, is the scope of the corrective knowledge found in the scriptures. Otherwise, scriptures would lose their corrective power of removing ignorance. The illusion of a snake disappears when the rope, on which this illusion of a snake rests, shines in its completeness. If even a single attribute (particularity) of a self-evident entity (e.g. whether it is concealed or revealed), is expressible through words, then it would become an adjective (quality) of Supreme Being. Then, one can assign the Supreme Being all the attributes mentioned in all the texts of the Vedas. So, for those who follow the authority of the valid sources of knowledge, there is no proof of any kind for the existence of an attributeless entity without particularities.

[If ignorance hides the attributeless reality completely, this reality itself comes under bondage, which is inadmissible. On the other hand, if ignorance hides a part of this reality, this part must be addressable as well as removable by scriptures and must have a particularity associated with it since words can only signify the particularities. It contradicts the assumption of attributeless reality.]

[Then, what is the correct way to understand reality? Ramanuja explains it for us.]

निर्विकल्पकप्रत्यक्षेऽपि सविशेषमेव वस्तु प्रतीयते । अन्यथा सविकल्पके सोऽयमिति पूर्वावगत -प्रकारविशिष्टप्रत्ययानुपपत्तेः । वस्तुसंस्थानविशेषरूपत्वाद्रोत्वादेर्निर्विकल्पदशायामपि ससंस्था -नमेव वस्त्वित्थमिति प्रतीयते । द्वितीयादिप्रत्ययेषु तस्य संस्थानविशेषस्यानेकवस्तुनिष्ठतामात्रं

प्रतीयते । संस्थानरूपप्रकाराख्यस्य पदार्थस्यानेकवस्तुनिष्ठतयानेकवस्तुविशेषणत्वं द्वितीयादिप्र
-त्ययावगम्यमिति द्वितीयादिप्रत्ययाः सविकल्पका इत्युच्यन्ते ॥

Even the perception of an attributeless entity appears as an entity possessing attributes. Otherwise, in the absence of perception with attribute (recognition) for an object that it is the same object would not be possible. 'Cowness' (or the distinctive nature of the cow) consists of a specific configuration of the object. Therefore, even at the time of its attributeless perception, it appears that the object possesses a specific configuration. In the second and other later perceptions of the object, the same configuration appears to also exist in many other objects. What is peculiar to the second and later perceptions is that the same configuration is seen to persist in many other objects and so it is an attribute of many objects not just one. Therefore, the second and other perceptions are called perceptions with attributes.

[Suppose a person sees a cow for the first time in his life. After seeing it, he will have a mental cognition of the cow. When he sees other cows later, he realizes the similarity between them and identifies them also as cows. Basically, his mind compares the intrinsic qualities of these cows with the first cow he has seen to conclude that these later ones are also cows. We can say that the first perception of a cow is attributeless and the subsequent ones as with attributes. The first perception is a limited perception whereas the subsequent perceptions make him aware that cow is a species and these cows are similar to the first one. This recognition of similarity is present only in the later perceptions. So, it would be appropriate if we define attributeless as a negation of some attributes and not all.]

[In Bhaskar's view, species and an object belonging to it are considered different as well as non-different. They say that a cow and cowness (the essential characteristics of a cow) can be different as well as non-different. Now, Ramanuja discards this view.]

अत एवैकस्य पदार्थस्य भिन्नाभिन्नत्वरूपेण द्व्यात्मकत्वं विरुद्धं प्रत्युक्तम् । संस्थानस्य संस्थानिनः प्रकारतया पदार्थान्तरत्वम् । प्रकारत्वादेव पृथक्सिद्ध्यनर्हत्वं पृथगनुपलम्भश्चेति न द्व्यात्मकत्वसिद्धिः ॥

This also refutes the perception of a single object in two different ways, viz. with its attributes and without them. The specific configuration (species, outline, structure, etc.) of an object that characterizes it, is different from an object. We can say it exists as a type (or attribute) of the object. But, since it is an essential or inseparable attribute, it cannot exist apart from the object and is also incapable of being perceived separately. Due to these two reasons, a configuration cannot be considered a material entity.

[Ramanuja says since cowness cannot be perceived distinctly from a cow, it does not have a material existence. It is just an abstract concept since it solely depends on the object 'cow'. Hence, we cannot say that cow and cowness are both different and non-different as both are not objects.]

[Now, Ramanuja asks the non-dualists to mention those negations, which makes them assume reality as completely attributeless.]

अपि च निर्विशेषवस्तुवादिना स्वयंप्रकाशे वस्तुनि तदुपरागविशेषाः सर्वैः शब्दैर्निरस्यन्त इति वदता के ते शब्दा निषेधका इति वक्तव्यम् । 'वाचारम्भणं विकारो नामधेयं मृत्तिकेत्येव सत्यम्' (छा० उ० ६/१/४) इति विकारनामधेययोर्वाचारम्भणमात्रत्वात् । यत्त्र कारणतयोपलक्ष्यते वस्तुमात्रं तदेव सत्यमन्यदसत्यमितीयं श्रुतिर्वदतीति चेन्नैतदुपपद्यते । 'एकस्मिन् विज्ञाते सर्व विज्ञातं भवति' इति प्रतिज्ञातेऽन्यज्ञानेनान्यज्ञानासंभवं मन्वानस्यैकमेव वस्तु विकाराद्यवस्था-विशेषेण पारमार्थिकेनैव नामरूपमवस्थितं चेत्तत्रैकस्मिन् विज्ञाते तस्माद्भिलक्षणसंस्थानान्तर-मपि तदेवेति तत्र दृष्टान्तोऽयं निदर्शितः । नात्र कस्यचिद्विशेषस्य निषेधकः कोऽपि शब्दो दृश्यते । वाचारम्भणमिति वाचा व्यवहारेणारभ्यत इत्यारम्भणम् । पिण्डरूपेणावस्थितायाः मृत्तिकाया

नाम वान्यद्व्यवहारश्रान्यः । घटशरावादिरूपेणावस्थितायास्तस्या एव मृत्तिकाया अन्यानि नामधेयानि व्यवहाराश्रान्यद्दशाः । तथापि सर्वत्र मृत्तिकाद्रव्यमेकमेव नानासंस्थाननानानामधेया -भ्यां नानाव्यवहारेण चारभ्यत इत्येतदेव सत्यमित्यनेनान्यज्ञानेनान्यज्ञानसंभवो निदर्शितः । नात्र किंचिद्वस्तु निषिध्यत इति पूर्वमेवायमर्थः प्रपञ्चितः ॥

Moreover, non-dualists maintain the existence of an attributeless self-luminous object (Supreme Reality) and reject all illusory appearances which conceal it as false based on the statements of the Veda. Then, they should mention those statements which reject other objects as false. They might quote the text "Modification and name like 'pot' and 'dish' are only for the purpose of speech, the clay alone is real" (Chhandogya Upanishad 6/1/4), and say that, since modification and name are only in speech, the mere substance (clay) that is seen there as the material cause that alone is true (real) and the rest (pot, etc.) are untrue (unreal).

If they interpret the Vedic statement like this, it cannot be sustained. When it is declared that by knowing One (Supreme Being), all else becomes known," Svetaketu does not think it possible that, by knowing one thing, another thing could be known. (To explain how this is possible his guru answers). If the same substance exists in varied but real (and true) states, owing to specific modifications, etc., when one thing (basis) is known, though it has acquired configurations different from it, they remain the same substance and may therefore be stated to be known as well.

It is to explain this that example (of the clay) is employed. In this passage, there is not a single word that denies any attribute. The use of various names for clay is based on practical (worldly) purposes. Clay, which exists in the form of a lump, has a certain name and usefulness. The same clay, when it exists in the state of pot, dish, etc., has different names and different uses. In spite of this, the substance, clay is the same in all. Using different configurations and different names means that clay is utilized for different purposes. Therefore, this illustration alone is the true meaning as it explains the possibility of knowing one thing by knowing another. No attribute or (particularity) of any kind has been rejected here. This has already been explained at length.

[Ramanuja asserts that clay as the cause and pots as the effects are both real, otherwise, knowledge of a real cause cannot provide the knowledge of unreal effects. Since clay is present in all pots, knowing it would make one aware of the constitution of all pots.]

[Now, Ramanuja discards another incorrect interpretation of non-dualitsts.]

अपि च 'येनाश्रुतं श्रुतम्' (छा० उ० ६/१/३) इत्यादिना ब्रह्मव्यतिरिक्तस्य सर्वस्य मिथ्यात्वं प्रतिज्ञातं चेत् 'यथा सोम्यैकेन मृत्पिण्डेन' (छा० उ० ६/१/४) इत्यादिदृष्टान्तः साध्यविकलः स्यात् । रज्जुसर्पादिवन्मृत्तिकाविकारस्य घटशरावादेरसत्यत्वं श्वेतकेतोः शुश्रूषोः प्रमाणान्तरेण युक्त्या चासिद्धमित्येतदपि सिषाधयिषितमिति चेत् । यथेति दृष्टान्तयोपादानं न घटते ॥

Besides, if you (non-dualist) say that passages like, "By hearing of which, what is unheard of becomes heard" (Chhandogya Upanishad 6/1/3), declares that everything except Supreme Being is illusory, then the illustrative example like "just as, my dear, by one lump of clay all other clay objects are known" (Chhandogya Upanishad 6/1/4) will be of no use. Since the illusoriness of modifications of clay, pot, dish, etc. is not (false) like the illusion of the serpent in the rope, even after hearing it Shvetaketu cannot understand it either by reason or by any other valid source of knowledge. If non-dualists say that they sought to show even the illusoriness of pot, dish, etc., thereby they are used as an example here. Then, we say that the introduction (of them) as an example by the use of the word "just as" would be improper for Svetaketu was not already aware of their falseness.

[The example of snake and rope as given by the non-dualist is not similar to the example given in the Upanishad. The clay and pots are both real whereas in their example rope is real and snake is unreal. So, they incorrectly conclude that only the Supreme Being is real and this world is unreal.]

[Non-dualists say that ultimate reality is devoid of any differences either homogeneous or heterogeneous or intrinsic. For example, if a cow is different from another cow, we call it homogeneous difference. A cow is also different from a horse, we term it heterogeneous difference. A cow has different organs that differ from each other, we call it intrinsic difference. Non-dualists negate all the differences. Ramanuja, now, counters this interpretation.]

'सदेव सोम्येदमग्र आसीदेकमेवाद्वितीयम्' (छा० उ० ६/२/१) इत्यत्र सदेवैकमेवेत्यवधारणद्वये -नाद्वितीयमित्यनेन च सन्मात्रातिरेकिसजातीयविजातीयाः सर्वे विशेषा निषिद्धा इति प्रतीयत इति चेन्नेतदेवम् । कार्यकारणभावावस्थाद्वयावस्थितस्यैकस्य वस्तुन एकावस्थावस्थितस्य ज्ञानेनावस्थान्तरावस्थितस्यापि वस्त्वैक्येन ज्ञाततां दृष्टान्तेन दर्शयित्वा श्वेतकेतोरप्रज्ञातं सर्वस्य ब्रह्मकारणत्वं च वक्तुं सदेव सोम्येदमित्यारब्धम् । इदमग्रे सदेवासीदिति । अग्र इति कालविशेषः । इदंशब्दवाच्यस्य प्रपञ्चस्य सदापत्तिरूपां क्रियां सद्द्रव्यतां च वदति । एकमेवेति चास्य नानानामरूपविकारप्रहाणम् । एतस्मिन् प्रतिपादितेऽस्य जगतः सदुपादानता प्रतिपादिता भवति । अन्यत्रोपादानकारणस्य स्वव्यतिरिक्ताधिष्ठात्रपेक्षादर्शनेऽपि सर्वविलक्षणत्वादस्य सर्वज्ञस्य ब्रह्मणः सर्वशक्तियोगो न विरुद्ध इत्यद्वितीयपदमधिष्ठात्रन्तरं निवारयति । सर्वशक्ति-युक्त्वादेव ब्रह्मणः । काश्चन श्रुतयः प्रथममुपादानकारणत्वं प्रतिपाद्य निमित्तकारणमपि तदेवेति प्रतिपादयन्ति । यथेयं श्रुतिः ।

The non-dualist might refer to the statement "O serene one, in the beginning, (Surpeme) Reality alone was present, without a second." (Chhandogya Upanishad 6/2/1) And say that here the two terms 'without a second' and 'alone' emphasize the presence of reality and so it appears to negate the presence of other entities whether of the same kind or of a different kind.

We say that it is not so. The same substance can exist in two different states, as the cause in one state and as the effect in another state. By understanding the causal state of the substance, one can also understand its existence in another state. The presence of the same substance in the two states is explained to Shvetaketu by an example. Since Shvetaketu does not know that the Supreme Being is the cause of all, he is introduced to it by the words, 'O serene, the reality itself existed at the beginning of this'.

The meaning of, 'The reality itself existed in the beginning of this" is as follows. The word, 'beginning' signifies a particular period of time, and the term 'this' signifies this world, which was fused in the Supreme Being along with its activity and as its substantive essence (material cause). The words 'One alone' signify that differentiations of names and forms (of this world) were non-existent then. When we interpret it thus, it becomes clear that the world has the Supreme Being (truth, reality) as its material cause. In other cases of worldly causation, the material cause is seen to be different from the efficient cause. But for Supreme Being, who is distinguished from everything else and is omniscient no contradiction arises if he does not require an efficient cause different from him because he is omnipotent.

The words 'without a second' affirm the absence of another efficient cause. Some Vedic texts first state that the Supreme Being is the material cause due to his omnipotence and then add that the same Supreme Being is also the efficient cause. To this class of texts belongs the present passage.

It is only because the Supreme Being is omnipotent that some Vedic passages first declare Him to be the material cause and then state that He is also the instrumental cause as the present statement "the reality alone ..." does.

[Ramanuja interprets the statement 'the reality alone ...' in a different way. According to him, this sentence shows that the

Supreme Being is the material as well as the efficient cause of everything. He also says that a cause can exist in different states. For example, before creation, everything was present in a subtle invisible form in the Supreme Being and after creation, it manifested into this vast world, though still existing in him.]

[Ramanuja further cites statements of similar type from other Upanishads to support his interpretation.]

अन्याश्च श्रुतयो ब्रह्मणो निमित्तकारणत्वमनुज्ञायास्यैवोपादानतादि कथमिति परिचोद्य, सर्वशक्तियुक्तत्वादुपादानकारणं तदितराशेषोपकरणं च ब्रह्मैवेति परिहरन्ति । 'किंस्विद्वनं क उ स वृक्ष आसीद्यतो द्यावापृथिवी निष्टतक्षुर्मनीषिणो मनसा पृच्छतेदुत्द्यादध्यतिष्ठद्भुवनानि धारयन्' (तै० ब्रा० २/८/१५), 'ब्रह्म वनं ब्रह्म स वृक्ष आसीद्यतो द्यावापृथिवी निष्टतक्षुर्मनीषिणो मनसा विब्रवीमि वः ब्रह्माध्यतिष्ठद्भुवनानि धारयन्' (तै० ब्रा० २/८/१६) इति सामान्यतो दृष्टेन विरोधमाशङ्क्य ब्रह्मणः सर्वविलक्षणत्वेन परिहार उक्तः ॥

Some other Vedic passages first admit the Supreme Being as the instrumental cause, and then they ask how he could (at the same time) be the material cause. They answer (the question) by saying that, owing to his possession of all forms of power, the Supreme Being can be the material cause and also other accessory aids (required for the production of the effect). Thus they negate the existence of all other aids. (Consider) this text "O Sages, search in your mind, with what trees did He build up the sky and the earth? Where was the forest from which the trees were brought? Where does it stand to support the world?" (Taittiriya Brahman 2/8/15); Supreme Being is the forest. The Supreme Being is the tree (timber) for the creation of the sky and the earth. I tell you, in reply, that He supports the world on himself." (Taittiriya Brahman 2/8/16) Here, doubt on the oneness of material and instrumental cause is first raised as a possible objection from what is commonly seen, and then the objection is resolved on the grounds of the extraordinariness of the Supreme Being from everything else.

[These statements show that, unlike ordinary objects, the Supreme Being can be a material and instrumental cause of the world.]

[After explaining his view, Ramanuja discards the interpretation of the non-dualists.]

अतः 'सदेव सोम्येदमग्र आसीत्' (छा० उ० ६/२/१) इत्यत्राप्यग्र इत्याद्यनेकविशेषा ब्रह्मणो प्रतिपादिताः । भवदभिमतविशेषनिषेधवाची कोऽपि शब्दो न दृश्यते । प्रत्युत जगद्ब्रह्मणोः कार्यकारणभावज्ञापनायाग्र इति कालविशेषसद्भावः । आसीदिति क्रियाविशेषो, जगदुपादानता जगन्निमित्तता च, निमित्तोपादानयोर्भेदनिरसनेन तस्यैव ब्रह्मणः सर्वशक्तियोगश्चेत्यप्रज्ञातः सहस्रशो विशेषा एव प्रतिपादिताः ॥

Therefore in the passage, "The reality itself existed in the beginning of this, my dear," (Chhandogya Upanishad 6/2/1) many attributes of the Supreme Being like 'at first' are indicated. There is not a single word that expresses the denial of attributes, which you (non-dualists) favor. On the contrary, in order to explain the cause-and-effect relation between the Supreme Being and the world, the text indicates the existence of a particular time, as in the words at first. The word 'existed' indicates a specific kind of action (verb). Moreover, this statement also specifies that the Supreme Being is the material as well as the instrumental cause. It also answers the objection that the instrumental cause is (usually) different from the material cause by bringing in the omnipotence of the Supreme Being. Therefore, it shows thousands of attributes (or particular features) of the Supreme Being, not known before.

[Ramanuja showed that none of the words that can signify the view of non-dualists is present in the text.]

[Ramanuja now shows that his interpretation is correct by citing other statements in the same section of the Upanishad.]

यतो वास्तवकार्यकारणभावादिविज्ञाने प्रवृत्तमत एव 'असदेवेदमग्र आसीत्' (छा० उ० ६/२/१) इत्यारभ्यासत्कार्यवादनिषेधश्च क्रियते – 'कुतस्तु खलु सोम्यैवं स्यात्' (छा० उ० ६/२/२) इति । प्रागसत उत्पत्तिरहेतुकेत्यर्थः । तदेवोपपादयति – 'कथमसतः सज्जायेत' (छा० उ० ६/२/२) इति । असत उत्पन्नमसदात्मकमेव भवतीत्यर्थः । यथा मृदुत्पन्नं घटादिकं मृदात्मकम् । सत उत्पत्तिर्नाम व्यवहारविशेषहेतुभूतोऽवस्थाविशेषयोगः ॥

Since this passage aims to explain the essence of the cause-and-effect relationship between the Supreme Being and the world, it refutes the view that the effect arises without a cause. In the passage beginning with "This (world), at first, was non-existent." (Chhandogya Upanishad 6/2/1) Then it asks the question, "How could this be true, my dear?" (Chhandogya Upanishad 6/2/2) It means "The origin of the world from non-existence is impossible, as there would be no basis for this world." Then it explains it again "How could a thing that really exists arise from something that has no real existence?" (Chhandogya Upanishad 6/2/2) What arises from a thing that does not really exist must also be unreal, in the same way as a thing like a pot, etc. that is made of clay has the qualities of clay. The origin of something that already exists means its transformation from one state to another so that it becomes fit for a new use.

[Other statements of the section show that this section aims to establish the cause-and-effect relation between the Supreme Being and the world, consisting of living and non-living beings. All these entities were already present in their subtle form in the Supreme Being. The creation only means their change from a subtle state to a gross or visible state. It also says that the origin of existence (reality) is not possible from non-existence (unreality). Those, who accept this possibility, are called non-existentialists. This view is not supported in any Vedic view.]

[Vaiseshikas says that this world of living and non-living beings is composed of insentient atoms, which combine in various ways to produce this world. According to them, this combination leads to the birth of new entities, which were earlier non-existent. Ramanuja discards their view first before refuting the non-dualists.]

एतदुक्तं भवति । एकमेव कारणभूतं द्रव्यमवस्थान्तरयोगेन कार्यमित्युच्यत इत्येकविज्ञानेन सर्व-विज्ञानं प्रतिपिपादयिषितम् । तदसत्कार्यवादे न सेत्स्यति । तथा हि निमित्तसमवाय्यसमवायि-प्रभृतिः कारणैरवयव्याख्यं कार्यं द्रव्यान्तरमेवोत्पद्यत इति कारणभूताद्वस्तुनः कार्यस्य वस्त्वन्तर-त्वान्न तज्ज्ञानेनास्य ज्ञातता कथमपि संभवतीति । कथमवयवि द्रव्यान्तरं निरस्यत इति चेत् । कारणगतावस्थान्तरयोगस्य द्रव्यान्तरोत्पत्तिवादिनः संप्रतिपन्नस्यैवैकत्वनामान्तरादेरुपपादक-त्वाद्द्रव्यान्तरादर्शनाच्चेति कारणमेवावस्थान्तरापन्नं कार्यमित्युच्यत इत्युक्तम् ॥

What has been said so far means this - The same substance which, at first, was the cause and later became associated with a different state is said to be the effect. Based on this reasoning, the knowledge one can lead to the knowledge of all. This would be impossible to explain if one assumes that the effect did not exist before (in the cause). Those, who assume this (the Vaiseshikas), state that there are three kinds of causes: the instrumental cause, the material cause, and the aggregative cause, which produce the effect or result. From these three, they say that a new substance with the name of a composite or a whole consisting of parts is produced as an effect. It would follow (on this view) that the effect is different from the cause. If it is so, by knowledge of the cause, knowledge of the effect could not result. The Vaiseshikas might ask, "How do you say that the effect, which is a composite or whole consisting of parts, is not a new substance?" The answer is as follows: "That the effect is a new substance is denied on two grounds. What you call a new substance is the same substance that has acquired a new state or condition. The same substance, having acquired a new state or condition, is called by a new name and serves a different purpose. Moreover, we do not see a new substance (different from its cause).

So, there is no need to postulate a new substance. Therefore, it has been stated that the cause itself is called an effect when it has acquired a new state or condition."

[Ramanuja says that if the effect is entirely different from the cause, the knowledge of the cause cannot produce the knowledge of the effect. So, Vaiseshikas cannot explain this fundamental premise of the Upanishads. Since we see the presence of clay in the pots made from it, it is unnecessary to accept the creation of a new substance; rather, it is only a change of state for the clay.]

[Now, Ramanuja rejects the explanation of the non-dualists.]

ननु निरधिष्ठानभ्रमासंभवज्ञापनायासत्कार्यवादनिरासः क्रियते । तथा ह्येकं चिद्रूपं सत्यमेवाविद्या -च्छादितं जगद्रूपेण विवर्तते इत्यविद्याश्रयत्वाय मूलकारणं सत्यमित्यभ्युपगन्तव्यमित्यसत्कार्य- वादनिरासः । नैतदेवम् । एकविज्ञानेन सर्वविज्ञानप्रतिज्ञादृष्टान्तमुखेन सत्कार्यवादस्यैव प्रसक्त- त्वादित्युक्तम् । भवत्पक्षे निरधिष्ठानभ्रमासंभवस्य दुरुपपादत्वाच्च । यस्य हि चेतनगतदोषः पारमार्थिको, दोषाश्रयत्वं च पारमार्थिकं, तस्य पारमार्थिकदोषेण युक्तस्यापारमार्थिकगन्धर्व नगरादिदर्शनमुपपन्नं, यस्य तु दोषश्चापारमार्थिको दोषाश्रयत्वं चापारमार्थिकं तस्यापारमार्थिके- नाप्याश्रयेण तदुपपन्नमिति भवत्पक्षे न निरधिष्ठानभ्रमासंभवः ॥

The non-dualists might object to it and say: Here, the Upanishad refutes the non-existentialist's doctrine that the effect did not exist before in the cause (or as the cause). They establish that no illusion can take place without a (real) substrate or basis. The single conscious Reality, when shadowed by ignorance, is illusorily seen as the world. This ignorance requires, for its function as a shadow, something that is real as the ultimate cause. Thus, Upanishad refutes the view of non-existentialists that there is no such ultimate and real cause as Supreme Reality.

We say this explanation of the non-dualists is not valid. The proposition, by the knowledge of one, all things become known and the illustrative example of clay shows that this context aims to prove that the effect existed before as the cause and does not arise as a new substance. Moreover, by employing the view of non-dualists, it is impossible to refute non-existentialist philosophy (or Madhyamika, a Buddhist doctrine). This doctrine says a permanent basis (substrate) is not necessary for the occurrence of an illusion.

In our view (distinguished non-duality), we hold that the defect in an individual conscious being is real and the basis of a defect is also real, so for us, illusory appearances like the city of the Gandharvas, mirages, etc, are easy to explain as they are associated with real defects.

But, a non-dualist, who considers that the defect in an individual conscious being is unreal and the basis of this defect is also unreal, may well accept that, even when the basis (substrate) is unreal, illusions might take place. Therefore, in the non-dual system, it is quite possible to have an occurrence of illusions without a real (permanent) basis.

[Ramanuja rejects the non-dualist explanation for the presence of permanent reality as the substrate of illusion because, for them, everything is unreal, the illusion and its experiencer. So, it would be very much possible for the underlying basis of all to be unreal. The non-dualists cannot easily show the reality of basis when everything else is unreal.]

[Now, Ramanuja demonstrates that the statements of other Upanishads are also in accordance with his explanation.]

शोधकेष्वपि – 'सत्यं ज्ञानमनन्तं ब्रह्म' (तै० उ० २/१), आनन्दो ब्रह्म' (तै० उ० ३/६) इत्यादिषु वाक्येषु सामान्याधिकरण्यव्युत्पत्तिसिद्धानेकगुणविशिष्टैकार्थावबोधनमविरुद्धमिति सर्वगुण-विशिष्टं ब्रह्माभिधीयत इति पूर्वमेवोक्तम् ॥

The clarifying statements such as "Supreme Being is true, conscious, and infinite" (Taittiriya Upanishad 2/1) and "Supreme

Being is bliss," (Taittiriya Upanishad 3/6), etc. determine the true nature of the Supreme Being. It has already been said that all these statements refer to the sole Supreme Being that consists of all of these distinguished qualities. This is possible as he is the common basis of all such attributes. Hence, this interpretation does not contradict anything we have said before.

[Other Upanishads also do not support the view of the attributeless reality of non-dualists.]

[Non-dualists cite some other statements of the Upanishads in support of attributeless reality.]

'अथात आदेशो नेति नेति' (बृ॰ उ॰ ४/३/६) इति बहुधा निषेधो दृष्यत इति चेत् । किमत्र निषिध्यत इति वक्तव्यम् । 'द्वे वाव ब्रह्मणो रूपे मूर्तं चैवामूर्तं च' (बृ॰ उ॰ ४/३/१) इति मूर्तामूर्तात्मकः प्रपञ्चः सर्वोऽपि निषिध्यत इति चेन्नैवम् । ब्रह्मणो रूपतयाप्रज्ञातं सर्वं रूपतयोपदिश्य पुनर्तदेव निषेद्धुमयुक्तम् । प्रक्षालनाद्धि पङ्कस्य दूरादस्पर्शनं वरमिति न्यायात् । कस्तर्हि निषेधवाक्यार्थः । सूत्रकारः स्वयमेव वदति – 'प्रकृतैतावत्त्वं हि प्रतिषेधति ततो ब्रवीति च भूय' (ब्र॰ सू॰ ३/२/१) इति । उत्तरत्र – 'अथ नामधेयं सत्यस्य सत्यं प्राणा वै सत्यं तेषामेष सत्यम्' (बृ॰ उ॰ ४/३/६) इति सत्यादिगुणगणस्य प्रतिपादितत्वात्पूर्वप्रकृतैतावन्मात्रं न भवति ब्रह्मेति, ब्रह्मण एतावन्मात्रता प्रतिषिध्यत इति सूत्रार्थः ॥

Now, non-dualists might say: In the instruction "(He is) not so, not so.," (Brihat Aranyaka Upanishad 4/3/6) there is a repeated denial (of the world). (We ask): What is denied' here must be stated. The non-dualists might reply: "Supreme Being has two forms, tangible (visible) and intangible (invisible) - world having a visible material form (like earth and water) and that with an (invisible) intangible form like air, ether, etc. The existence of both forms is denied here." (Brihat Aranyaka Upanishad 4/3/1)

We say it is not so. After describing the world as His form that was previously not known, it would be improper (for the text) to deny its existence immediately afterward. The common logic prevails here -

"Better not to touch sludge (dirt) at all than to wash it off after getting stained with it."

Then, you might ask what the meaning of negation in this sentence is. The author of the Brahma Sutras (Vyasa) has himself stated the meaning. "The denial is used so that one does not limit Supreme Being's nature to only two forms stated before in the context." (Brahma Sutra 3/2/1) Therefore, the text, after specifying just two forms of the Supreme Being, proceeds again to state (a number of his qualities). Immediately after the sentence "(He is) not so, not so.", the Upanishad says, "His name is the True of the True; the individual souls are true and He is truer than they are". (Brihat Aranyaka Upanishad 4/3/6) In this way, a number of attributes are declared of the Supreme Being, so it is only the limiting of the Supreme Being to the mentioned attributes that is objected to here (and not the attributes themselves). This is the meaning of the Sutra.

[Ramanuja says that the use of negation in the Upanishad is to emphasize that the attributes of the Supreme Being are not limited to what is being said here, rather, they are infinite. The negation does not at all mean that the Supreme Being is attributeless because the same section of the Upanishad says that he is the truth of the truth, thus, mentions his attribute.]

[Now, non-dualists cite one more statement of the Upanishad to show that reality is attributeless.]

'नेह नानास्ति किंचन' (बृ० उ० ६/४/१९) इत्यादिना नानात्वप्रतिषेध एव दृश्यत इति चेत् ।
अत्राप्युत्तरत्र – 'सर्वस्य वशी सर्वस्येशान' (बृ० उ० ६/४/२२) इति सत्यसङ्कल्पत्वसर्वेश्वरत्व-
प्रतिपादनाच्चेतनवस्तुशरीर ईश्वर इति सर्वप्रकारसंस्थितः स एक एवेति तत्प्रत्यनीकाब्रह्मात्मक-
नानात्वं प्रतिषिद्धं न भवदभिमतम् । सर्वास्वेवंप्रकारासु श्रुतिष्विययेव स्थितिरिति न क्वचिदपि
ब्रह्मणः सविशेषत्वनिषेधकवाची कोऽपि शब्दो दृश्यते ॥

The non-dualists might say, "There is no such thing as plurality here." (Brihat Aranyaka Upanishad 6/4/19), and say - in this and other Vedic sentences, the denial of plurality (of the world) alone is seen."

Our answer to it is as follows: "Here also, immediately afterward, the Upanishad says, "He has all under His power, He rules over all." (Brihat Aranyaka Upanishad 6/4/22) This brings out the Supreme Being's irresistible will and lordship over all. He has all things, whether sentient (living) or non-sentient (non-living) as his body and has them as his modes (types). He is the sole Lord of all that exists." What is denied here is the existence of any entity other than those that have the Supreme Being as their soul. The plurality (of souls) that non-dualists have in mind is not denied here. This is the real meaning of all such statements. Therefore, nowhere do we find any statement which denies the attributes of the Supreme Being.

[Here also, the subsequent statements in the same section of the Upanishad mention the Supreme Being as all-powerful and the ruler of all. Thus, it is never described as attributeless. The denial here is to negate the plurality of the existence not sustained or ensouled by the Supreme Being because it will contradict the absolute supremacy and control of the Supreme Being over them.]

[After refuting the claims of the non-dualists, Ramanuja points out the flaws in their viewpoint. At first, he refutes their view of hiding the Supreme Being by ignorance.]

अपि च निर्विशेषज्ञानमात्रं ब्रह्म तच्चाछादिकाविद्यातिरोहितस्वरूपं स्वगतनानात्वं पश्यतीत्ययमर्थो न घटते । तिरोधानं नाम प्रकाशनिवारणम् । स्वरूपातिरेकिप्रकाशधर्मानभ्युपगमेन प्रकाशस्यैव स्वरूपत्वात्स्वरूपनाश एव स्यात् । प्रकाशपर्यायं ज्ञानं नित्यं स च प्रकाशोऽविद्यातिरोहित इति बालिशभाषितमिदम् । अविद्यया प्रकाशतिरोहित इति प्रकाशोत्पत्तिप्रतिबन्धो विद्यमानस्य विनाशो वा । प्रकाशस्यानुत्पाद्यत्वाद्विनाश एव स्यात् । प्रकाशो नित्यो निर्विकार-

स्तिष्ठतीति चेत् । सत्यामप्यविद्यायां ब्रह्मणि न किंचित्तिरोहितमिति नानात्वं पश्यतीति भवतामयं व्यवहारः सत्स्वनिर्वचनीय एव ॥

Further, the non-dualists' view that the Supreme Being is pure consciousness without any attributes, and ignorance conceals its real nature, due to which the Supreme Being (illusorily) sees plurality imposed on it, is unsustainable. Concealment means veiling of light. However, you do not admit that the Supreme Being has consciousness (light) as its attribute; rather assume it is his essential nature. If you say that there is obstruction of this consciousness, it would mean that the Supreme Being itself ceases to exist. To say that consciousness (Supreme Being), which is a synonym for luminosity, is eternal and, at the same time, to say that this luminosity is concealed by ignorance is childish, (due to inherent contradiction in your reasoning). When it is said that luminosity is concealed by ignorance, it can mean either of two things - obstruct the origin of luminosity or destroy already existing luminosity. Since luminosity is not something that has been newly created, it would follow that already existing luminosity perishes. (How then you could say it to be eternal?). If, on the other hand, you maintain that luminosity is eternal and unchanging, ignorance, even though it exists, could not conceal the Supreme Being. Hence, to say that, owing to ignorance, the Supreme Being suffers obscuration and sees plurality is inconsistent. This position of the non-dualists is indeed not sayable in the presence of the wise.

[Non-dualists do not accept conscious light as an attribute of the Supreme Being; rather they say it is his intrinsic nature. Since this consciousness is the intrinsic nature of the Supreme Being and not an attribute, ignorance cannot diminish it. So ignorance has to either destroy it or stop its birth. Both options are impossible to exist in an eternal Supreme Being. Hence, ignorance cannot hide the luminosity of the Supreme Being.]

[The non-dualists counter-attack the interpretation of Ramanuja.]

ननु च भवतोऽपि विज्ञानस्वरूप आत्माभ्युपगन्तव्यः । स च स्वयंप्रकाशः । तस्य च देवादिस्व-रूपात्माभिमाने स्वरूपप्रकाशतिरोधानमवश्यमाश्रयणीयम् । स्वरूपप्रकाशे सति स्वात्मन्याका-रान्तराध्यासायोगात् । अतो भवतश्चायं समानो दोषः । किं चास्माकमेकस्मिन्नेवात्मनि भवदुदी-रितं दुर्घटत्वं भवतामात्मानन्त्याभ्युपगमात्सर्वेष्वयं दोषः परिहरणीयः ॥

The non-dualists might argue, "You also have to postulate an individual self whose nature is knowledge or consciousness and state that this consciousness is self-luminous. When this self imagines that it is a deity, human, etc., you have to also admit that this self-luminosity undergoes obscuration, for if there is self-luminosity, it would be impossible to imagine the super-imposition on itself of any other form (like that of deity, human, etc.). Therefore, the untenability that you have pointed out in our doctrine is common to you as well. Furthermore, the untenability pointed out by you against us is only in relation to a single self (viz., Supreme Being), whereas, since you postulate an infinity of souls (individual or embodied souls), this untenability will, in your case, have to be disproved in all of them".

[The non-dualists say that for us this inconsistency which you have shown is for just one soul in our viewpoint whereas for you it exists for infinitely many individual souls since you also accept, like us, that the individual souls are intrinsically conscious.]

[Ramanuja now explains, at length, why this inconsistency does not arise in his viewpoint. He describes how his viewpoint has arrived at.]

अत्रोच्यते स्वभावतो मलप्रत्यनीकानन्तज्ञानानन्दैकस्वरूपं स्वाभाविकानवधिकातिशयापरि-मितोदारगुणसागरं निमेषकाष्ठाकलामुहूर्तादिपरार्धपर्यन्तापरिमितव्यवच्छेदरूपसर्वोत्पत्तिस्थिति-विनाशादिसर्वपरिणामनिमित्तभूतकालकृतपरिणामास्पृष्टानन्त महाविभूतिस्वलीलापरिकरस्वां-

शभूतानन्तबद्धमुक्तनानाविधचेतनतद्द्योग्यभूतानन्तचित्रपरिणामशक्तिचेतनेतरवस्तुजातान्तयामि
-त्वकृतसर्वशरीरत्वसर्वप्रकारावस्थानावस्थितं परं ब्रह्मैव वेद्यं, तत्साक्षात्कारक्षमभगवद्वैपायन-
पराशरवाल्मीकिमनुयाज्ञवल्क्यगौतमापस्तम्बप्रभृतिमुनिगणप्रणीतविविध्यर्थवादमन्त्रस्वरूपवेदमू-
लेतिहासपुराणधर्मशास्त्रोपबृंहितपरमार्थभूतानादिनिधनाविच्छिन्नपाठसंप्रदायगर्य्यजु:सामाथ-
र्वरूपानन्तशाखं वेदं चाभ्युपगच्छतामस्माकं किं न सेत्स्यति ।

To this, we reply, "There is nothing difficult for us to prove since we believe that the aim of Vedanta is to know the Supreme Being, who, by nature, is free from all imperfections. His intrinsic nature is of infinite knowledge and bliss. He is the ocean of boundless, unsurpassed, and innumerable noble qualities by his very nature. The Supreme Being has two regions of magnificence, eternal (spiritual) and natural (materialistic). His eternal magnificence is infinite and untouched by the modifications or changes due to time which is the accessory cause of all modifications like the origin, continuance, and perishing of all material things. His natural magnificence is subject to modifications due to various time units like nimesha, kashta, kala, muhurtha, and other measures extending up to the epoch (parardha). The eternal magnificence consists of infinite sentient beings (individual souls), bound and free, which are His parts. Likewise, his natural magnificence consists of all nonsentient entities, which are subject to infinite, wonderful, and varied changes and are the objects of enjoyment for the sentient beings. Supreme Being has all these (living and non-living) entities as accessories for His sportful activity. He is their inner ruler and has all entities as His body and as His attributes. We believe also that the sources of our knowledge are the Vedas, Rik, Yaju, Sama, and Atharva, which consist of endless branches and have come down to us in a continuous oral tradition without beginning and without end. These Vedas find their elucidation and elaboration in the Puranas, historical and religious scriptures, which themselves are based on the Vedas. These texts have three parts, injunctions (vidhi), explanations (arthavada), and hymns (mantra). These texts were composed by many sages like Bhagavan Dvaipayana (Vyasa), Parasara, Valmiki, Manu, Yajnavalkya, Goutama, and Apastamba, all capable of realizing the Supreme Being.

[Ramanuja says since his viewpoint is entirely based on the teachings of many great sages, it is not difficult for him to resolve this inconsistency.]

[Ramanuja cites some of the fundamental teachings which he will later use to resolve the inconsistency cited by the non-dualists.]

यथोक्तं भगवता द्वैपायनेन महाभारते – 'यो मामजमनादिं च वेत्ति लोकमहेश्वरम् ।' (गीता १०/३), 'द्वाविमौ पुरुषौ लोके क्षरश्चाक्षर एव च । क्षरः सर्वाणि भूतानि कूटस्थोऽक्षर उच्यते ॥' (गीता १५/१६), 'उत्तमः पुरुषस्त्वन्यः परमात्मेत्युदाहृतः । यो लोकत्रयमाविश्य बिभर्त्यव्यय ईश्वरः ॥' (गीता १५/१७), 'कालं च पचते तत्र न कालस्तत्र वै प्रभुः ।' (म० भा० शा० १९५/९), 'एते वै निरयास्तात स्थानस्य परमात्मनः ॥' (म० भा० शा० १९६/६), 'अव्यक्तादिविशेषान्तं परिणामर्द्धिसंयुक्तम् । क्रीडा हरेरिदं सर्वं क्षरमित्यवधार्यताम् ॥' (म० भा० शा० २०६/५८), 'कृष्ण एव हि लोकानामुत्पत्तिरपि चाप्ययः । कृष्णस्य हि कृते भूतमिदं विश्वं चराचरम् ॥' (म० भा० स० ३८/२३) इति । कृष्णस्य हि कृत इति कृष्णस्य शेषभूतं सर्वमित्यर्थः ।

For instance, Lord Dvaipayana (Vyasa) says in the Mahabharata, "He who knows that I have no birth, that I am always free from birth and that I am the Supreme Ruler of the world (he will be made pure of all sins)". Gita 10/3. "In this world, there are two kinds of beings – destructible and indestructible. The destructible living beings are bound to this world. The indestructible souls are released from their bondage, "There is a third kind of being, who is different (from these two) and who is called the Supreme Being) (in the Vedas). He has entered into the three worlds and supports them as their eternal ruler". Gita 15/16 & 17

"Time (which changes all things here) is itself worn out there (in the transcendental world of Supreme Being) and has no control at all there". Mahabharata, Shantiparva 196/6.

"Compared to that (transcendental world of Supreme Being), these things (that we see) here are hells." Mahabharata Shantiparva 198-6. "All this, beginning from the unmanifested to a particular object in the creation, which changes is a (cosmic) sport of Hari." Mahabharata, Shantiparva 206/58.

"Krishna is indeed the origin of the worlds and, likewise, of their dissolution. This universe with all moving and non-moving things exists for Krishna." Mahabharata, Sabhaparva 38/23

The phrase "for Krishna" means that everything fulfills its purpose by being his instrument.

[According to Gita and Mahabharata, there are three types of entities – individual soul, insentient matter, and their controller Supreme Being (Lord Krishna). This creation is just a cosmic sport of Krishna. In his abode, time has no power.]

[Now, he cites references from the holy Vishnu Purana.]

भगवता पराशरेणाप्युक्तम् – 'शुद्धे महाविभूत्याख्ये परे ब्रह्मणि शब्द्यते । मैत्रेय भगवच्छब्दः सर्वकारणकारणे ॥' (वि० पु० ६/५/७५), 'ज्ञानशक्तिबलैश्वर्यवीर्यतेजांस्यशेषतः । भगवच्छब्दवाच्यानि विना हेयैर्गुणादिभिः ॥' (वि० पु० ६/५/७९), 'एवमेष महाशब्दो मैत्रेय भगवानिति । परमब्रह्मभूतस्य वासुदेवस्य नान्यगः ॥' (वि० पु० ६/५/७६), 'तत्र पूज्यपदार्थोक्तिपरिभाषासमन्वितः । शब्दोऽयं नोपचारेण त्वन्यत्र ह्युपचारतः ॥' (वि० पु० ६/५/७७), 'एवंप्रकारममलं सत्यं व्यापकमक्षयम् । समस्तहेयरहितं विष्णवाख्यं परमं पदम् ॥' (वि० पु० १/२२/५३), 'कलामुहूर्तादिमयश्च कालो न यद्विभूतेः परिणामहेतुः ॥' (वि० पु० ४/१/८४), 'क्रीडतो बालकस्येव चेष्टास्तस्य निशामय ॥' (वि० पु० १/२/२०) इत्यादि ।

And Lord Parashara says: "O Maitreya, the word 'Bhagavan' (Lord, God) denotes the Supreme Being, who is ever pure, for whom exist the two (great) magnificences and who is the (final) cause of all causes." Vishnu Purana 6/5/72.

Wisdom, power, strength, lordship, prowess, and splendor are, without any exception, expressed by the word "Bhagavan (the Supreme Being)" without any imperfections whatsoever." Vishnu Purana 6/5/79

O Maitreya, this great word "Bhagavan" refers only to Vasudeva, who is the Supreme Being". Vishnu Purana 6/5/76.

"To Him, this word (Bhagavan) is applicable in its primary and direct sense and not for mere courtesy. To others (it is applicable only) for courtesy's sake". Vishnu Purana 6/5/77.

"That supreme abode (goal) of Lord Vishnu is pure, eternal, all-pervasive, and imperishable. It is ever opposite to all that is impure." Vishnu Purana 1/22/53.

"Time, which has units like kala, muhurta, etc., has no power to cause any modification in His transcendental world". Vishnu Purana 4/1/84

"Look, his activities are like the plays of a child." Vishnu Purana 1/2/20, etc.

[It again corroborates what is mentioned in Gita and Mahabharata. It also says the Supreme Being consists of infinite auspicious qualities as well as none of inauspicious qualities. And, his control reigns supreme over all, including time (or death).]

[Ramanuja gives further references from the illustrious Smritis and Dharma Sutra.]

मनुनापि – 'प्रशासितारं सर्वेषामणीयांसमणीयसाम्' (म॰ स्मृ॰ १२/१२२) इत्युक्तम् ।
याज्ञवल्क्येनापि – 'क्षेत्रस्येश्वरज्ञानाद्विशुद्धिः परमा मता' (या॰ स्मृ॰ ३४) इति ।

आपस्तम्बेनापि – 'पूः प्राणिनः सर्व एव गुहाशयस्य' (आप॰ धर्मसू॰ २२/४) इति । सर्वे
प्राणिनो गुहाशयस्परमात्मनः पूः - पुरं शरीरमित्यर्थः । प्राणिन इति सजीवात्मभूतसंघातः ॥

Manu also says: "He (Supreme Being) controls all and is more subtle
than the subtlest". 12/122

Yajnavalkya says: "The purification of an individual soul which
results from a knowledge of the Supreme Being is considered the
greatest of all purifications."

So also Apastamba: "All living beings are the city (body) of Him who
takes His repose in them as its cave". The living beings here mean
all the individual souls, which consist of a body structure,
constituted of the (five) elements.

[These establish that all living and non-living beings are the body of
the Supreme Being. And, by knowing him, one attains liberation.]

[Now, Ramanuja resolves the inconsistency in his doctrine cited by
the non-dualists.]

ननु च किमनेनाडम्बरेण । चोद्यं तु न परिहृतम् । उच्यते । एवमभ्युपगच्छतामस्माकमात्मधर्म-
भूतस्य चैतन्यस्य स्वाभाविकस्यापि कर्मणा पारमार्थिकं संकोचं विकासं च ब्रुवतां सर्वमिदं
परिहृतम् । भवतस्तु प्रकाश एव स्वरूपमिति प्रकाशो न धर्मभूतस्तस्य संकोचविकासौ वा
नाभ्युपगम्यते । प्रकाशप्रसारानुत्पत्तिमेव तिरोधानभूताः कर्मादयः कुर्वन्ति । अविद्या चेत्तिरोधानं
तिरोधानभूततयाविद्यया स्वरूपभूतप्रकाशनाश इति पूर्वमेवोक्तम् । अस्माकं त्वविद्यारूपेण
कर्मणा स्वरूपनित्यधर्मभूतप्रकाशः संकुचितः । तेन देवादिस्वरूपात्माभिमानो भवतीति विशेषः
॥

"Well", the non-dualists perhaps say, "What is the use of this
verbose speech? Our objection still remains unanswered".

Here is the answer (to him): In our view the self has knowledge
(luminosity or consciousness) as its intrinsic attribute, which as the
result of (past) actions undergoes expansion or contraction. With

this view, the objection is easily resolved for us. According to you (non-dualist), luminosity is the essential nature (of self) and is not his attribute. You do not believe in its expansion or contraction. In our system, actions, etc. are the factors that obscure the spread of luminosity (of the self). The ignorance that you postulate conceals the luminosity. If so, it has already been pointed out by us that the very nature of the self would perish; whereas, for us, ignorance, which is really (past) actions, causes contraction of only the luminosity of the self (and not the self itself). Due to this ignorance or actions, the self identifies itself with (the body of) a deity, a man, etc. This is the difference between the two views.

[In Ramanuja's view, consciousness is an attribute of an individual soul so it can increase or decrease. It is similar to hiding a light source with a cloth having holes. This also explains the variation of consciousness among different species and even within them. More ignorance means less consciousness. This change of an attribute (consciousness) does not destroy an individual soul. However, for non-dualists, these changes are not possible because they assume consciousness as the essential nature of the self which is invariant.]

[Non-dualists might ask what the evidence for contraction and expansion of consciousness in an individual self is.]

यथोक्तम् – 'अविद्या कर्मसंज्ञान्या तृतीया शक्तिरिष्यते ॥ यथा क्षेत्रशक्तिः सा वेष्टिता नृप सर्वगा ।' (वि० पु० ६/७/६२), 'संसारतापानखिलानवाप्नोत्यतिसंततान्' (वि० पु० ६/७/६३) , 'तया तिरोहितत्वाच्च शक्तिः क्षेत्रज्ञसंज्ञिता । सर्वभूतेषु भूपाले तारतम्येन वर्तते ॥' (वि० पु० ६/७/६३) इति । क्षेत्रज्ञानां स्वधर्मभूतस्य ज्ञानस्य कर्मसंज्ञाविद्यया संकोचं विकासं च दर्शयति ॥

The same view is mentioned in the following verses of Vishnu Purana 6/7/61, 62, 63

"The third power (of the Supreme Being) is ignorance or past actions. This power overpowers the individual self within a body. (Being thus overpowered by actions), the individual self, O king, becomes subject to persistent afflictions of the world. Thus, obscured consciousness of the individual self, O king is seen in different degrees in different beings."

This verse (Vishnu Purana 6/7/63) thus shows how the intrinsic knowledge of the individual self undergoes contraction and expansion as a consequence of ignorance, which we also call action.

[Ramanuja concludes his response after showing verses from Vishnu Purana, which supports his interpretation. It shows that tenets of his doctrine conform to the authoritative scriptures.]

[Now, Ramanuja shows the second vulnerability in the view of non-dualists. He says that they cannot demonstrate the existence of ignorance, which hides the essential nature of the Supreme Being.]

अपि चाच्छादिकाविद्या श्रुतिभिश्चैक्योपदेशबलाच्च ब्रह्मस्वरूपतिरोधानहेयदोषरूपाश्रीयते तस्याश्च मिथ्यारूपत्वेन प्रपञ्चवत्स्वदर्शनमूलदोषापेक्षत्वात् । न सा मिथ्या दर्शनमूलदोषः स्यादिति ब्रह्मैव मिथ्यादर्शनमूलं स्यात् । तस्याश्चानादित्वेऽपि मिथ्यारूपत्वादेव ब्रह्मदृश्यत्वेनैवा-नादित्वात्तद्दर्शनमूलपरमार्थदोषानभ्युपगमाच्च ब्रह्मैव तद्दर्शनमूलं स्यात् । तस्य नित्यत्वादनि-र्मोक्ष एव ॥

Moreover, non-dualists postulate a concealing entity called ignorance as a defect or fault that obscures the Supreme Being. They have to do it to prove non-duality (of individual and Supreme Self) as is mentioned in the Upanishad. Since, according to you, this ignorance is itself illusory like the world; its appearance would also require an explanatory cause in the form of a defect (in the same way as you postulated the fault called ignorance to explain the illusion of the world). (This defect of ignorance, by itself, cannot explain its own illusory appearance). So, you will have to postulate another defect to explain this illusory ignorance. If this defect were real, there would be two entities, the Supreme Being and the defect, and the central doctrine of unity (nonduality or advaita) would go to pieces. If, on the other hand, you say that this defect is unreal, it would require, for its own illusory appearance, another defect, and so on. Thus, there would be infinite regress in the argument. To avoid these two undesirable results, you may have to maintain that the Supreme Being itself is the cause of the illusory appearance of the (original) ignorance.

Even if (you maintain that) ignorance is beginningless and therefore requires no explanatory defect as its cause, the very circumstance of it being illusory would imply that the Supreme Being sees the illusion as beginningless. As you do not admit any real defect in the Supreme Being on seeing this illusory ignorance, it would follow that the Supreme Being is itself the cause of the (illusion). As the Supreme Being is eternal, the illusion would also be eternally there, and there would, in this view, be no such thing as release from the bondage of ignorance.

[Here, Ramanuja argued that the existence of ignorance is not justified in any way as it would lead to an inconsistency in all cases.]

[Ramanuja now shows the third inconsistency in the viewpoint of non-dualists. Non-dualists say that there is just one (Supreme) soul, which is real, and all other individual souls are unreal. We can compare the situation with a single object and its multiple images.]

अत एवेदमपि निरस्तम् एकमेव शरीरं जीववत्, निर्जीवानीतराणि शरीराणि स्वप्नदृष्टनानाविधा-नन्तशरीराणां यथा निर्जीवत्वम् । तत्र स्वप्ने द्रष्टुः शरीरमेकमेव जीववत् । तस्य स्वप्नवेलायां दृश्यभूतनानाविधशरीराणां निर्जीवत्वमेव । अनेनैकेनैव परिकल्पितत्वाज्जीवा मिथ्याभूता इति । ब्रह्मणा स्वस्वरूपव्यतिरिक्तस्य जीवभावस्य सर्वशरीराणां च कल्पितत्वादेकस्मिन्नपि शरीरे शरीरवज्जीवभावस्य च मिथ्यारूपत्वात्सर्वाणि शरीराणि मिथ्यारूपाणि, तत्र जीवभावश्च मिथ्यारूप इत्येकस्य शरीरस्य तत्र जीवभावस्य च न कश्चिद्विशेषः । अस्माकं तु स्वप्ने द्रष्टुः

स्वशरीरस्य तस्मिन्नात्मसद्भावस्य च प्रबोधवेलायामबाधितत्वानन्येषां शरीराणां तद्वर्तजीवानां च
बाधितत्वात्ते सर्वे मिथ्याभूताः स्वशरीरमेकं तस्मिञ्जीवभावश्च परमार्थ इति विशेषः ॥

The above argument is enough to disprove another doctrine of the
non-dualists, namely: "One only of all the bodies (that are seen) has
a self within it; the other bodies have no souls like the bodies or
beings that are seen in dreams. In dreams, only the body of the
person that dreams has a self within it; the other bodies seen by
him in his dream are just bodies created (by his imagination) and
have no souls, being illusory bodies", (This doctrine is called the
doctrine of a single individual self). Since, according to non-duality,
the individual self as apart from the Supreme Being, as well as all
bodies, are just false or imaginary creations of the Supreme Being, it
would follow that the existence of a self even in one body is illusory,
in the same way as all the bodies are illusory; there is no special
reason to hold that one body alone is peculiar and has a self in it
(while all others have none). According to our system, on the other
hand, the person who dreams finds that his body and the existence
of the self in it are not contradicted on waking, while the other
bodies (seen in his dream) and the souls imagined in them during
the dream are contradicted (as they do not persist). So, they are all
illusory, while his body and the existence of the self in it are real.
This is the difference between the view of the non-dualists and
ours.

[In non-dualist view, there is no way in which one can decide which
body is real. However, in Ramanuja's view, every living being, after
waking up, knows that all other bodies seen in the dream were
false. Moreover, there are a lot of differences between the practical
world and dreams whereas non-dualists treat dreams and this
world in the same manner. Hence, their interpretation is
inconsistent.]

[Ramanuja now shows the fourth inconsistency in non-dualist doctrine. He argues that cessation of ignorance is not possible in their view.]

अपि च केन वा विद्यानिवृत्तिः सा कीदृशीति विवेचनीयम् । ऐक्यज्ञानं निवर्तकं निवृत्तिश्चानिर्वच-नीयप्रत्यनीकाकारेति चेत् । अनिर्वचनीयप्रत्यनीकं निर्वचनीयं तच्च सद्वासद्वा द्विरूपं वा कोट्यन्तरं न विद्यते । ब्रह्मव्यतिरेकेणैतदभ्युपगमे पुनरविद्या न निवृत्ता स्यात् । ब्रह्मैव चेन्निवृत्ति -स्तत्प्रागप्यविशिष्टमिति वेदान्तज्ञानात्पूर्वमेव निवृत्तिः स्यात् । ऐक्यज्ञानं निवर्तकं तदभावा-त्संसार इति भवद्दर्शनं विहन्यते ॥

Further, how does the cessation of ignorance occur and what is the nature of this cessation? This has to be examined. Non-dualists might say that the knowledge of unity (that the Supreme Being and the individual self are one) causes the cessation of ignorance. And, the cessation of ignorance is the opposite of inexpressible (or indescribable) since ignorance itself is neither real (like the Supreme Being) nor unreal (like the flower in the sky) nor both real and unreal and is therefore also inexpressible.

If you say, ignorance is indescribable, what is opposed to it must be expressible (or capable of description). Is the opposite of ignorance real or unreal or both real and unreal? There can not be any other alternative. If you hold that this cessation of ignorance is something real and other than the Supreme Being, there would be two entities that are real viz. Supreme Being and cessation of ignorance. This would be, against the doctrine of unity and as it could be possible only due to ignorance, (which) therefore would not cease to exist. If, on the other hand, you hold that the cessation of ignorance is due to the Supreme Being itself (or identical to it), since the Supreme Being already existed, the cessation of ignorance must have occurred even before the knowledge was acquired from the Vedanta. Therefore, your doctrine that the knowledge of unity causes cessation of ignorance and that the world (or bondage) is due to the absence of that knowledge falls apart.

[Ramanuja argues that the cessation of ignorance has to be real after the knowledge of unity, otherwise, it is of no use. If it is real, it is either different from the Supreme Being or identical to it. If it is different from the Supreme Being, there would be two real entities and the doctrine of non-duality will fall apart. If they say it is identical to the Supreme Being, the Supreme Being was always present then why did it occur? Thus, cessation of ignorance is not possible in view of non-dualists.]

[Ramanuja shows the fifth inconsistency in non-dualist philosophy. He argues that in their view, knowledge of unity cannot overpower ignorance.]

किञ्च निवर्तकज्ञानस्याप्यविद्यारूपर्वात्तन्निवर्तनं केनेति वक्तव्यम् । निवर्तकज्ञानं स्वेतरसमस्त-भेदं निवर्त्य क्षणिकत्वादेव स्वयमेव विनश्यति दावानलविषनाशनविषान्तरवदिति चेन्न । निवर्तकज्ञानस्य ब्रह्मव्यतिरिक्तत्वेन तत्स्वरूपतदुत्पत्तिविनाशानां मिथ्यारूपत्वात्तद्विनाशरूपा विद्या तिष्ठत्येवेति तद्विनाशदर्शनस्य निवर्तकं वक्तव्यमेव । दावाग्न्यादीनामपि पूर्वावस्थाविरोधि-परिणामपरंपरावर्जनीयैव ॥

Furthermore, if you assume that knowledge that causes the cessation of ignorance has the nature of ignorance (illusory), then non-dualist has to explain by what means that knowledge, too, would cease to exist. He might state in reply, "This knowledge, which causes the cessation of ignorance, removes all differences other than it and then perishes of itself since all knowledge is momentary. As illustrative examples, the non-dualists might cite the examples of (self-extinguishing) forest fire and the poison which destroys the effect of other poison and then destroys itself."

But this cannot be a proper reply. Since this knowledge which causes cessation of ignorance is other than the Supreme Being, its existence, origin, and destruction are illusory (according to non-dualists). After its destruction, the knowledge of its cessation still stands and a remedy for its destruction will have to be thought of. In the case of the forest fire, etc., what disappears continues to exist in a non-conflicting new state different from those chains of states that respectively precede them.

[In the view of non-dualists, the knowledge that is the opposite of ignorance remains after ignorance is destroyed. Ramanuja asks how this knowledge will be destroyed. In the case of forest fire, fire remains in an unmanifested form within the ashes. So, how do non-dualists get away with this knowledge, which is other than the Supreme Being, as it is the opposite of ignorance? Supreme Being is neither opposed to ignorance nor to knowledge as it can co-exist with both in their view.]

[Now, Ramanuja talks about the sixth inconsistency in non-dualist doctrine. He asks who the knower of this knowledge of unity, which causes the cessation of ignorance, is.]

अपि च चिन्मात्रब्रह्मव्यतिरिक्तकृत्स्ननिषेधविषयज्ञानस्य कोऽयं ज्ञाता । अध्यासरूप इति चेन्न । तस्य निषेधतया निवर्तकज्ञानकर्मत्वात्तत्कर्तृत्वानुपपत्तेः । ब्रह्मस्वरूप एवेति चेन्न । ब्रह्मणो निवर्तकज्ञानं प्रति ज्ञातृत्वं किं स्वरूपमुताध्यस्तम् । अध्यस्तं चेदयमध्यासतन्मूलविद्यान्तरं च निवर्तकज्ञानविषयतया तिष्ठत्येव । तन्निवर्तकान्तराभ्युपगमे तस्यापि त्रिरूपतयानवस्थैव । सर्वस्य हि ज्ञानस्य त्रिरूपकत्वविरहे ज्ञानत्वमेव हीयते । कस्यचित्कंचनार्थविशेषं प्रति सिद्धिरूपत्वात् । ज्ञानस्य त्रिरूपत्वविरहे भवतां स्वरूपभूतज्ञानवन्निवर्तकज्ञानमप्यनिवर्तकं स्यात् । ब्रह्मस्वरूपस्यैव ज्ञातृत्वाभ्युपगमेऽस्मदीय एव पक्षः परिगृहीतः स्यात् । निवर्तकज्ञान-स्वरूपज्ञातृत्वं च स्वनिवर्त्यान्तर्गतमिति वचनं भूतलव्यतिरिक्तं कृत्स्नं छिन्नं देवदत्तेनेत्यस्यामेव छेदनक्रियायामस्याश्छेदनक्रियायाश्छेत्तृत्वस्य च छेद्यान्तर्भाववचनवदुपहास्यम् ॥

Besides this knowledge, which is pure consciousness and denies the reality of all objects other than the Supreme Being, the non-dualists have to specify who the knower of this knowledge is. If they say that the individual self falsely superimposed on the Supreme Being is its knower, it would be illogical; for this knowledge denies the very existence of the illusory superimposition (of the individual self). Hence, this illusory superimposition is the object of the action for the knowledge of unity. Since it is the object of knowledge, it cannot, at the same time, be the subject who owns that knowledge (i.e.) it cannot be the knower.

If, on the other hand, you say the Supreme Being itself is the knower of this knowledge, you must tell if this knowledge exists in the Supreme Being as his intrinsic nature or is superimposed on him illusorily.

If you accept this (second) knowledge to be superimposed on the Supreme Being, then this illusory superimposition (of second knowledge) and the ignorance which causes it (second knowledge) will stand unaffected by the knowledge of unity. For, they are not within the scope of that knowledge, which removes the original ignorance. If you admit another knowledge, which could dispel this (second) ignorance, there would be a further difficulty. This knowledge, too, would require the three essential components of all knowledge, viz., a knower, a thing to be known, and the action of knowing. The question would then again arise "Who is its knower?" and thus you will be stuck in infinite regress. Without these three essentials (knower, knowing, and what is known), there could be no such thing as knowledge at all. For knowledge is that which illumines something to a knower.

If you hold that this knowledge of unity which dispels ignorance has none of these three essentials, rather, it is mere consciousness and an intrinsic nature of the Supreme Being; it would then be incapable of dispelling ignorance like the intrinsic nature of the Supreme Being.

If, on the other hand, you accept that the Supreme Being itself is really the knower, then you have accepted our position, namely, that the Supreme Being is not mere consciousness or knowledge, but is also the knower who has knowledge as an attribute of His.

If you say that the knowledge which causes cessation of ignorance dispels itself as well as its knower, it would be laughable. For it would be similar to say that if Devadatta has cut down everything except the ground, he has cut down the action of cutting, the person who cuts, and those things which are cut down.

[Here, Ramanuja shows that neither an individual self nor a Supreme Being can be a knower for non-dualists in a consistent manner. He also shows that even if they assume the identity of knower, knowledge, and knowable, they cannot overcome this problem. And, if they accept the Supreme Being as a knower, their viewpoint is not different from that of Ramanuja.]

[Ramanuja points out the seventh inconsistency in non-dualist doctrine. He questions the validity of the means through which illusory appearance, due to ignorance, is dispelled. Non-dualists maintain this world is unreal so after self-realization this world should cease to be visible.]

अपि च निखिलभेदनिवर्तकमिदमैक्यज्ञानं केन जातमिति विमर्शनीयम् । श्रुत्यैवेति चेन्न । तस्या ब्रह्मव्यतिरिक्ताया अविद्यापरिकल्पितत्वात्प्रपञ्चबाधकज्ञानस्योत्पादकत्वं न संभवति । तथा हि दुष्टकारणजातमपि रज्जुसर्पज्ञानं न दुष्टकारणजन्येन रज्जुरियं न सर्प इति ज्ञानेन बाध्यते । रज्जुसर्पज्ञानभये वर्तमाने केनचिद्भ्रान्तेन पुरुषेण रज्जुरियं न सर्प इत्युक्तेऽप्ययं भ्रान्त इति ज्ञाते सति तद्वचनं रज्जुसर्पज्ञानस्य बाधकं न भवति भयं च न निवर्तते । प्रयोजकज्ञानवतः श्रवणवेलायामेव हि ब्रह्मव्यतिरिक्तत्वेन श्रुतेरपि भ्रान्तिमूलत्वं ज्ञातमिति । निवर्तकज्ञानस्य ज्ञातुस्तत्सामग्रीभूतशास्त्रस्य च ब्रह्मव्यतिरिक्तया यदि बाध्यत्वमुच्यते हन्त तर्हि प्रपञ्च-निवृत्तेर्मिथ्यात्वमापततीति प्रपञ्चस्य सत्यता स्यात् । स्वप्नदृष्टपुरुषवाक्यावगतपित्रादि मरणस्य -मिथ्यात्वेन पित्रादिसत्यतावत् । किञ्च तत्त्वमस्यादिवाक्यं न प्रपञ्चस्य बाधकम् । भ्रान्तिमूल-त्वाद्भ्रान्तप्रयुक्तरज्जुसर्पबाधकवाक्यवत् ॥

Moreover, one should carefully consider the means that produce this knowledge of unity that enables one to realize Supreme Being alone is real and that all differences we perceive in the world are illusory. If you say Upanishads are the source of this knowledge, it cannot be a proper answer in your system because everything except the Supreme Being is the creation of ignorance. Therefore, it would follow that the Upanishads, who are different from the Supreme Being, cannot dispel the illusory appearance of the world, being themselves the products of ignorance.

For example, the illusion of a serpent in a rope, which is caused by some error in perception, cannot be dispelled by the knowledge if it comes from a defective source. If a person who is afraid due to the illusion of the serpent in the rope, and another person, whom he knows to be of unsound mind, tells him "This is a rope and not a serpent", his words would not dispel the illusion of the first person, and his fear due to it will also not vanish. Similarly, if a person hears the words of the Upanishads that everything except the Supreme Being is illusory, he knows that the Upanishads, being different from the Supreme Being, are themselves a product of illusion. Therefore, the knowledge imparted by the Upanishads that the Supreme Being alone is real cannot dispel his ignorance.

If you say "The knowledge of unity which dispels ignorance, a scripture which provides that knowledge and, so also, the person who has that knowledge are all illusory and false, since they are different from Supreme Being", then, indeed, the illusory nature of the world and its disappearance in liberation would also become false. This would only mean that the world is real. Suppose someone tells a person in his dream that his father is dead and he afterward comes to know that it was all a dream, and then realizes that the knowledge imparted to him in the dream about his father's death is false and that his father is really alive. Moreover, the texts of the Upanishads like "you are that" cannot negate the reality of the world, because these words are the product of illusion, just as the speech of a deluded person, trying to correct the illusory cognition of the serpent in a rope.

[Here, Ramanuja shows by a counter-example of snake, rope, and a deluded person that a non-authoritative means of knowledge cannot produce knowledge. Since non-dualists do not accept the authority of anything, except non-duality, for them, the Upanishads would also cease to be a valid source of knowledge.]

[Non-dualists counter the interpretation of Ramanuja.]

ननु च स्वप्ने कस्मिंश्चिद्द्वये वर्तमाने स्वप्नदशायामेवायं स्वप्न इति ज्ञाते सति पूर्वभयनिवृत्तिर्दृष्टा ।
तद्वदत्रापि संभवतीति । नैवम् । स्वप्नवेलायामेव सोऽपि स्वप्न इति ज्ञाते सति पुनर्भयानिवृत्तिरेव
दृष्टेति न कश्चिद्विशेषः । श्रवणवेलायामेव सोऽपि स्वप्न इति ज्ञातमेवेत्युक्तम् ॥

But the non-dualists might say, "Suppose some fear persists in a person in a dream. If knowledge arises, even during the dream, that it is a dream, the previous fear is seen to disappear. In the same way, here also (the knowledge imparted by the illusory Upanishads may dispel the erroneous notion of duality due to ignorance)".

We say it is not so. During the dream itself, if one knows that the knowledge that removed his fear was itself a dream, his previous fear is seen to recur again. Thus, this explanation does not improve your position. It has been already stated that even while we listen to the Upanishads, we are aware (according to the non-dualists) that the Upanishads are as illusory as dreams so they cannot remove our ignorance.

[Ramanuja shows again that if someone is aware that the source of knowledge is not authoritative, it cannot create a lasting impact.]

[Non-dualists bring forth another argument to justify their position.]

यदपि चेदमुक्तं भ्रान्तिपरिकल्पितत्वेन मिथ्यारूपमपि शास्त्रमद्वितीयं ब्रह्मेति बोधयति तस्य सतो ब्रह्मणो विषयस्य पश्चात्तनबाधादर्शनाद्ब्रह्म सुस्थितमेवेति । तदयुक्तम् । शून्यमेव तत्त्वमिति वाक्येन तस्यापि बाधितत्वात् । इदं भ्रान्तिमूलवाक्यमिति चेत् । सदद्वितीयं ब्रह्मेति वाक्यमपि भ्रान्तिमूलमिति त्वयैवोक्तम् । पश्चात्तनबाधादर्शनं तु सर्वशून्यवाक्यस्यैवेति विशेषः । सर्वशून्यवादिनो ब्रह्मव्यतिरिक्तवस्तुमिथ्यात्ववादिनश्च स्वपक्षसाधनप्रमाणपारमार्थ्यानभ्युपग-मेनाभियुक्तैर्वादानधिकार एव प्रतिपादितः । अधिकारोऽनभ्युपायत्वान्न वादे शून्यवादिनः । इति ॥

The non-dualists say though the scripture is illusory, being a product of delusion (or error), it declares that the Supreme Being exists without a second. That existence of the Supreme Being is true because it is not contradicted by its experience.

This statement, too, cannot hold good. For, the existence or reality of the Supreme Being is contradicted by (a school of Buddhists, nihilists), who declare reality is non-existent. If the non-dualist says that this contention of the Buddhists is due to error, it may be replied. "You have yourself stated that the words in the Upanishad, "Supreme Being is real and without a second" are due to illusion". The contention here is that nothing really exists (not even the Supreme Being) has the superiority of having no later contradiction. Both the Buddhist, who does not believe in the reality of anything and the non-dualist, who contends that everything except the Supreme Being is unreal, are equally unfit, in the opinion of the wise, to be a part of the discussion. This is so because neither of them accepts the truth of any authority which could prove their contention to be right. It has been said that disputation is at all possible only with those who accept the truth (authority) of the valid sources of knowledge. It is of no use to argue with someone, who does not believe in the reality of anything.

[Ramanuja argues that since non-dualists and nihilists do not accept any valid source of knowledge, they cannot prove anything and are, therefore, unfit for any discussion.]

[Ramanuja asks non-dualists how they have decided this world to be unreal. It is the eighth inconsistency in the non-dualists view.]

अपि च प्रत्यक्षदृष्टस्य प्रपञ्चस्य मिथ्यात्वं केन प्रमाणेन साध्यते । प्रत्यक्षस्य दोषमूलत्वेनान्यथासिद्धिसंभवान्निर्दोषं शास्त्रमनन्यथासिद्धं प्रत्यक्षस्य बाधकमिति चेत् । केन दोषेण जातं प्रत्यक्षमनन्तभेदविषयमिति वक्तव्यम् । अनादिभेदवासनाख्यदोषजातं प्रत्यक्षमिति चेत् । हन्त तर्ह्यनेनैव दोषेण जातं शास्त्रमपीत्येकदोषमूलत्वाच्छास्त्रप्रत्यक्षयोर्न बाध्यबाधक-भावसिद्धिः ॥

Furthermore, on what authority (basis) do you establish the unreality of the world that we perceive with our senses?

The non-dualists may say, "Sense perception arises from a defect or fault. So, what sense perception brings before us can be explained to be false (as it is arising due to faults), whereas the scripture, which is faultless and could not be explained to be false otherwise, should be considered superseding to sense-perception".

If he says so, (we ask), "By what fault does sense-perception reveal to us (this world so full of) endless differences? If you say, in reply, error in sense-perception is due to the false attachment to differences that persists from beginningless time", we reply, "The same fault is also present in scripture (which, too, recognizes differences).

How, then, do you establish the superiority of the scripture over sense perception (as a valid source of knowledge) and state that it contradicts the sense perception?

[Ramanuja argues that scriptures cannot negate the sense perception as both of them recognize differences (dualities) and there is no way we can say one is superior to the other.]

[Ramanuja puts forth his view on the matter. According to him, sense-perception and Scripture have different scopes (domains) and cannot, therefore, conflict with each other.]

आकाशवाय्वादिभूततदारब्धशब्दस्पर्शादियुक्तमनुष्यत्वादिसंस्थानसंस्थितपदार्थग्राहि प्रत्यक्षम् ।
शास्त्रं तु प्रत्यक्षाद्यपरिच्छेद्यसर्वान्तरात्मत्वसत्यत्वाद्यनन्तविशेषणविशिष्टब्रह्मस्वरूपतदुपासना-
द्याराधनप्रकारतत्प्राप्तिपूर्वकतत्प्रसादलभ्यफलविशेषतदनिष्टकरणमूलनिग्रहविशेषविषयमिति
न शास्त्रप्रत्यक्षयोर्विरोधः । अनादिनिधनाविच्छिन्नपाटसंप्रदायताद्यनेकगुणविशिष्टस्य शास्त्रस्य
बलीयस्त्वं वदता प्रत्यक्षपारमार्थ्यमवश्यमभ्युपगन्तव्यमित्यलमनेन श्रुतिशतवितिततवातवेगपरा-
हतकुदृष्टिदुष्टयुक्तिजालतूलनिरसनेनेत्युपरम्यते ॥

Perception is the apprehension of elements like space (sky) and air and their properties like hearing, touch, etc., which exist in various forms like humans, animals, etc. Scripture, on the other hand, deals with the matters not apprehended by perception, viz., the nature of the Supreme Being, His being the innermost soul of all, His being the eternal Reality, and His being endowed with countless attributes, the ways of worship and meditation on Supreme Being, and the various benefits accruing from His grace, such as attaining Him, and likewise also, the punishments that will be incurred by doing things displeasing to Him. (As sense perception and Scripture concern themselves with entirely different matters, there cannot be any conflict between them). You, too, admit that Scripture, which is a superior authority, has no beginning and no end and has the merit of a continuous tradition (regarding its text and delivery). You should necessarily also admit the reality of what we experience by sense perception. Enough of this refutation of flimsy cotton-like light arguments brought forward by the perverse minds, which are thrown and swept away by the strong wind of hundreds of passages in the Upanishads.

[Sense perception deals with various experiences related to sight, sound, touch, taste, and smell. The scriptures, on the other hand, are concerned with matters that are non-worldly, e.g. what happens after death, how to experience the soul, etc. This clearly shows their domains of operations are different. Since their scopes are different, there can be no conflict between them. This ends the refutation of non-dualist philosophy by Ramanuja.]

Refutation of Bhaskara Philosophy

[Bhaskara's system of Bhedabheda accepts the presence of a wrapper beside the Supreme Being. Due to the presence of this wrapper, difference, and non-difference in Supreme Being can occur.]

द्वितीये तु पक्ष उपाधिब्रह्मव्यतिरिक्तवस्त्वन्तरानभ्युपगमाद्ब्रह्मण्येवोपाधिसंसर्गादौपाधिकाः सर्वे दोषा ब्रह्मण्येव भवेयुः । ततश्चापहतपाप्मत्वादिनिर्दोषत्वश्रुतयः सर्वे विहन्यन्ते ॥

According to the second view, there is nothing else besides the Supreme Being and the limiting adjuncts (finite wrappers). Since there is nothing else the wrappers associate with Supreme Being itself. Hence, all imperfections of the wrappers (such as body, senses, etc.) would affect the Supreme Being. The statements of the Upanishads like the Supreme Being is free from all faults and imperfections, etc. would then be contradicted.

[Since they do not accept the presence of individual souls, Ramanuja says all the defects due to the wrapper will occur in the Supreme Being. This contradicts the statements of the Upanishads. Hence, this view is also inconsistent.]

[Bhaskarites now explain through an example how the arrangement of bound souls and Supreme Being exists in their view.]

यथा घटाकाशादेः परिच्छिन्नतया महाकाशाद्वैलक्षण्यं परस्परभेदश्च दृश्यते तत्रस्था गुणा वा दोषा वानवच्छिन्ने महाकाशे न संबध्यन्ते एवमुपाधिकृतभेदव्यवस्थितजीवगता दोषा अनुपहिते परे ब्रह्मणि न संबध्यन्त इति चेत् । नैतदुपपद्यते । निरवयवस्याकाशस्यानवच्छेद्यस्य घटादिभि-श्छेदासंभवात्तेनैवाकाशेन घटादयः संयुक्ता इति ब्रह्मणोऽप्यच्छेद्यत्वाद्ब्रह्मैवोपाधिसंयुक्तं स्यात् । घटसंयुक्ताकाशप्रदेशोऽन्यस्मादाकाशप्रदेशाद्भिद्यत इति चेत् । आकाशस्यैकस्यैव प्रदेशभेदेन घटादिसंयोगाद्घटादौ गच्छति तस्य च प्रदेशभेदस्यानियम इति तद्वद्ब्रह्मण्येव प्रदेशभेदानियमे-नोपाधिसंसर्गादुपाधौ गच्छति संयुक्तवियुक्तब्रह्मप्रदेशभेदाच्च ब्रह्मण्येवोपाधिसंसर्गः क्षणे क्षण

बन्धमोक्षौ स्याताभिति सन्तः परिहसन्ति ॥

The Bhaskarites might defend their position by saying "Universal space (sky) is all-pervasive, but the space within a jar, etc. is limited and thus looks different from the all-pervasive space as it possesses different attributes. The merits and demerits associated with the limited space do not affect the universal space. In the same way, the faults and imperfections of the individual self (embodied soul) who is marked off from the rest (of Supreme Being) by the differences due to the wrappers may not affect Supreme Being".

If it is so stated, it cannot be considered correct. Space is partless and non-composite so it cannot be divided. So, the jars, etc. cannot divide it and are, therefore, connected only with the pervasive space. Likewise, the Supreme Being cannot be divided (into parts) and its wrappers must be connected with the Supreme Being itself (and are not any part of it.)

The Bhaskarite might say, "The region of space which is connected with the jar is different from the other region which is not so connected". We reply: "Space is a single (non-composite) entity and becomes connected with the jar, etc. through a part or region of it. If you do not accept it when the jar is moved (from one place to another), it is some other region (that becomes connected), and thus there is no fixed connection to a region. Similarly, there will be no fixed region of the Supreme Being (which becomes connected with its wrappers. When the wrappers move, the part of the Supreme Being (newly) connected with the wrappers becomes differentiated from the region (now) not connected with it. So, you (the Bhaskarite) would be forced to admit that, at one moment, when connected with wrappers, the Supreme Being is bound in the world and that, at another moment, when the wrappers have moved away, it has attained release. An admission of this kind would be ridiculous in the eyes of impartial thinkers.

[Ramanuja shows that if Bhaskarites divide space in regions, and treat them differently, the movement of a container will change the underlying space. Thus, if they imagine individual souls within the Supreme Being like this, the arrangement of souls will become inconsistent.]

[Bhaskarites offer a further justification of their view.]

निरवयवस्यैवाकाशस्य श्रोत्रेन्द्रियत्वेऽपीन्द्रियव्यवस्थावद्ब्रह्मण्यपि व्यवस्थोपपद्यत इति चेत् । न वायुविशेषसंस्कृतकर्णप्रदेशसंयुक्तस्यैवाकाशप्रदेशस्येन्द्रियत्वात्तस्य च प्रदेशान्तराभेदेऽपीन्द्रिय-व्यवस्थोपपद्यते । आकाशस्य तु सर्वेषां शरीरेषु गच्छत्स्वनियमेन सर्वप्रदेशसंयोग इति ब्रह्मण्युपाधिसंयोगप्रदेशानियम एव ॥

The Bhaskarite might argue as follows: "Although space is without parts, it is considered as the sense organ of hearing and it is possible to distinguish between that region which is called the sense of hearing and the rest of space which is not the organ of hearing. (In the same manner, it may be possible to distinguish between Supreme Being with wrappers and Supreme Being without wrappers."

But this argument is fallacious. Space by itself is not the sense organ of hearing. It is only the region of the space that is connected with the cavity of the ear, modifiable by a special kind of air (sound vibrations due to others), called the sense of hearing. Though there is no distinguishing feature between this region of space and the rest of space, it can still be distinguished as the sense of hearing due to the presence of a special kind of modifiable air. Just as any region of space can come into contact with the bodies of living beings when they move without any fixed rule, likewise there will be no definite rule for association of wrappers with Supreme Being in all regions of space.

[Ramanuja contradicts their explanation again by citing there can be no general rule for association of space with the wrappers. The same is true for individual souls.]

[Now, Ramanuja, on the basis of scriptures, discards their view that space is the sense organ of hearing.]

आकाशस्य स्वरूपेणैव श्रोत्रेन्द्रियत्वमभ्युपगम्यापीन्द्रियव्यवस्थोक्ता । परमार्थतस्त्वाकाशो न श्रोत्रेन्द्रियम् । वैकारिकादहंकारादेकादशेन्द्रियाणि जायन्त इति हि वैदिकाः । यथोक्तं भगवता पराशरेण – 'तैजसानीन्द्रियाण्याहुर्देवा वैकारिका दश । एकादशं मनश्चात्र देवा वैकारिकाः स्मृताः ॥' (वि० पु० १/२/४७) इति । अयमर्थः । वैकारिकस्तैजसो भूतादिरिति त्रिविधोऽहंकारः । स च क्रमात्सात्त्विको राजसस्तामसश्च । तत्र तामसाद्भूतादेराकाशादीनि भूतानि जायन्त इति सृष्टिक्रममुक्त्वा तेजसाद्राजसादहंकारादेकदशेन्द्रियाणि जायन्त इति परमतमुपन्यस्य सात्त्विका -हंकाराद्वैकारिकानीन्द्रियाणि जायन्त इति स्वमतमुच्यते   देवा वैकारिकाः स्मृता इति । देवा इन्द्रियाणि । एवमिन्द्रियाणामाहंकारिकाणां भूतैश्चाप्यायनं महाभारत उच्यते । भौतिकत्वेऽपी-न्द्रियाणामाकाशादिभूतविकारत्वादेवाकाशादिभूतपरिणामविशेषा व्यवस्थिता एव शरीरवत्पुरु-षाणामिन्द्रियाणि भवन्तीति ॥

Here, we have explained the contradiction in assigning distinct sense organs to living beings, assuming that the sense of hearing is not intrinsically different from space. As a matter of fact, however, space does not form the sense of hearing at all. Vedic scholars hold that the eleven senses arise from the Vaikarika or (sattvika) ego. For instance, Lord Parashara says:-

"It is (sometimes) said that the senses arise from Taijasa (Rajasic) ego. But, the ten senses (and their controlling deities) along with the mind as the eleventh, arise from Vaikarika or (sattvika) ego". (Vishnu Purana 1/2/47)

This is the meaning of the verse: Ego is of three kinds: Vaikarika, Taijasa, and Bhutadi, which are respectively called also Sattvika, Rajasika, and Tamasika. The sage (Parashara) states that from the Tamasika ego, the five fundamental elements like space, etc. are produced. He then cites the opinion of others that the eleven sense organs are produced from the Rajasika Ego and indicates his own opinion that the senses arise from the Sattvika ego. The word deva (deities) in the verse means the senses. In the Mahabharata as well, it is similarly stated that the senses are produced by the Sattvika ego and nourished (or strengthened) by the fundamental elements (space, etc.). Even if we accept that the senses are the modifications of the five fundamental elements, the Bhaskarite contention does not gain anything. The senses are distinguished from the fundamental elements like space etc. as being their modifications (products), in the same way the body is distinguished from the five fundamental elements out of which it is built up. The treatment of the senses will be similar to the bodies.

[Ramanuja demonstrates that scriptures do not accept space as the sense of hearing. So, the contention of Bhaskarites is incorrect.]

[Now, Ramanuja cites some more inconsistencies in their viewpoint.]

ब्रह्मण्यच्छेद्दे निरवयवे निर्विकारे त्वनियमेनानन्तहेयोपाधिसंसर्गदोषो दुष्परिहर एवेति श्रद्धाना-
नामेवायं पक्ष इति शास्त्रविदो न बहु मन्यन्ते । स्वरूपपरिणामाभ्युपगमादविकारत्वश्रुतिर्बाध्यते
। निरवद्यता च ब्रह्मणः शक्तिपरिणाम इति चेत् । केयं शक्तिरुच्यते । किं ब्रह्मपरिणामरूपा ।
उत ब्रह्मणोऽनन्या कापीति । उभयपक्षेऽपि स्वरूपपरिणामोऽवर्जनीय एव ॥

However, this cannot be said to be true for the individual self, who is not a modification (defect) of the Supreme Being because the Upanishad says that the Supreme Being is without any modification or change. Therefore, since the Supreme Being is indivisible, without parts and without changes or modifications, it would be impossible to disprove the presence of innumerable imperfections due to contact with the wrappers in Bhaskara's view. Those, who are well-versed in the Scripture, have, therefore, scant regard for this system, which could be accepted only by those who are guided by mere faith.

Further, you (Bhaskarites) hold that the Supreme Being's essential nature evolves into non-sentient things. This is opposed to the Upanishad statement which declares that Supreme Being is without any changes or modifications. If you maintain, (in order to avoid this difficulty) that it is not the Supreme Being that evolves into non-sentient things but that His power undergoes the evolution, we ask, "What is this power? Is it a modification of the Supreme Being? Or is it something not different from the Supreme Being? In either case, it would follow, in your view, that the Supreme Being itself undergoes change (which is against the Upanishad).

[Ramanuja shows that in Bhaskarite's view, the Supreme Being is not devoid of imperfections. Moreover, since the Supreme Being, through his power, changes into insentient entities, changes in its nature are inevitable. This is also against the spirit of Vedanta texts. Hence, this viewpoint should also be discarded.]

Refutation of Yadavaprakasa Philosophy

[Bhaskara accepts the difference between an individual soul and the Supreme Soul as artificial and non-difference as natural. It is created due to the presence of a wrapper. After liberation it ceases to exist, so only non-difference between them remains. He accepts the difference between insentient matter and Supreme Soul natural as it always persists, even after liberation. The view of Yadavaprakasha is a slight modification of Bhaskara's view. He accepts the difference between an individual soul and the Supreme Soul also as natural. So, he treats the living and non-living entities in the same manner.]

तृतीयेऽपि पक्षे जीवब्रह्मणोर्भेदवदभेदस्य चाभ्युपगमात्तस्य च तद्द्वारात्सौभरिभेदवच्च स्वावतार -भेदवच्च सर्वस्येश्वरभेदतात्सर्वे जीवगता दोषास्तस्यैव स्युः । एतदुक्तं भवति । ईश्वरः स्वरूपेणैव सुरनरतिर्यक्स्थावरादिभेदेनावस्थित इति हि तदात्मकत्ववर्णनं क्रियते । तथा सत्येक -मृत्पिण्डारब्धघटशरावादिगतान्युदकाहरणादीनि सर्वकार्याणि यथा तस्यैव भवन्ति, एवं सर्वजीवगतसुखदुःखादि सर्वमीश्वरगतमेव स्यात् ॥

The third view (of Yadavaprakasha) also maintains that the individual self and Supreme Being are both really different and non-different. It says that the Supreme Being becomes the individual self. The situation is similar to that of sage Saubhari, said to have embodied several bodies simultaneously. It is also similar to differences among multiple incarnations of the Supreme Being. From this, it would follow that the imperfections of the individual self would only belong to the Supreme Being. The meaning of the above is this: This view maintains that the Supreme Being, itself, in his own essential nature, assumes different forms like those of deities, humans, animals, and plants as their souls. If this position is taken up, just as all actions, such as the holding of water, which pertain to jars, dishes, etc., made of a single lump of clay, belongs to clay itself, even so, all the pleasures and pains of all the embodied souls would pertain to Supreme Being himself.

[Ramanuja says the situation of difference and non-difference in the case of this view is similar to a yogi Saubhari assuming multiple bodies or a Supreme Being incarnating as various gods like Rama, Krishna, etc. Thus, the Supreme Being has intrinsically changed into everything living and non-living. Since the underlying (Supreme) soul is the same in all, all the problems associated with individual selves will also occur in the Supreme Being. This is inadmissible.]

[The Yadavaites suggest their counterargument for this.]

घटशरावादिसंस्थानानुपयुक्तमृद्द्रव्यं यथा कार्यान्तरान्वितमेवमेव सुरपशुमनुजादिजीवत्वानुपयु-क्तेश्वरः सर्वज्ञः सत्यसंकल्पत्वादिकल्याणगुणाकर इति चेत्सत्यं स एवेश्वर एकेनांशेन कल्याण-गुणगणाकरः स एवान्येनांशेन हेयगुणाकर इत्युक्तम् । द्वयोरंशयोरीश्वराविशेषात् । द्वंशौ व्यवस्थितविति चेत् । कस्तेन लाभः । एकस्यैवानेकांशेन नित्यदुःखित्वादंशान्तरेण सुखित्वमपि नेश्वरत्वाय कल्पते । यथा देवदत्तस्यैकस्मिन् हस्ते चन्दनपङ्कानुलेपकेयूरकटकाङ्गुलीयालंका-रस्तस्यैवान्यस्मिन् हस्ते मुद्राभिघातः कालानलज्वालानुप्रवेशश्च तद्वद्देवेश्वरस्य स्यादिति ब्रह्मा-ज्ञानपक्षादपि पापीयानयं भेदाभेदपक्षः । अपरिमितदुःखस्य पारमार्थिकत्वात्संसारिणामनन्त-त्वेन दुस्तरत्वाच्च ॥

(The followers of Yadavaprakasha) might argue: "That part of the clay which has not been used for making of jars, dishes, etc., is not associated with the effect of any action (like the holding of water). In the same way, that part of the Supreme Being, which is not involved in the formation of such individual souls as deities, beasts, and humans, is the abode of omniscience, omnipotence, and other such auspicious qualities".

Reply – Even if we accept it, it would imply that one part of the Supreme Being has an abundance of auspicious qualities, while another part is full of imperfections since both have the quality of being Supreme Being.

They might reply, "The two parts are distinguished or differentiated from each other. If the Supreme Being is positioned in two such parts, what is the problem?"

Reply - We ask, "What do you gain by it? It is not suitable for the Supreme Being to be eternally miserable in one part, and be happy in another part. It is like Devadatta, having one arm smeared with sandal paste and adorned with a bracelet, armlet, and ring, while the other arm of the same (Devadatta) is beaten with a wooden mortar and put into the flames of an all-consuming fire. That would be the condition of the Supreme Being. This deduction of your view (Bhedabheda) is even more blasphemous than the non-dualistic view that the Supreme Being is associated with ignorance, for, according to you, this unbounded suffering is real (and not illusory as in non-duality) and insurmountable as individual souls are innumerable (and not single as in non-duality).

[Even if, they suggest various parts in Supreme Being, they cannot remove the presence of afflictions in Supreme Being.]

[If they further claim that the Supreme Being is distinguished from its parts, they have come within the scope of our viewpoint.]

तस्माद्द्विलक्षणोऽयं जीवांश इति चेत् । आगतोऽसि तर्हि मदीयं पन्थानम् । ईश्वरस्य स्वरूपेण तादात्म्यवर्णने स्यादयं दोषः । आत्मशरीरभावेन तु तादात्म्यप्रतिपादने न कश्चिद्दोषः । प्रत्युत निखिलभुवननियमनादिर्महानयं गुणगणः प्रतिपादितो भवति । सामानाधिकरण्यं च मुख्यवृत्तम् ॥

If the Yadavaprakasha school says, "Therefore we hold that this part, namely, the individual self, is different in nature from Supreme Being", they will have come to our way (of thinking). The objection pointed out (so far) will arise only if it is held that the Supreme Being himself (intrinsically) changes into the individual soul and is identical to it. If, like us, they say that the relationship between the

Supreme Being and the individual soul is that between the soul and the body, there cannot be any such objection. In fact, far from there being any objection, a number of great qualities like the control of all individual souls by the Supreme Being will be explained. Here, the Supreme Being becomes the common basis of all auspicious attributes and everything follows in a direct way.

[Ramanuja says that if they assume the Supreme Being is distinguished from an individual soul, Yadavaites have to describe the relationship between them as well. According to the scriptures, it cannot be different from the soul and body relationship. This is identical to what we say.]

[Now, Ramanuja points out the error in their reasoning.]

अपि चैकस्य वस्तुनो भिन्नाभिन्नत्वं विरुद्धत्वान्न संभवतीत्युक्तम् । घटस्य पटाद्भिन्नत्वे सति तस्य तस्मिन्नभावः । अभिन्नत्वे सति तस्य च भाव इति । एकस्मिन् काले चैकस्मिन् देशे चैकस्य हि पदार्थस्य युगपत्सद्भावावोऽसद्भावावश्च विरुद्धः ॥

Moreover, it is already stated that an entity cannot be both different and nondifferent (from another) as it would be a contradiction. If a jar is different from a piece of cloth, the jar cannot exist in the cloth. If two entities are not different from each other, one is present in another and vice versa. The existence and the non-existence of the same object at the same time and place contradict each other.

[According to Ramanuja, this view suffers from logical inconsistency. This is obvious to all.]

[Now, Yadavaites defend their position with an example. Two cows, one without horns and the other with broken horns are the same if we look at their species, but they are different if we see them as individual living entities. Ramanuja says if they define equality in this way, they have to show difference and non-difference between species and individuals also.]

जात्यात्मना भावो व्यक्त्यात्मना चाभाव इति चेत् । जातेर्मुण्डेन चाभावे सति खण्डे मुण्डस्यापि सद्भावप्रसङ्गः । खण्डेन च जातेरभिन्नत्वे सद्भावो भिन्नत्वे चासद्भावः अश्वे महिषत्वस्यैवेति विरोधो दुष्परिहर एव । जात्यादेर्वस्तुसंस्थानतया वस्तुनः प्रकारत्वात्प्रकारप्रका -रिणोश्च पदार्थान्तरत्वं प्रकारस्य पृथक्सिद्ध्यनर्हत्वं पृथगनुपलम्भश्च तस्य च संस्थानस्य चानेक- वस्तुषु प्रकारतयावस्थितश्चेत्यादि पूर्वमुक्तम् ॥

The Bhedabheda schools might say, "As a species, two cows might be the same but as individual living beings they are different."

Reply – If the species is stated to be not different from the individual, it would follow that in the cow with broken horns, the cow without horns would be present for both of them belong to the same species 'cow'. (We are equating two objects as they belong to the same species.) This would be against reason. If the species is held as both different and non-different from the individual, owing to non-difference, the species (cowness) should be present in the cow with broken horns, and owing to its difference with the other cow, it would not be present in it, in the same way as buffaloes is not present in a horse. Such contradictions would be difficult to address in this view.

The species is really a mode (type) or attribute of an object, being the common configuration of the object. The mode or attribute of an object is different from the object possessing the attribute. It has already been stated that the attribute is inseparable from the object possessing it and incapable of being apprehended apart from the object. Moreover, such a configuration is present as an attribute in several objects.

[The right view is that species and individuals do not exist separately. The individual has certain essential characteristics that define them as belonging to a specific species.]

[Ramanuja explains how equality among objects should be interpreted.]

सोऽयमिति बुद्धिः प्रकारैक्यादयमपि दण्डीति बुद्धिमत् । अयं च जात्यादिप्रकारो वस्तुनो भेद इत्युच्यते । तद्योग एव वस्तुनो भिन्नमिति व्यवहारहेतुरित्यर्थः । स च वस्तुनो भेदव्यवहारहेतुः स्वस्य च संवेदनवत् । यथा संवेदनं वस्तुनो व्यवहारहेतुः स्वस्य व्यवहारहेतुश्च भवति ॥

The idea "This person is the same as seen before" arises from the commonality of attributes in both perceptions. When we say, "This man, too, has a stick", it means though this person and stick are different from the previously seen person with a stick, they share some common attributes. It is these common attributes or differentiating features that define its species. The association with these differentiating features is the cause of the object being considered as different (from others). Just as knowledge makes other objects known as well as itself, these differentiating features, which define a species, make an object known as well as its difference from other objects.

[It is through differentiating features of an object, we assess its similarity or difference from other objects. When one sees a cow for the first time, along with the cow, these different features are also perceived by his mind.]

[If someone says that one perceives just the existence of an object and not the differentiating features, it is not acceptable due to its conflict with sense perception.]

अत एव सन्मात्रग्राहि प्रत्यक्षं न भेदग्राहीत्यादिवादा निरस्ताः । जात्यादिसंस्थानसंस्थितस्यैव
वस्तुनः प्रत्यक्षेण गृहीतत्वात्तस्यैव संस्थानरूपजात्यादेः प्रतियोग्यपेक्षया भेदव्यवहारहेतुत्वाच्च ।
स्वरूपपरिणामदोषश्च पूर्वमेवोक्तः ॥

This argument also refutes the contention that sense perception
apprehends mere existence and not differentiating features. For
perception to apprehend the object, its species possesses its
specific configuration (distinctive feature). It is this distinctive
feature that reveals the object having a particular species and its
differences from other objects. The objection to the view that the
Supreme Being intrinsically modifies into non-sentient beings has
already been dealt with.

[This ends the refutation of the rival systems of philosophy.]

Description of Vishishta Advaita Philosophy

[After showing the inconsistency in other prevalent views of his time, Ramanuja now gives a detailed explanation of Vishishta-Advaita or distinguished non-duality. First, he lists those statements from the Upanishads, which are the basis of the core principles in his philosophy.]

'यः पृथिव्यां तिष्ठन् पृथिव्या अन्तरो यं पृथिवी न वेद यस्य पृथिवी शरीरं यः पृथिवीमन्तरो यमयति एष त आत्मान्तर्याम्यमृतः ।' (बृ० उ० ५/७/३), 'य आत्मनि तिष्ठन्नात्मनोऽन्तरो य आत्मा न वेद यस्यात्मा शरीरं य आत्मानमन्तरो यमयति एष त आत्मान्तर्याम्यमृतः ।' (बृ० उ० ५/७/२६), 'यः पृथिवीमन्तरे संचरन् यस्य पृथिवी शरीरं यं पृथिवी न वेद' (सु० उ० ७) इत्यादि । 'योऽक्षरमन्तरे संचरन् यस्याक्षरं शरीरमक्षरं न वेद यो मृत्युमन्तरे संचरन् यस्य मृत्युः शरीरं यं मृत्युर्न वेद एष सर्वभूतान्तरात्मापहतपाप्मा दिव्यो देव एको नारायणः ।' (सु० उ० ७), 'द्वा सुपर्णा सयुजा सखाया समानं वृक्षं परिषस्वजाते । तयोरन्यः पिप्पलं स्वाद्वत्त्यनश्नन्नन्योऽभि- चाकशीति ॥' (मु० उ० ३/१/१), 'अन्तः प्रविष्टः शास्ता जनानां सर्वात्मा ।' (तै० आ० ३/११/३), 'तत्सृष्ट्वा तदेवानुप्राविशत् । तदनुप्रविश्य सच्च त्यच्चाभवत्' (तै० उ० आन० ६/२-३), 'सत्यं चानृतं च सत्यमभवत् ।' (तै० उ० आन० ६/३), 'अनेन जीवेनात्मना' (छा० उ० ६/३/२) इत्यादि । 'पृथगात्मानं प्रेरितारं च मत्वा जुष्टस्ततस्तेनामृतत्वमेति ।' (श्वे० उ० १/६), 'भोक्ता भोग्यं प्रेरितारं च मत्वा सर्वं प्रोक्तं त्रिविधं ब्रह्ममेतत् ।' (श्वे० उ० १/१२), 'नित्यो नित्यानां चेतनश्चेतनानामेको बहूनां यो विदधाति कामान् ।' (क० उ० २/५/१३), 'प्रधानक्षेत्रज्ञपतिर्गुणेशः ।', 'ज्ञाज्ञौ द्वावजावीशनीशौ' (श्वे० उ० १/९) इत्यादिश्रुतिशतैस्तदुप- बृंहणैः ।

"He who dwells in the earth and is intrinsic to earth, which the earth is not aware of; the earth is whose body and who controls the earth from within - He is your soul, the inner-controller, who is immortal". (Brihadaranyaka Upanishad 5/7/3, Kanva recension) "He who dwells in the soul and who is intrinsic to the soul, whom the soul is not aware of, the soul is whose body and who controls the soul from within - He is your soul, the inner controller, who is immortal". (Brihadaranyaka Upanishad 5/7/26, Madhyandina recension)

"He who accompanies the earth, to whom the earth is the body, and whom the earth is not aware of" and etc. (Subala Upanishad 7) "He who accompanies the imperishable soul, to whom the soul is the body, and whom the soul is not aware of. He who accompanies Death, to whom Death is the body, and whom Death is not aware of; he is the inner soul of all beings and is untouched by (their) imperfections. He is the supreme Deity, Narayana, who is without a second". (Subala Upanishad 7)

"Two birds with beautiful wings, similar qualities, and mutually attached to each other rest on the same Pipal (holy fig) tree. One of them (the individual self) eats the ripe fruit, while the other (the Supreme Self) shines without eating it". (Mundaka Upanishad 3/1/1)

"He has entered within all beings and controls them (from within). He is the soul of all. (Taittiriya Aranyaka 3/11/3) "He created it all; having created it, He entered into it; having entered into it, He became the individual self which remains ever the same without any change, and also the non-sentient, which is subject to change. Though He became the sentient (living) and the insentient (non-living), He never changes is always the unchanging truth". (Taittiriya Upanishad 2/6/2-3)

"I will enter with the individual living being as his soul and will create the various forms and give them their names". (Chhandogya Upinishad 6/3/2). "The individual self realizes that the Supreme Self directs him (in the wheel of the world) and that he is different from the Supreme Self that directs him. By winning the grace of the Supreme Self thereby, he attains immortality." (Shvetashvatara Upanishad 1/6). "Having realized the one, who experiences (pleasures and pains), the object of experience and Him who directs all, I have described to you the three-fold nature of things". (Shvetashvatara Upanishad 1/12) "The Eternal of the Eternals, the Soul of all souls, He who fulfills the desires of many, is himself single". (Katha Upanishad (2/5/13). "He is the Lord of matter and souls and the qualities". "He (Supreme Self), whose knowledge has no limits and he (individual self) whose knowledge is limited, they are the Ruler and the Ruled". (Svetasvetara Upanishad 6/33 & 1/17) From hundreds of such texts in the Upanishad and also, by their explanations such as the following-

[Brihadaranyaka and Subala Upanishad mention that the Supreme Being is the inner soul of the earth, etc. the non-living entities as well as the soul individual selves or living entities. He is their controller and is devoid of any imperfections. He is non-dual.

Mundaka Upanishad says that he is untouched by the actions or their results. Taittiriya Upanishad and Aranyaka, in addition, say that he has created this world and entered into it as its soul. Chhandogya Upanishad says that he classified this world into various names and forms by becoming the soul of all.

Shvetashvatara Upanishad says that there are three types of fundamental entities in this world – Supreme Being, Individual souls, and insentient nature. The Supreme Being lords over the other two. An individual soul can attain the Supreme Being through his grace after serving him.

Katha Upanishad says that there are many individual souls (not just one), and so on.]

[Now, Ramanuja points out other scriptures in whose light or accordance, he interprets the statements of the Upanishads.]

'जगत्सर्वं शरीरं ते स्थैर्यं ते वसुधातलम् ॥' (वा० रा० ६/१२६/१६), 'यत्किंचित्सृज्यते येन सत्त्वजातेन वै द्विज । तस्य सृज्यस्य संभूतौ तत्सर्वं वै हरेस्तनुः ॥' (वि० पु० १/२२/३८), 'अहमात्मा गुडाकेश सर्वभूताशयस्थितः ॥' (गीता १०/१०), 'सर्वस्य चाहं हृदि संनिविष्टो मत्तः स्मृतिर्ज्ञानमपोहनं च ॥' (गीता १५/१५) इत्यादिवेदविदग्रेसरवाल्मीकिपराशरद्वैपायनवचोभिश्च परस्य ब्रह्मणः सर्वस्यात्मत्वावगमाच्चिदचिदात्मकस्य वस्तुनस्तच्छरीरत्वावगमाच्च शरीरस्य शरीरिणं प्रति प्रकारतयैव पदार्थत्वाच्छरीरशरीरिणोश्च धर्मभेदेऽपि तयोरसंकरात्सर्वशरीरं ब्रह्मेति

ब्रह्मणो वैभवं प्रतिपादयद्भिः सामानाधिकरण्यादिभिर्मुख्यवृत्तै: सर्वचेतनाचेतनप्रकारं ब्रह्मैवाभि-
धीयते । सामानाधिकरण्यं हि द्वयो: पदयो: प्रकारद्वयमुखेनैकार्थनिष्ठत्वम् । तस्य चैतस्मिन् पक्षे
मुख्यता । तथा हि तत्त्वमिति सामानाधिकरण्ये तदित्यनेन जगत्कारणं सर्वकल्याणगुणगणाकरं
निरवद्यं ब्रह्मोच्यते । त्वमिति च चेतनसामानाधिकरण्यवृत्तेन जीवान्तर्यामिनिरूपि तच्छरीरं तदात्म
-तयावस्थितं तत्प्रकारं ब्रह्मोच्यते । इतरेषु पक्षेषु सामानाधिकरण्यहानिर्ब्रह्मण: सदेषता च स्यात्
॥

"The whole world is your body; the stability of the earth is
dependent on you". Ramayana 6/126/16)

"Whatever is created by whomsoever it may be, Hari is the cause of
it all and everyone (of these creations) is His body". (Vishnu Purana
1/22/38

"I am, O Arjuna, the soul of all beings and abide within their hearts. I
am seated in the heart of everyone. From me arise memory,
perception, and their loss as well." (Gita 10/10);

From these and other such utterances of Valmiki, Parashara, and
Vyasa, who are the foremost in those who know the real meaning of
the Vedas, we learn that the Supreme Being is the soul of all and
that everything, sentient and non-sentient, is His body. The body is
the inseparable attribute of the soul, which owns the body; it is,
therefore, its type (mode). Therefore, the word denoting the body
denotes also the soul whose mode the body is. Since the body and
the soul have different attributes, the two do not get mixed up with
each other. Since the Supreme Being has everything as its body, all
of them reveal his magnificence as their common basis
(samanadhikarana). When interpreted like this, all sentient and non-
sentient objects refer to the Supreme Being as his mode in a
principal and direct manner.

Common basis (Samana-adhikarana) is said to be present when two
words refer to the same object in two different ways and this
coordination into an object follows directly in our interpretation. It
also has primary significance in our view. Thus, we can explain the

presence of the common basis in the statement "you are that", using our view. 'That' refers to the Supreme Being the (material) cause of the world, the abode of all auspicious qualities, (the one) who is free from all imperfections. The word 'you' refers to the Inner Ruler within the individual self as its common basis, who has the individual self as His body, who is its soul, and who has the individual self as His mode or inseparable attribute. In the interpretations of other systems, there exists no such (direct) interpretation of the Supreme Being as a common basis. Thus, they also associate the Supreme Being with faults or imperfections.

[Valmiki Ramayana, Vishnu Purana, and Gita show that the relation between an individual soul and the Supreme Being is similar to that of a body and a soul. What is the meaning of this statement? Even though our bodies change, our souls do not. Similarly, individual souls might come under ignorance, accept various bodies, and ultimately be liberated but the underlying Supreme Being does not undergo any change.

Now, let us talk about the most important concept 'common basis (samana-adhikarana) in Ramanuja philosophy. Suppose we see a beautiful rose and describe it as 'a red, scented flower'. Here, we have used two different adjectives 'red' and 'scented' to describe a single flower. These two adjectives depict two entirely different properties of the flower. However, both adjectives point to a single rose. We say that the basis of these two properties is a common rose. So, rose is a common basis of various attributes. Similarly, in the case of the Supreme Being, we ascribe to it various attributes like omniscient, almighty, creator, inner-controller, etc in various contexts; all of these attributes refer to a single Supreme Being.

When we refer to a person by a name, this name refers to his body as well as to his soul. This is done almost all the time, though unconsciously. We can say that the body is a mode (type, attribute) of a soul so we identify them together, or interchangeably.

However, it becomes clear from the context whether the body is being referred to or the soul. A similar relationship exists between an individual soul and the Supreme Being. Hence, a common word such as soul, Brahman, self, etc. can be used for both of them. However, we need to identify the correct referrer by the context, without contradicting the statements of the other Upanishads.

This grand unification of all scriptures, without any underlying inconsistency, is one of the greatest hallmarks of Ramanuja philosophy.]

[Now, Ramanuja summarizes the import of all scriptures to describe the characteristics of the Supreme Being.]

एतदुक्तं भवति । ब्रह्मैवमवस्थितमित्यत्रैवंशब्दार्थभूतप्रकारतयैव विचित्रचेतनाचेतनात्मक-
प्रपञ्चस्य स्थूलस्य सूक्ष्मस्य च सद्भावः । तथा च बहु स्यां प्रजायेयेत्ययमर्थः संपन्नो भवति ।
तस्यैवेश्वरस्य कार्यतया कारणतया च नानासंस्थानसंस्थितस्य संस्थानतया चिदचिद्वस्तुजातम-
वस्थितमिति ॥

This interpretation means this: (When the Upanishads, etc. say) the Supreme Being exists thus (in this world), it means that the Supreme Being exists as all sentient (living) and non-sentient (non-living) beings either in their subtle or gross forms. Only then can the text "I will become the many" have any real meaning. Therefore, it follows that all sentient and non-sentient beings exist as various configurations or inseparable attributes of the Supreme Being, who is their cause and they are his effect (products).

[Supreme Being has created this world of living and non-living entities from within; earlier all this world was in a subtle form within him, and he manifested it in its current form. He remains within all as their inner souls and all entities are his type.]

[After describing his views broadly, Ramanuja, now, addresses the common doubts on it. The first one is how can we refer to an individual soul as a type of Supreme Being.]

ननु च संस्थानरूपेण प्रकारतयैवंशब्दार्थत्वं जातिगुणयोरेव दृष्टं न द्रव्यस्य । स्वतन्त्रसिद्धियोग्य-स्य पदार्थस्यैवंशब्दार्थतयेश्वरस्य प्रकारमात्रत्वमयुक्तम् । उच्यते द्रव्यस्यापि दण्डकुण्डलादेर्द्रव्या -न्तरप्रकारत्वं दृष्टमेव । ननु च दण्डादेः स्वतन्त्रस्य द्रव्यान्तरप्रकारत्वे मत्वर्थीयप्रत्ययो दृष्टः । यथा दण्डी कुण्डलीति । अतो गोत्वादितुल्यतया चेतनाचेतनस्य द्रव्यभूतस्य वस्तुन ईश्वरप्रकार-तया सामानाधिकरण्येन प्रतिपादनं न युज्यते । अत्रोच्यते गौरश्वो मनुष्यो देव इति भूतसंघात-रूपाणां द्रव्याणामेव देवदत्तो मनुष्यो जातः पुण्यविशेषेण, यज्ञदत्तो गौर्जातः पापेन, अन्यश्चेतनः पुण्यातिरेकेण देवो जात इत्यादिदेवादिशरीराणां चेतनप्रकारतया लोकवेदयोः सामानाधिकर-ण्येन प्रतिपादनं दृष्टम् ॥

An objection might arise that only the species and the qualities of an entity and not the entity itself are usually seen as modes of another object. An entity that can exist by itself (independent of others) cannot rightly be considered as an attribute or mode of Supreme Being.

Well, the reply is as follows: Even substances like the stick and the ear-ring are often seen as attributes of another substance (say, a man, when we speak of a man with a stick or with an ear-ring).

But this answer might be said to be unsatisfactory, and the objector might say, "When one substance, such as stick and ear-ring, which can also have an independent existence, is an attribute of another substance, we (invariably) speak of that other substance possessing the substance and do not speak of it as a common basis for the first substance. For example, we speak of Devadatta possessing a stick and not Devadatta as being a stick. Therefore, it will not be proper to consider substances like sentient and nonsentient beings as being similar to species like 'cowness' and speak of them as modes or attributes of the Supreme Being so the terms standing for them cannot signify the Supreme Being.

The reply to this objection is as follows: The words 'cow', 'horse', 'man', 'deity', etc. denote the respective bodies, which are substances built up of non-sentient matter. And yet it is often said, "Devadatta was born as a man owing to certain meritorious actions (in his past life)". "Yagnadatta was born as a cow owing to sinful actions". "Another sentient being was born as a deity owing to meritorious deeds of a superior character". In all these instances, the bodies of these, men, deities, etc. are used as modes or attributes of the individual souls. Thus, the individual souls are the common basis of the substances (namely, the five elements that build up the body) as Devadatta is a man', Yagnadatta is a cow, etc. This coordination is quite common in (ordinary interaction) and the Vedas.

[Till here, Ramanuja has shown that soul and body are used interchangeably in worldly interaction as well as Vedas.]

[Now, he extends this similarity to Supreme Being and other entities.]

अयमर्थः - जातिर्वा गुणो वा द्रव्यं वा न तत्रादरः । कंचन द्रव्यविशेषं प्रति विशेषणतयैव यस्य सद्भावस्तस्य तदपृथक्सिद्धेस्तत्प्रकारतया तत्सामानाधिकरण्येन प्रतिपादनं युक्तम् । यस्य पुनर्द्रव्यस्य पृथक्सिद्धस्यैव कदाचित्क्वचिद्द्रव्यान्तरप्रकारत्वमिष्यते तत्र मत्वर्थीयप्रत्यय इति विशेषः । एवमेव स्थावरजङ्गमात्मकस्य सर्वस्य वस्तुन ईश्वरशरीरत्वेन तत्प्रकारतयैव स्वरूप-सद्भाव इति । तत्प्रकारीश्वर एव तत्तच्छब्देनाभिधीयत इति तत्सामानाधिकरण्येन प्रतिपादनं युक्तम् । तदेवैतत्सर्वं पूर्वमेव नामरूपव्याकरणश्रुतिविवरणे प्रपञ्चितम् ॥

The meaning is as follows: It does not matter whether it is a species, a quality, or a substance. When any of them exists as an inseparable attribute of a particular substance, they might signify that other substance. But, if a substance that can stand independently by itself, is considered at any time and in any place as an attribute or of another substance, then they cannot signify that other substances and usage will require "being with" or 'possessing" as "Davadatta is with a stick" and not "Devadatta is a stick". In the same way, all objects, either moving or non-moving, being the body of the Supreme Being, can exist only as inseparable attributes of His. Therefore, the Supreme Being who has them as His inseparable attributes is referred to also by the respective words denoting them in a primary sense as their common basis. All this has been explained at length during the explanation of the Vedic text related to the creation of names and forms.

[The crux of the matter is if two entities are inseparable, then we can refer them interchangeably. If a man holds a stick, it can exist separately from him, so a stick is not a type of a man. However, as long as the body is not separate from the soul, we can refer to them interchangeably.]

[Since the Supreme Being is the inner soul of all living and non-living entities of the world at all times, nothing is inseparable from him. Hence, we can refer to all entities as his type.]

अतः प्रकृतिपुरुषमहदहंकारतन्मात्रभूतेन्द्रियतदारब्धचतुर्दशभुवनात्मकब्रह्माण्डतदन्तर्वर्तिदेव-तिर्यङ्मनुष्यस्थावरादिसर्वप्रकारसंस्थानसंस्थितं कार्यमपि सर्वं ब्रह्मैवेति कारणभूतब्रह्मविज्ञाना-देव सर्वं विज्ञातं भवतीत्येकविज्ञानेन सर्वविज्ञानमुपपन्नतरम् । तदेवं कार्यकारणभावादिमुखेन कृत्स्नस्य चिदचिद्वस्तुनः परब्रह्मप्रकारतया तदात्मकत्वमुक्तम् ॥

Therefore, the self or soul, nature, cosmic intellect, ego, the five tanmatras, the five fundamental elements (earth, water. fire, air, and sky), and the eleven senses, are the twenty-five entities that make up the fourteen worlds of the universe. This universe consists of various types of deities, animals, birds, humans, and nonmoving things like plants. All these are inseparable attributes of the Supreme Being. These are all effects of the Supreme Being. Hence, when Supreme Being, their ultimate (material) cause is known, everything becomes known; "by the knowledge of one, all become known", says the Upanishad. So it has been declared (by the Upanishad) that the Supreme Being is the soul of all sentient and non-sentient entities, which are His attributes because He is their (material) cause and they are the effects.

[Since the Supreme Being is the material cause of all entities, they cannot be separated from it and hence, there is no issue with their common reference.]

[Some might raise another doubt; since the Supreme Being is said as the material cause of the world, it would mean that the Supreme Being itself evolves into nature and the individual souls. This implies that the Supreme Being will incur defects.]

ननु च परस्य ब्रह्मण: स्वरूपेण परिणामास्पदत्वं निर्विकारत्वनिरवद्यत्वश्रुतिव्याकोपप्रसङ्गेन निवारितम् । 'प्रकृतिश्च प्रतिज्ञादृष्टान्तानुपरोधात्' (ब्र॰ सू॰ १/४/२३) इत्येकविज्ञानेन सर्व-विज्ञानप्रतिज्ञानमृत्तत्कार्यदृष्टान्ताभ्यां परमपुरुषस्य जगदुपादानकारणत्वं च प्रतिपादितम् । उपादानकारणत्वं च परिणामास्पदत्वमेव । कथमिदमुपपद्यते ?

You have ruled out the possibility of the Supreme Being intrinsically evolving (in the form of the world) on the ground that it would be against the Vedic texts which declare that the Supreme Being is not subject to any change and that it is free from imperfections. But, Brahma Sutra 1/4/23 states that the Supreme Being is also the material cause (of the world), and cites the illustrative example (clay and its effect jar, etc.). If the Supreme Self is the material cause of the world, only then by his knowledge of him, all other things become known. Whatever is the material cause of the world must change. How can you resolve this inconsistency of change in Supreme Being?"

[The central point of the doubt is that an entity that undergoes changes cannot be the Supreme Being as it is declared to be changeless.]

[Ramanuja gives his interpretation to address this doubt in the next few paragraphs.]

अत्रोच्यते - सजीवस्य प्रपञ्चस्याविशेषेण कारणत्वमुक्तम् । तत्रेश्वरस्य जीवरूपपरिणामाभ्युप-गमेन 'नात्मा श्रुतेर्नित्यत्वाच्च ताभ्यः' (ब्र० सू० २/३/१८) इति विरुध्यते । वैषम्यनैर्घृण्यपरि-हारश्च जीवानामनादित्वाभ्युपगमेन तत्कर्मनिमित्ततया प्रतिपादितः 'वैषम्यनैर्घृण्ये न सापेक्ष-त्वात्' (ब्र० सू० २/१/३४), 'न कर्मविभागादिति चेन्न अनादित्वादुपपद्यते चाप्युपलभ्यते च' (ब्र० सू० २/१/३५) इत्यकृताभ्यागमकृतविप्रणाशप्रसङ्गश्चानित्यत्वेऽभिहितः ॥

The answer to this is as follows: The Upanishad says that the Supreme Being is the (material) cause of the insentient world including the individual selves (living beings) without any exception. (When this is so), if someone says that the Supreme Being evolves into the form of the individual selves it would be in conflict with the Brahma Sutra (2/3/18) which says: "The soul is not created because it is denied by the Upanishads as they proclaim that the soul is eternal."

Further, the Supreme Self is declared to be free from partiality and cruelty in its dealings with the different individual selves in Brahma Sutra 2/1/34 in these words: "Supreme Self is neither partial nor cruel, in the creation of individual selves as it is in accordance with their past actions." Just like the beginningless nature of the individual selves, their actions are also beginningless and are the reason (for the inequalities seen among different living beings and the cruel suffering which some are subjected to). Vyasa raises a possible objection to this and answers it in Brahma Sutra 2/1/35 thus: "If you object to the existence of actions before creation as there is no division (of Supreme Being into individual selves), the answer is "because the individual selves have no beginning, they exist even before creation. However, this existence is without any distinction from the Supreme Self (in an unmanifested form). If you accept the beginning of the individual self, it would imply that he enjoys the fruit of what was not done by him. And, since you have accepted his beginning, you have to accept his end also. This would imply the destruction of the results of his actions without experiencing them. So, you have to accept the individual self as eternal."

[Here, Ramanuja first shows that all individual souls are eternal i.e. they always exist. Even before the explicit creation of the world, they exist in the Supreme Being though not distinctly visible. It is as per the statements of the Upanishads. Like their existence, their actions and their results are also without a beginning. If we do not accept it, we have to accept that an individual has to experience the results of actions during its association with a body, which it has not done. Likewise, after death, if actions and their effects do not remain, then it is possible that the soul has not experienced the results of some of its actions.]

[Now, Ramanuja says that nature is also without a beginning. He shows various references for it.]

तथा प्रकृतेरप्यनादिता श्रुतिभिः प्रतिपादिता – 'अजामेकां लोहितशुक्लकृष्णां बह्वीं प्रजां जनयन्तीं सरूपाम् । अजो ह्येको जुषमाणोऽनुशेते जहात्येनां भुक्तभोगामजोऽन्यः ॥' (श्वे॰ उ॰ ४/५) इति प्रकृतिपुरुषयोरजत्वं दर्शयति । 'अस्मान्मायी सृजते विश्वमेतत्तस्मिंश्चान्यो मायया संनिरुद्धः ।' (श्वे॰ उ॰ ४/९), मायां तु प्रकृतिं विद्यान्मायिनं तु महेश्वरम्' (श्वे॰ उ॰ ४/१०) इति प्रकृतिरेव स्वरूपेण विकारास्पदमिति च दर्शयति । 'गौरनाद्यन्तवती सा जनित्री भूतभाविनी' (मन्त्रिक उ॰ ५) इति च । स्मृतिश्च भवति – 'प्रकृतिं पुरुषं चैव विद्ध्यनादी उभावपि । विकारांश्च गुणांश्चैव विद्धि प्रकृतिसंभवान् ॥' (गीता १३/१९), 'भूमिरापोऽनलो वायुः खं मनो बुद्धिरेव च । अहंकार इतीयं मे भिन्ना प्रकृतिरष्टधा ॥ अपरेयमितस्त्वन्यां प्रकृतिं विद्धि मे पराम् । जीवभूतां

महाबाहो ययेदं धार्यते जगत् ॥' (गीता ७/४-५), 'प्रकृतिं स्वामवष्टभ्य विसृजामि पुनः पुनः ।
(गीता ९/८), 'मयाध्यक्षेण प्रकृतिः सूयते सचराचरम् ॥' (गीता ९/१०) इत्यादिका ॥

Just as the individual self is without any beginning, nature (matter) also is declared by the Upanishads to be without a beginning. That nature and the individual self were not created is also brought out in the following Vedic text:-

"A certain entity, nature, which has no beginning produces many things of the same type (namely, things constituted of the five fundamental elements) and is red, white, and black (i. e. it has the colors, respectively, of the elements, fire, water, and earth). Another entity, the individual self, which has no beginning, imagines (in ignorance) that it is the same as the other (viz., nature) and follows its ways. Another being, also without beginning (a wise person), enjoys it (i. e. nature for a short time) and then abandons it (in disgust). Shvetashvatara Upanishad 4/5

Another Upanishadic statement also shows that only nature is subject to change in essential characteristics. "The one (Supreme Being) who controls nature creates the world out of it; another (the individual self) is bound by nature (Maya)". "It should be known that nature (with its three qualities, sattva, rajas, and tamas) is Maya and that He who controls nature is Supreme Being". Shvetashvatara Upanishad 4/9-10.

"Nature, which has neither beginning nor end, like a cow, produces (fire, water, and earth) and creates also the world." - Mantrika Upanishad 5

Smriti text (Bhagavad Gita) also states that only nature evolves into the world: "Know that nature and the individual self (which are associated with each other) are both without a beginning. – Gita 13/19

"Earth, water, fire, air, space (sky), the mind, cosmic intellect, and ego these eight forms of nature are mine. Know also that there is another nature (splendor) of mine different from this inferior nature. It is of the nature of the individual self and is superior. O Arjun, by it (the individual self), the world of matter (nature) is supported". – Gita 7/4-5

"I create the world again and again by evolving my nature (of eight forms)". – Gita 9/8

"Under my control, nature gives birth to this world consisting of moving and non-moving beings". - Gita 9/10, etc.

[These statements show that nature is also without a beginning. However, there is a small difference between individual soul and nature. An individual soul is eternal whereas the nature (and actions) associated with it (bondage) ends after its liberation. So, nature associated with an individual is without a beginning but it has an end. The cosmic form of nature remains for other individual souls which are not yet liberated.]

[Since both living and non-living entities remain as the body of the Supreme Being, before and after creation, they are inseparable from Him. Just as the body can change without any change in the underlying soul, the Supreme Being is also unchanged during changes in nature or individual selves.]

एवं च प्रकृतेरपीश्वरशरीरत्वात्प्रकृतिशब्दोऽपि तदात्मभूतस्येश्वरस्य तत्प्रकारसंस्थितस्य वाचकः । पुरुषशब्दोऽपि तदात्मभूतस्येश्वरस्य पुरुषप्रकारसंस्थितस्य वाचकः । अतस्तद्विकाराणामपि तथेश्वर एवात्मा । तदाह – 'व्यक्तं विष्णुस्तथाव्यक्तं पुरुषः काल एव च ।' (वि० पु० १/२/१८), 'स एव क्षोभको ब्रह्मन् क्षोभ्यश्च परमेश्वरः ॥' (वि० पु० १/२/३१) इति । अतः प्रकृतिप्रकार-संस्थिते परमात्मनि प्रकारभूतप्रकृत्यंशे विकारः प्रकार्यंशे चाविकारः । एवमेव जीवप्रकार-संस्थिते परमात्मनि च प्रकारभूतजीवांशे सर्वे चापुरुषार्थाः प्रकार्यंशो नियन्ता निरवद्यः सर्वकल्याणगुणाकरः सत्यसंकल्प एव ॥

Thus, nature is the body of the Supreme Being and therefore the word nature denotes (also) the Supreme Being, who is its soul and who has it as His mode or inseparable attribute. Similarly, the word individual self also denotes the Supreme Being who is its soul and who has the individual self as His mode. Hence, the Supreme Being is also the soul of the world constituted of the changes in the individual self and nature. So, the Vishnu Purana says:

"Vishnu (Supreme Being) is both the causal (subtle, invisible) reality and the reality which is called the effect (gross, visible). He is the individual self and also Time." Vishnu Purana 1/2/18

"He is the agitator (of the changes) as well as the agitated and he is the Supreme Ruler." Vishnu Purana 1/2/31

Hence, it is nature that is the mode or attribute of the Supreme Self who has it as His attribute - it is only this part or aspect that undergoes change. He who has nature as His mode does not undergo any change. In the same way, in the Supreme Self who has the individual self as His mode, it is only the individual self, the attributive part, that is subject to the ills of the world, whereas the Supreme Self is the controller, stainless and full of all auspicious qualities and His will is omnipotent.

[Since both living and non-living entities are the modes or attributes of the Supreme Being, they can change without causing any change in the Supreme Being. Just as a spider creates its web from within and withdraws it without any change in it, likewise, the Supreme Being also creates this world without undergoing any change or defect.]

[Thus, Ramanuja has demonstrated the changeless nature of the Supreme Being amidst all the changes. Now, he tells how creation takes place from its subtle or invisible (unmanifested) form to gross or visible (manifested) form.]

तथा च सति कारणावस्थ ईश्वर एवेति तदुपादानकजगत्कार्यावस्थोऽपि स एवेति कार्यकारणयो-
रनन्यत्वं सर्वश्रुत्यविरोधश्च भवति । तदेवं नामरूपविभागानर्हसूक्ष्मदशापन्नप्रकृतिपुरुषशरीरं
ब्रह्म कारणावस्थं, जगतस्तदापत्तिरेव च प्रलयः । नामरूपविभागविभक्तस्थूलचिदचिद्वस्तुशरीरं
ब्रह्म कार्यावस्थम्, ब्रह्मणस्तथाविधस्थूलभाव एव जगतः सृष्टिरित्युच्यते । यथोक्तं भगवता
पराशरेण – 'प्रधानपुंसोरजयोः कारणं कार्यभूतयोः ।' (वि० पु० १/९/३७) इति ॥

And, thus it follows that the Supreme Self, with the individual self
and nature as His attributes, is the cause and that He is, at the same
time, the effect (namely the world), which has the former as its
material cause. In this way, one can explain that the effect is none
other than the cause and all the Vedic texts would find
reconciliation. Thus, the Supreme Being in the causal state has
nature and individual self as His body, and they are then in such a
subtle condition that they cannot be distinguished by names and
forms. The passage of the world to this phase of existence is termed
dissolution. The state of the effect in the Supreme Being shows up
when the individual self and nature manifest in their gross
condition as His body, where they can be distinguished by names
and forms. The attainment of this gross condition by the Supreme
Being is called the creation of the world. So says Lord Parashara:
"Nature and individual self are both beginningless. Supreme Being is
both their cause and the effect". – Vishnu Purana 1/9/37

[Since all entities always exist, it is only their attaining a visible or
manifested form that is what we call creation. When these entities
become invisible or unmanifested, we say it to be their destruction
or dissolution. However, it is just a change of state from the
existential perspective. At all times, all entities remain as a mode of
Supreme Being. So, we can refer to them interchangeably.]

[One can ask what the primary meaning of a word, the object for
which it is used in worldly context or the Supreme Being is.]

तस्मादीश्वरप्रकारभूतसर्वावस्थप्रकृतिपुरुषवाचिनः शब्दास्तत्प्रकारविशिष्टतयावस्थिते परमात्म-
नि मुख्यतया वर्तन्ते । जीवात्मवाचिदेवमनुष्यशब्दवत् । यथा देवमनुष्यादिशब्दा देवमनुष्यादि-
प्रकृतिपरिणामविशेषाणां जीवात्मप्रकारतयैव पदार्थत्वात्प्रकारिणि जीवात्मनि मुख्यतया वर्तन्ते
। तस्मात्सर्वस्य चिदचिद्वस्तुनः परमात्मशरीरतया तत्प्रकारत्वात्परमात्मनि मुख्यतया वर्तन्ते सर्वे
वाचकाः शब्दाः ॥

Therefore, since all existing things are modes or attributes of the
Supreme Being, the words denoting nature and individual self in
whatever state they may be, denote, primarily, the Supreme self,
just as the words denoting the bodies of demi-god, human, etc.
primarily denote their individual selves. Words like 'demi-god' and
'human' denote the bodies of individual selves, which are specific
modifications of matter that denote, primarily, the individual souls,
since these bodies are only the modes or attributes of the the
individual souls. In the same way, all things, the sentient and the
non-sentient are the bodies of the Supreme Self, and are, therefore,
His modes or attributes and, for that reason, the words that denote
the sentient and the non-sentient entities denote (also) the
Supreme Self primarily.

[Since Suprme Being is the cause of all entities in their causal
(subtle) state as well as in their effect (gross) state, all words
primarily refer to the changeless Supreme Being. The entity
associated with a word in a worldly context is its secondary
meaning. It is the essence one talks about first.]

[Now, Ramanuja explains the soul and body relationship between
Supreme Being and individual souls.]

अयमेव चात्मशरीरभावः पृथक्सिद्ध्यनर्हाधाराधेयभावो नियन्तृनियाम्यभावः शेषशेषिभावश्च ।
सर्वात्मनाधारतया नियन्तृतया शेषितया च आप्नोतीत्यात्मा सर्वात्मनाधेयतया नियाम्यतया
शेषतया च अपृथक्सिद्धं प्रकारभूतमित्याकारः शरीरमिति चोच्यते । एवमेव हि जीवात्मनः
स्वशरीरसंबन्धः । एवमेव परमात्मनः सर्वशरीरत्वेन सर्वशब्दवाच्यत्वम् ॥

The relationship between the soul and the body is of the support and the supported, controller and the controlled, primary and secondary, in which the body is incapable of existing independently of the other (viz., the soul). The soul has its purposes fulfilled by the body and is therefore called primary and the body exists solely for fulfilling the purposes of the soul and is called secondary. The word soul (atma) means etymologically "that which obtains". It is so called because it obtains the body and acts as its support and as its directing agent, for the fulfillment of its own purposes. The body is a shape, being an inseparable attribute or mode (of the soul), as it is supported and controlled by the other and exists for the satisfaction of its purposes. It is this kind of relationship that exists between the individual self and its body. Similarly, the Supreme Self has all entities as His body and is therefore denoted by all words.

[Just as the body is completely dependent on the soul for its fulfillment in every sense, in the same way, an individual soul depends on the Supreme Being for its fulfillment. Serving the Supreme Being, through all actions, is its highest fulfillment.]

[Now, Ramanuja certifies this soul and body relationship between the Supreme Being and individual souls on the basis of scriptural evidence.]

तदाह श्रुतिगणः – ‘सर्वे वेदा यत्पदमामनन्ति’ (क० उ० २/१५), ‘सर्वे वेदा यत्रैकं भवन्ति’ (तै० आ० ३/११/१) इति । तस्यैकस्य वाच्यत्वादेकार्थवाचिनो भवन्तीत्यर्थः । ‘एको देवो बहुधा सन्निविष्टः’ (तै० आ० ३/१४/१), ‘सहैव सन्तं न विजानन्ति देवा’ इत्यादि । देवा इन्द्रियाणि । देवमनुष्यादीनामन्तर्यामितयात्मत्वेन निविश्य सहैव सन्तं तेषामिन्द्रियाणि मनःपर्यन्तानि न विजानन्तीत्यर्थः । तथा च पौराणिकानि वचांसि – ‘नताः स्म सर्ववचसां प्रतिष्ठा यत्र शाश्वती ।’ (वि० पु० १/१४/२३) वाच्ये हि वचसः प्रतिष्ठा । ‘कार्याणां कारणां पूर्वं वचसां वाच्यमुत्तमम् ।’ (जित० स्तो० ७/४), ‘वेदैश्च सर्वैरहमेव वेद्यः ।’ (गीता १५/१५) इत्यादीनि सर्वाणि हि वचांसि सशरीरात्मविशिष्टमन्तर्यामिणमेवाचक्षते । ‘हन्ताहमिमास्तिस्रो देवता अनेन जीवेनात्मानुप्रविश्य

नामरूपे व्याकरवाणि' (छा० उ० ६/३/२) इति हि श्रुतिः । तथा च मानवं वचः - 'प्रशासितारं सर्वेषामणीयांसमणीयसाम् रुक्माभं स्वप्नधीगम्यं विद्यात्तं पुरुषं परम् ॥' (म० स्मृ० १२/१२२) अन्तः प्रविश्यान्तर्यामितया सर्वेषां प्रशासितारं नियन्तारम् अणीयांस आत्मनः कृत्स्नस्याचेतन-स्य व्यापकतया सूक्ष्मभूतास्ते तेषामपि व्यापकत्वात्तेभ्योऽपि सूक्ष्मतर इत्यर्थः । रुक्माभः आदित्यवर्णः स्वप्नकल्पबुद्धिप्राप्यः, विशदतमप्रत्यक्षतापन्नानुध्यानैकलभ्य इत्यर्थः । 'एनमेके वदन्त्यग्निं मारुतोऽन्ये प्रजापतिम् । इन्द्रमेके परे प्रमाणमपरे ब्रह्म शाश्वतम् ॥' (म० स्मृ० १२/१२३) इति । एके वेदा इत्यर्थः । उत्तरीत्या परस्यैव ब्रह्मणः सर्वस्य प्रशासितृत्वेन सर्वान्तरात्मतया प्रविश्यावस्थितत्वादग्न्यादयः शब्दा अपि शाश्वतब्रह्मशब्दवत्तस्यैव वाचका भवन्तीत्यर्थः । तथा च स्मृत्यन्तरम् - 'ये यजन्ति पितृन् देवान् ब्राह्मणान् सहुताशनान् । सर्वभूतान्तरात्मानं विष्णुमेव यजन्ति ते ॥' (दक्ष स्मृ०) इति । पितृदेवब्राह्मणहुताशनादिशब्दा-स्तन्मुखेन तदन्तरात्मभूतस्य विष्णोरेव वाचका इत्युक्तं भवति ॥

Many Vedic texts declare this truth: "All the Vedas point to Supreme Being as that which is to be attained." (Katha Upanishad 2/15)

"All the Vedas (knowledge) become one in Him". (Taittiriya Aranyaka 3/11/1)

The meaning is that since the Supreme Being is the only thing that is expressed by all words, the meanings of all words express one and the same thing or attain unity in Him.

"The one Supreme Being exists in varied forms (like demi-gods, humans, etc.), being their inmost self." (Taittiriya Aranyaka 3/14/1)

"The senses (deva) of these beings are not aware of Him though He exists with them".

The word deva (presiding deities) in the Upanishad quoted here means the senses. The Upanishad means that He exists within demi-gods, humans, etc. as their inmost soul and is therefore (always) with them and (yet) the senses of these beings are not aware of Him.

There are passages in the Puranas which state the same thing:

"We bow to Him wherein all words find their final and eternal resting place (meaning)". (Vishnu Purana 1/14/23)

The resting place of a word is of course that thing which is expressed by it.

"That which is the first cause of all effects is the primary and chief significance of all words". (Jitanta Stotram 7/4)

"By all the Vedas (knowledge), it is I that is to be known." (Gita 15/15)

These and other passages refer to the Inner Self that has, as His attributes, individual souls with their bodies. The Upanishad declares: "So. I will enter into these three deities fire, water, earth, and the individual self as their souls and create names and forms (such as demi-gods, humans, animals, plants, etc.)." (Chhandogya Upanishad 6/3/2)

So are the words of Manu: "He, who rules over all, who is subtler than the subtlest, know Him as the Supreme Being with the radiance of the gold and capable of being realized by intelligence similar to that in a dream". (Manu Smriti 12/123)

The meaning is as follows: "He, who rules over all." means "He who directs and controls all, having entered into them as their Inner Self". Souls are said to be subtlest because they pervade all non-sentient things. The Supreme Being is said to be subtler than the souls because He pervades even the souls. The word "radiance of the gold" in the verse means "having the color of the sun". "Realised by intelligence similar to that in a dream" means "he is capable of being realized only by constant meditation, which has attained the highest clarity of sense perception".

"Some call Him Fire, others call Him Wind, and others still call Him Prajapati (Lord of population), some others call Him Indra (Lord of demi-gods), while others call Him Prana (breath). He is called also by others the Eternal Supreme Being". Manu Smriti 12/123

"Some" means some Vedas. On the line of reasoning stated before, since the Supreme Being has entered into all things as their Inner Self for controlling and directing them, words like Fire also denote Him just like the words "Eternal Supreme Being".

So also another Smriti says:-

"Those, who perform fire-worships to the spirits of their forefathers, to the demi-gods and to Brahmins as well as to Fire, perform these fire-worships only to Vishnu who is the Inner Self of all". (Daksha Smriti)

Words like "the spirits of forefathers", 'demi-gods', 'Brahmins,' and 'Fire' denote only Vishnu who is their Inner Self".

[Thus, various scriptures refer to Supreme Beings as the ultimate meaning of all words. This axiom of Ramanuja philosophy is, therefore, derived on the basis of these authoritative statements.]

[Ramanuja now explains how an individual soul comes under bondage, what changes occur in its intrinsic attributes like knowledge, etc.]

अत्रेदं सर्वशास्त्रहृदयम् - जीवात्मानः स्वयमसंकुचितापरिच्छिन्ननिर्मलज्ञानस्वरूपाः सन्तः कर्म-रूपाविद्यावेष्टितास्तत्तत्कर्मानुरूपज्ञानसंकोचमापन्नाः, ब्रह्मादिस्तम्बपर्यन्तविविधविचित्रदेहेषु प्रविष्टास्तद्देहोचितलब्धज्ञानप्रसरास्तत्तद्देहात्माभिमानिनस्तदुचितकर्माणि कुर्वाणस्तदनुगुण-सुखदुःखोपभोगरूपसंसारप्रवाहं प्रतिपद्यन्ते । एतेषां संसारमोचनं भगवत्प्रपत्तिमन्तरेण नोपपद्यत इति । तदर्थः प्रथममेषां देवादिभेदरहितज्ञानैकाकारतया सर्वेषां साम्यं प्रतिपाद्य, तस्यापि स्वरूपस्य भगवच्छेषतैकरसतया भगवदात्मकतामपि प्रतिपाद्य, भगवत्स्वरूपं च हेयप्रत्यनीककल्याणैकतानतया सकलेतरविसजातीयमनवधिकातिशयासंख्येयकल्याणगुण-गणाश्रयं स्वसंकल्पप्रवृत्तसमस्तचिदचिद्वस्तुजाततया सर्वस्यात्मभूतं प्रतिपाद्य, तदुपासन साङ्गं तत्प्रापकं प्रतिपादयन्ति शास्त्राणीति ॥

This is the heart (essence) of all scriptures - "The individual souls have pure knowledge as their attribute; this knowledge is, in its (essential) nature, without any contraction or limits. (But) owing to ignorance which is of the nature of actions, this knowledge has undergone contraction in accordance with their respective actions. (As a consequence), they enter into the bodies of created beings from Brahma downwards to the (smallest) grass and obtain an extent of knowledge that is in accordance with their respective bodies. They identify themselves with their respective bodies and perform actions suited to them and, in virtue of these actions, are caught up in the stream of the world, which consists of the experience of pleasures and pains adapted to their nature. Their release from the world is impossible except by devout self-surrender to the Lord. For this purpose, the scriptures teach that all souls are of the nature merely of knowledge and are therefore exactly alike. Their essential nature is to solely subserve the purposes of the Lord as they have the Lord as their soul. They teach, further, that the essential nature of the Lord is different from all else, being absolutely opposed to all that is imperfect and being of the nature of bliss. He is the abode of boundless, wonderful, and innumerable auspicious qualities. He, by His mere will, is the soul of all, directing all things, sentient, and non-sentient. The scriptures finally teach that the means to attain Him is devotion to Him along with the supplementary rites.

[Since knowledge is an attribute of a soul, it can expand and contract without causing any change in the eternal state of a soul. When a soul is bound, its knowledge is contracted under the influence of its actions; it is as if the sun has come behind the clouds. The higher the contraction of this knowledge, the lower will be the species a soul would be acquiring. How can a soul come out of its bondage? An unceasing devotion or refuge in the Supreme Being can free a soul from its bondage. When an individual soul serves the Supreme Being, considering him as his very own inner soul, He graces him with knowledge, which then frees him from his afflictions forever.]

[If you ask how Ramanuja has come to this conclusion, he shows multiple references that support his view.]

यथोक्तम् – 'निर्वाणमय एवायमात्मा ज्ञानमयोऽमलः । दुःखाज्ञानमला धर्मा प्रकृतेस्ते न चात्मनः ।' (वि॰ पु॰ ६/७/२२) इति प्रकृतिसंसर्गकृतकर्ममूलत्वान्नात्मस्वरूपप्रयुक्ता धर्मा इत्यर्थः । प्राप्ताप्राप्तिविवेकेन प्रकृतेरेव धर्मा इत्युक्तम् । 'विद्याविनयसंपन्ने ब्राह्मणे गवि हस्तिनि । शुनि चैव श्वपाके च पाण्डिताः समदर्शिनः ।' (गीता ५/१८) इति । देवतिर्यङ्मनुष्यस्थावररूपप्रकृति -संसृष्टस्यात्मनः स्वरूपविवेचनी बुद्धिरेषां ते पण्डिताः । तत्तत्प्रकृतिविशेषवियुक्तात्मयाथात्म्य- ज्ञानवन्तस्तत्र तत्रात्यन्तविषमाकारे वर्तमानमात्मानं समानाकारं पश्यन्तीति समदर्शिन इत्युक्तम् । तदिदमाह – 'इहैव तैर्जितः सर्गो येषां साम्ये स्थितं मनः । निर्दोषं हि समं ब्रह्म तस्माद्ब्रह्मणि ते स्थिताः ॥' (गीता ५/१९) इति । निर्दोषं देवादिप्रकृतिविशेषसंसर्गरूपदोषरहितं स्वरूपेणाव- स्थितं सर्वमात्मवस्तु निर्वाणरूपज्ञानैकाकारतया सममित्यर्थः ॥

As stated in the following verse: "The soul (self) is of the nature of bliss; it is of the nature of knowledge; it is stainless (pure). Suffering, ignorance and impurities are the qualities of nature and not of the soul." (Vishnu Purana 6/7/22)

This means that since the qualities (like suffering, ignorance, and impurities) are due to actions that arise from the soul's association with nature, they do not pertain to the essential nature of a soul. By association with nature, suffering, etc. occur. After dissociation from nature, they cease to exist. Hence, by this discernment, they are stated to be properties of nature.

Bhagavad Gita says:-

"The wise see all with equanimity, whether a Brahmana with wisdom and humility, or a cow, or an elephant, or a dog or an outcaste." Gita 5/18

"The wise" are those, who can distinguish the essential nature of the soul even though it is associated with any of the varied kinds of bodies, like demigods, humans, animals, and plants. They know the true nature of the self, distinctly from the specific and widely different forms of matter. Though these forms are widely different from each other, they see their underlying souls to be of the same nature. Therefore, they are the seers of equality.

Gita further declares as follows: "Those, whose minds are established in the equanimity, have conquered the cycle of birth and death in this world itself. For, the supreme reality is stainless and equanimous; therefore, they rest in that supreme reality." (Gita 5/19)

'Without faults' means "without the faults arising from association with specific forms of matter like the bodies of demigods and the rest". The soul of everyone, in its essential nature, has only the nature of bliss or knowledge and is, therefore, alike (in all) as it is after liberation.

[Vishnu Purana says that suffering or bondage is not an intrinsic attribute of the soul rather, it is an attribute of insentient nature, so a soul can come out of it. Gita says that those who know reality see knowledge as an intrinsic attribute of all souls, even if they differ in their external appearances. It further says that if someone practices to see this equanimity of knowledge in everything, he attains the Supreme Being.]

[Ramanuja says that the supreme duty of an individual soul is to serve, love, and meditate on the Supreme Being as He alone is its ultimate reality and Lord.]

तस्यैवंभूतस्यात्मनो भगवच्छेषतैकरसता तन्नियाम्यता तदेकाधारता च तच्छरीरतत्तनुप्रभृति-
भिः शब्दैस्तत्समानाधिकरण्येन च श्रुतिस्मृतीतिहासपुराणेषु प्रतिपाद्यत इति पूर्वमेवोक्तम् ॥

The soul that has been described so far exists only to subserve the purposes of the Lord, is controlled and directed by Him, and has Him as his sole support. Therefore the individual souls are referred to as the bodies of the Supreme Being as it is their common basis. The Upanishads, smritis (Memory-based texts), itihasas (history texts), and Puranas describe it similarly. This has already been stated by us.

[Just as we refer to our body and soul interchangeably in many day-to-day contexts, the scriptures also refer to an individual soul and Supreme Soul interchangeably. What we can infer from it? As a body functions as per the wish of its soul, an individual should act and think according to the wish of the Supreme Soul. This is the essence as per hundreds of Upanishads, 18 Smritis, 18 UpSmritis, 2 history texts (Ramayana and Mahabharata), 18 Puranas, and 18 UpPuranas, etc.]

[Now, Ramanuja shows explicit evidence for unconditional devotion or refuge in the Supreme Being for liberation. He also describes the infinite auspicious qualities of the Supreme Being and how he has pervaded it all.]

'दैवी ह्येषा गुणमयी मम माया दुरत्यया । मामेव ये प्रपद्यन्ते मायामेतां तरन्ति ते ॥' (गीता ७/१४) इति । तस्यात्मनः कर्मकृतविचित्रगुणमयप्रकृतिसंसर्गरूपात्संसारान्मोक्षो भगवत्प्रप-त्तिमन्तरेण नोपपद्यत इत्युक्तं भवति । 'नान्यः पन्था अयनाय विद्यते' (तै० आ० ३/१२/१७) इत्यादिश्रुतिभिश्च । 'मया ततमिदं सर्वं जगदव्यक्तमूर्तिना । मत्स्थानि सर्वभूतानि न चाहं तेषु अवस्थितः ॥ न च मत्स्थानि भूतानि पश्य मे योगमैश्वरम् ॥' (गीता ९/४-५) इति सर्वशक्तियोगात्स्वैश्वर्यवैचित्र्यमुक्तम् । तदाह – 'विष्टभ्याहमिदं कृत्स्नमेकांशेन स्थितो जगत् ।' (गीता १०/४२) इति, अनन्तविचित्रमहाश्चर्यरूपं जगन्ममायुतांशेनात्मतया प्रविश्य सर्वं मत्संकल्पेन विष्टभ्यानेन रूपेणानन्तमहाविभूतिपरिमितोदारगुणसागरो निरतिशयाश्चर्यभूतः स्थितोऽहमित्यर्थः । तदिदमाह – 'एकत्वे सति नानात्वं नानात्वे सति चैकता । अचिन्त्यं ब्रह्मणो रूपं कुतस्तद्धेदितुमर्हति ॥' इति । प्रशासितृत्वेनैक एव सन्विचित्रचिदचिद्वस्तुष्वन्तरात्मतया प्रविश्य तत्तद्रूपेण विचित्रप्रकारो विचित्रकर्म कारयन्नानारूपां भजते । एवं स्वल्पांशेन तु सर्वैश्वर्यं नानारूपं जगत्तदन्तरात्मतया प्रविश्य विष्टभ्य नानात्वेनावस्थितोऽपि सन्ननवधिकाति-शयासंख्येयकल्याणगुणगणः सर्वेश्वरः परब्रह्मभूतः पुरुषोत्तमो नारायणो निरतिशयाश्चर्यभूतो नीलतोयदसंकाशः पुण्डरीकदलामलायतेक्षणः सहस्रांशुसहस्रकिरणः परमे व्योम्नि । 'यो वेद निहितं गुहायां परमे व्योमन्' (तै० उ० २/१/१), 'तदक्षरे परमे व्योमन्' (तै० ना० उ० १/२) इत्यादिश्रुतिसिद्ध एक एवातिष्ठते ॥

Bhagavad Gita says: "This divine Maya (veil, nature) of mine, characterized by three qualities of nature, viz

sattva, rajas, and tamas, is very difficult to cross, but those who seek me alone, they overcome this divine veil." (Gita 7/14)

This means that the bondage of a soul occurs due to its actions. Through them it associates with nature, possessing varied qualities. The release of the embodied soul from the world is impossible without self-surrender to the Lord. The Upanishads also state, 'There is no other way to attain Supreme Being'. (Taittiriya Aranyaka 3/12/17)

Gita further says:-

"This world is all pervaded by me without revealing my form; all beings are situated within me, but I do not depend on them like this. Look at my divine Yoga to understand how those beings are not situated in me. (Gita 9/4-5)

Thus, the transcendentally wonderful nature of His divine Lordship is stated to arise from the possession of all powers.

The same idea is proclaimed again in the following verse: "I hold the whole world under my control with a fragment of my might". (Gita 10/42)

It means: "I enter into this wonderful and infinitely varied universe as its soul by an infinitesimal part of myself and hold it under my control by my mere will. Thus, I am the possessor of the boundless splendor of this universe. I am the abode of immeasurable noble qualities and stand as an object of unsurpassed wonder.

About him, it has been further said: "The Lord is manifold while (remaining) one; while He is manifold, He remains single. His form is beyond thought. Who is there capable of understanding it?"

As a ruler and controller, though He remains one, he enters into the varied forms of sentient and insentient entities as their inner self and thus appears in varied modes, directs them to perform varied deeds, and thus assumes many forms. Having entered into the world consisting of varied and wonderful forms with an extremely small fragment of His might, as their inner controlling self, He is seen as manifold. At the same time, Narayana, who is the Supreme Being and the most exalted among all souls, remains one, the Lord of all Lords, possessed of boundless, wonderful, and innumerable auspicious qualities. He is of unsurpassed splendor and has a complexion similar to that of a blue cloud. His eyes are clear and wide like the petals of a lotus; He has a form resembling the radiance of a thousand suns. He dwells in the transcendent realm (space), as the Upanishads declare, "Who knows the one, who stays in the cave of the Supreme Space" (Taittiriya Upanishad 2/1/1), "Situated in that imperishable and highest sky" (Taittiriya Narayana Upanishad 1/2) and still remains one.

[Various texts are unanimous in his Lordship, omniscience, omnipresence, inner-dwelling, his beautiful form, and unsurpassed splendor.]

[Since there is nothing that is comparable to the Supreme Lord, it is beyond the intuitive and analytical powers of anyone to comprehend Him in completeness. Ramanuja explains it through an example.]

ब्रह्मव्यतिरिक्तस्य कस्यचिदपि वस्तुन एकस्वभावस्यैककार्यशक्तियुक्तस्यैकरूपस्य रूपान्तर-योग: स्वभावान्तरयोग: शक्त्यन्तरयोगश्च न घटते । तस्यैतस्य परब्रह्मणः सर्ववस्तुविजातीयतया सर्वस्वभावत्वं सर्वशक्तियोगश्चेत्येकस्यैव विचित्रानन्तरूपता च पुनरप्यनन्तापरिमिताश्वर्ययोगनै-करूपता च न विरुद्धेति वस्तुमात्रसाम्याद्विरोधचिन्ता न युक्तेत्यर्थः । यथोक्तं – 'शक्तय: सर्वभावानामचिन्त्यज्ञानगोचराः । यतोऽतो ब्रह्मणस्तास्तु सर्गाद्या भावशक्तय: ॥ भवन्ति तपसां श्रेष्ठ पावकस्य यथोष्णता ॥' (वि० पु० १/३/२३) इति ।
एतदुक्तं भवति सर्वेषामग्निजलादीनां भावानामेकस्मिन्नपि भावे दृष्टैव शक्तिस्तद्विजातीयभावा-न्तरेऽपीति न चिन्तयितुं युक्ता जलादावदृष्टापि तद्विजातीयपावके भास्वरत्वोष्णतादिशक्तिर्यथा

दृश्यते, एवमेव सर्ववस्तुविसजातीये ब्रह्मणि सर्वसाम्यं नानुमातुं युक्तिमिति । अतो विचित्रानन्त-
शक्तियुक्तं ब्रह्मैवेत्यर्थः तदाह – 'जगदेतन्महाश्चर्यं रूपं यस्य महात्मनः । तेनाश्चर्यवरेणाहं भवता
कृष्ण संगतः ॥' (वि० पु० ५/१९/७) इति । तदेतन्नानाविधानन्तश्रुतिनिकरशिष्टपरिगृहीत-
तद्व्याख्यानपरिश्रमादवधारितम् ॥

For no entity, other than the Supreme Being, with a certain type of nature and certain capability to perform only one kind of action and having only a single form, it is possible to possess another type of form, another type of nature, and other capabilities to act. Only the Supreme Being, different from all other entities, has all the natures and capabilities. Though He is single, He has manifold forms, countless and varied. Since He has wonderful, infinite, and varied powers, manifoldness and singleness are not opposed to each other in Him. On the ground that He is also an object (like others), it is not proper to say that there is a contradiction in the Supreme Being for it has a diversity of forms, powers, and qualities as well as unity of being.

So has it been said: "O best among ascetics, the (unique) powers of all things (like fire, water, etc) cannot be explained by reason. For the same reason, (unique) powers such as that of creation, etc. that belong to the Supreme Being are inconceivable just as the heat possessed by fire." Vishnu Purana 1/3/23

It comes to mean this: It would be unreasonable to expect that a certain power found in any one of such substances as fire, water, etc. will be seen in other entities different from that substance. Just as qualities like light, heat, etc. are not seen in water but are found in fire which is a different substance from water. Similarly, in Supreme Being, which is different from all other things, it is unreasonable to infer the same type of qualities liken other things. Therefore, the Supreme Being consists of wondrously manifold and infinite powers. So says (Akrura to Sri Krishna): "O Krishna, I have now met you, the great Being, whose wonderful form this world is and you yourself are the greatest marvel". Vishnu Purana 5/19/7

All these insights are the outcome of a careful study of hosts of Vedic passages with diverse significance and of their meanings as accepted by the wise after a great deal of effort.

[Since the Supreme Being consists of infinitely many unsurpassable attributes, various scriptures describe Him in various ways, according to what they seek to establish and impart.]

[Ramanuja first shows some of the most common descriptions related to the Supreme Being mentioned in the scriptures. Later, he will discuss how to reconcile these differing descriptions in the same Supreme Being.]

तथा हि प्रमाणान्तरापरिदृष्टापरिमितपरिणामानेकतत्त्वनियतक्रमविशिष्टौ सृष्टिप्रलयौ ब्रह्मणोऽने -कविधाः श्रुतयो वदन्ति ।

There are several types of Upanishad passages, speaking of the creation and dissolution of the universe by the Supreme Being, proceeding in rigorous order, involving a multitude of fundamental entities, subject to infinite modifications. All these matters relating to creation and dissolution are beyond the bounds of other sources of knowledge.

[From Him, as the ultimate cause, everything emerges, and in Him, everything finds its dissolution. Besides these texts, there is no other way to know these attributes.]

[Some other descriptions list his various properties, e.g. he is without any inauspicious qualities, etc.]

निरवद्यं निरञ्जनं विज्ञानमानन्दं निर्विकारं निष्कलं निष्क्रियं शान्तं निर्गुणमित्यादिकाः निर्गुणं ज्ञानस्वरूपं ब्रह्मेति काश्चन श्रुतयोऽभिदधति ।

Some Vedic texts describe the Supreme Being as being without any attributes and with knowledge as its intrinsic nature: "It is pure, free from stain; it is knowledge and bliss; it suffers no change; it has no parts; it is actionless; it is peaceful; it has no attributes."

[Thus, these Upanishads say that the Supreme Being is just the knowledge without any attributes, faultless, changeless, etc.]

[Some other texts emphasize his non-duality.]

'नेह नानास्ति किंचन मृत्योः स मृत्युमाप्नोति य इह नानेव पश्यति' (बृ॰ उ॰ ६/४/१९), 'यत्र त्वस्य सर्वमात्मैवाभूत् तत्केन कं पश्येत्तत्केन कं विजातीयात्' (बृ॰ उ॰ ६/४/१७) इत्यादिका नानात्वनिषेधवादिन्यः सन्ति काश्चन श्रुतयः ।

There are some other Vedic texts that deny plurality (multiplicity, presence of other entities) in the Supreme Being. "There is no multiplicity of any kind in Supreme Being. He, who sees differences in Supreme Being, goes from death to death". (Katha Upanishad 4/10, Brihadaranyaka Upanishad 6/4/14) "When everything becomes his soul, how is it possible for one to see another? By what means can anything else be seen? What else remains there to be known"? (Brihadaranyaka Upanishad 4/4/14)

[These texts specifically negate the presence of multiplicity in a liberated state.]

[Other texts describe his auspicious attributes.]

'यः सर्वज्ञः सर्ववित् यस्य ज्ञानमयं तपः' (मु० उ० १/१/१०), 'सर्वाणि रूपाणि विचित्य धीरो नामानि कृत्वाभिवदन् यदास्ते' (तै० आ० ३/१२/७), 'सर्वे निमेषा जज्ञिरे विद्युतः पुरुषादधि' (तै० ना० उ० १/८), 'अपहतपाप्मा विजरो विमृत्युर्विशोको विजघत्सोऽपिपासः सत्यकामः सत्यसंकल्प' (छा० उ० ८/१/५) इति सर्वस्मिञ्जगति हेयतयावगतं सर्वगुणं प्रतिषिध्य निरतिशयकल्याणगुणानन्त्यं सर्वज्ञता सर्वशक्तियोगं सर्वनामरूपव्याकरणं सर्वस्यावधारतां च काश्चन श्रुतयो ब्रुवते ।

There are other Vedic passages that deny the presence of such qualities as are considered imperfections in the world and affirm the existence of countless auspicious qualities in Him. They affirm his omniscience and omnipotence. They describe him as the provider of forms and names to all things and that He is the support of everything. "He who knows all and their characteristics, He whose actions (in creating the world) are of the nature merely of His will which is knowledge (He is Supreme Being)" (Mundaka Upanishad 1/1/10); "He who creates all forms, He, in his wisdom, gives them their names and calls them by these names". (Taittiriya Aranyanka 3/12/7); "All moments (of time) arose from the luminous Supreme Being." (Taittiriya Narayana Upanishad 1/8). "He is free from all sin; old age does not afflict him nor Death; He is free from sorrow; He has neither hunger nor thirst; all desirable objects are ever with Him and His will is ever accomplished" (Chhandogya Upanishad 8/1/5)

[These texts describe his omniscience, lordship over time and death, etc.]

[Some texts describe the multiplicity of this world, which is single-handedly created by him.]

'सर्वं खल्विदं ब्रह्म तज्जलानिति' (छा० उ० ३/१४/१), 'ऐतदात्म्यमिदं सर्व' (छा० उ० ६/८/७), 'एकः सन् बहुधा विचार' (तै० आ० ३/११/१) इत्यादिका ब्रह्मसृष्टं जगन्नानाकारं प्रतिपाद्य तदैक्यं च प्रतिपादयन्ति काश्चन ।

Other Vedic passages declare that the world created by the Supreme Being is manifold and yet everything is one with the Supreme Being. "Everything is, indeed, Supreme Being, for everything arises from Supreme Being, is absorbed in Him, and subsists in Him. (Chhandogya Upanishad 3/14/1); "All this has Supreme Being as its soul." (Chhandogya Upanishad 6/8/7); "Being one he is spread manifold." (Taittiriya Aranyanka 3/11/1)

[Just as a small seed contains the blueprint of all parts of a tree, such as trunk, branches, leaves, roots, flowers, fruits, etc., the Supreme Being alone creates this multi-faceted world alone, without any assistance.]

[Some texts describe the difference between the Supreme Being and individual souls. They also describe the nature of this difference.]

'पृथगात्मानं प्रेरितारं च मत्वा' (श्वे॰ उ॰ १/६), 'भोक्ता भोग्यं प्रेरितारं च मत्वा' (श्वे॰ उ॰ १/१२), 'प्रजापतिरकामयत प्रजाः सृजेयेति' (तै॰ ब्रा॰ २/२/१/१), 'पतिं विश्वस्यात्मेश्वरं शाश्वस्तं शिवमच्युतं' (तै॰ ना॰ उ॰ ११/३) 'तमीश्वराणां परं महेश्वरं तं देवतानां परं च दैवतं' (श्वे॰ उ॰ ६/७), 'सर्वस्य वशी सर्वस्येशान' (बृ॰ उ॰ ६/४/२२) इत्यादिका ब्रह्मणः सर्वस्मादन्यत्वं सर्वस्येशितव्यमीश्वरत्वं च ब्रह्मणः सर्वस्य शेषतां पतित्वं चेश्वरस्य काश्चन ।

Some Upanishads declare that the Supreme Being is different from everything else, that everything (else) is subject to His rule, that He is the ruler of all, that everything (else) exists to subserve His purposes, and that the Supreme Being is the Lord (of all). "He who realizes that the individual self is different from Supreme Being who directs him he alone becomes worthy of His grace". (Shvetashvatara Upanishad 1/6); "He who knows these three the experiencing self, the object of experience, and the ruler who directs" (Shvetashvatara Upanishad 1/12); "The Lord of the creatures desired: 'I will create these beings'." (Taittiriya Brahmana 2/2/1/1); "The Lord of the

world, the Great Ruler, is Supreme, the Supreme Deity of all deities"
(Taittiriya Narayana Upanishad 11/3); "Him, who is the great Lord of
the Lords, the ultimate God of the Gods" (Shvetashvatara Upanishad
6/7); "He who has everything under His control and rules over
everything" (Brihadaranyaka Upanishad 6/4/22).

[These texts show his ultimate authority over all, without any
exception.]

[Some texts depict him as the inner soul of all living as well as non-
living entities.]

'अन्तः प्रविष्टः शास्ता जनानां सर्वात्मा' (तै० आ० ३/११/३), 'एष त आत्मान्तर्याम्यमृतः'
(बृ० उ० ५/७/३), 'यस्य पृथिवी शरीरं यस्यापः शरीरं यस्य तेजः शरीरमित्यादि यस्याव्यक्तं
शरीरं यस्याक्षरं शरीरं', 'यस्य मृत्युः शरीरम्' (सु० उ० ७), 'यस्यात्मा शरीरम्' (बृ० उ०
५/७/२६) इति ब्रह्मव्यतिरिक्तस्य सर्वस्य वस्तुनो ब्रह्मणश्च शरीरात्मभावं दर्शयन्ति काश्चनेति ॥

There are also a number of Vedic passages that show that the
relationship between every object other than the Supreme Being
and the Supreme Being is that between the body and the soul. "The
Ruler has entered into all beings and is the soul of all" (Taittiriya
Aranyaka 3/11/3). "He is your soul and the Inner Ruler who is
immortal" (Brihadaranyaka Upanishad 5/7/3); "He whose body is
the earth, He of whom water is the body; He to whom fire is the
body. He to whom primordial nature before it undergoes
transformation is the body, He to whom indestructible nature is the
body, He to whom Death is the body. (Subala Upanishad 7) "He, to
whom, the individual soul is the body." (Brihadaranyaka Upanishad
5/7/26)

[These texts show that he is the soul of all, or in other words, every
other entity is his body.]

[Now, Ramanuja discusses how to reconcile the apparent differences in various descriptions.]

नानारूपाणां वाक्यानामविरोधो मुख्यार्थपरित्यागश्च यथा संभवति तथा वर्णनीयम् । वर्णितं च अविकारश्रुतयः स्वरूपपरिणामपरिहारादेव मुख्यार्थाः । निर्गुणवादाश्च प्राकृतहेयगुणनिषेधपर-तया व्यवस्थिताः । नानात्वनिषेधवादाश्चैकस्य ब्रह्मणः शरीरतया प्रकारभूतं सर्वं चेतनाचेतनं वस्त्विति सर्वस्यात्मतया सर्वप्रकारं ब्रह्मैवावस्थितमिति सुरक्षिताः । सर्वप्रकारविलक्षणत्वपति-त्वेश्वरत्वसर्वकल्याणगुणगणाकारत्वसत्यकामत्वसत्यसंकल्पत्वादिवाक्यं तदभ्युपगमादेव सुरक्षि-तम् । ज्ञानानन्दमात्रवादि च सर्वस्मादन्यस्य सर्वकल्याणगुणगणाश्रयस्य सर्वेश्वरस्य सर्वशेषिणः सर्वाधारस्य सर्वोत्पत्तिस्थितिप्रलयहेतुभूतस्य निरवद्यस्य निर्विकारस्य सर्वात्मभूतस्य परस्य ब्रह्मणः स्वरूपनिरूपकधर्मो मलप्रत्यनीकानन्दरूपज्ञानमेवेति स्वप्रकाशतया स्वरूपमपि ज्ञानमे-वेति च प्रतिपादनादनुपालितम् । ऐक्यवादाश्च शरीरात्मभावेन सामानाधिकरण्यमुख्यार्थतोप-पादनादेव सुस्थिताः ॥

This being the case, these passages which are diverse in their meaning should be interpreted in such a way that they do not conflict with one another and their primary and direct meaning is not given up. They have been so interpreted by us. The Vedic texts which deny change or modification in the Supreme Being have their direct meaning in our interpretation because we state that the essential nature of the Supreme Being is not subject to modification (and that these modifications are only in His body consisting of sentient and insentient entities). The passages in the Upanishad, which say that the Supreme Being is without attributes or qualities, are interpreted (by us) as meaning that the Supreme Being is without those imperfections that are found in the world associated with matter. The texts that deny plurality are, in no way, disregarded because we hold that all things other than the Supreme Being, both sentient and insentient, are His bodies or modes (attributes) and that He is the inner self of all, who has them as His modes. In this sense (we hold) that there is only one entity, viz., Supreme Being. The passages that say that the Supreme Being is different from all else, that He is the Lord and Ruler, that He is the abode of all auspicious qualities, that the objects of desire are ever with Him, and that His will is supreme, these passages are accepted by us (just as they are) and stand unshaken. The texts which declare that Supreme Being is mere knowledge or bliss are interpreted by us as follows: The Supreme Being, who is other than everything else, who is the abode of all auspicious qualities, who is the Ruler over all, for whose purposes everything else exists, who is the support of all things, who is the cause of the origin, continuance, and dissolution of everything else, who is free from all imperfections, who is not subject to any change or modification, who is the soul of all, (this Supreme Being) possesses (in our doctrine) knowledge which is of the nature of bliss as His essential attribute (the attribute which defines Him) and which is opposed to all impurities and that His essential nature is also knowledge because He is self-evident or self-luminous. The declarations of unity (between the individual soul and Supreme Being found in the Upanishads like "You are that" bring out the relationship of the body and the soul that exists between them in a primary and direct sense using the Supreme Being as the common basis. In this sense, we accept the authority of these passages also.

[The best way to interpret various statements is such that we do not leave their primary or direct meaning. The texts, which say that he himself has become this world mean that these changes are not in his intrinsic nature but in his modes only just as our body might change but the soul does not. The texts that say that the Supreme Being is attributeless can be interpreted as the absence of all inauspicious qualities in him. Those statements that say this world is non-dual mean that since everything is his body, there is nothing besides Him; hence, we can denote it all by Him alone.]

[One might ask, what the viewpoint that Ramanuja himself supports is. Is it the difference between an individual soul and Supreme

Being, or their identity, or their difference and non-difference coexist? Put differently, this means in the liberated state, whether there is a difference between a soul and the Super-Soul or not.]

एवं च सत्यभेदो वा भेदो वा द्व्यात्मकता वा वेदान्तवेद्यः कोऽयमर्थः समर्थितो भवति । सर्वस्य वेदवेद्यत्वात्सर्वं समर्थितम् । सर्वशरीरतया सर्वप्रकारं ब्रह्मैवावस्थितमित्यभेदः समर्थितः । एकमेव ब्रह्म नानाभूतचिदचिद्वस्तुप्रकारं नानात्वेनावस्थितमिति भेदाभेदौ । अचिद्वस्तुनश्चिद्वस्तु-नश्चेश्वरस्य च स्वरूपस्वभाववैलक्षण्यादसंकराच्च भेदः समर्थितः ॥

By this interpretation, it may be asked, which of the doctrines is proved as true according to the Vedas, the doctrine of non-difference (Advaita, non-duality) or the doctrine of difference as well as non-difference (duality-nonduality, bheda-abheda, dvaita-advaita), or the doctrine of plurality (bheda, dvaita, duality). The answer is as follows: Since every one of them is taught in the Vedas, every one of them is accepted as true (in a sense). Since the Supreme Being has everything else as His body and as His mode, He is the only existing entity. Thus, non-difference (advaita) is proved as true (in this sense). The one Supreme Being, we maintain, has sentient and non-sentient things, which are many and varied, as His modes and stands manifold. Therefore, difference as well as non-difference is proved also to be true (in a sense). We hold that sentient and non-sentient are different both in their essential nature and in their attributes from Supreme Being and they do not mix with one another. Therefore, the doctrine of duality is also accepted as true.

[Ramanuja says that he supports whatever is supported by the scriptures. Since all entities are the body of the Supreme Being, we can refer to them as a single entity, which means there is non-duality. Just as various body parts are different, these entities are different, and hence, there is a duality present among them. Supreme Being is different from other entities due to his superlative qualities and he is non-different from them as their inner soul so he remains different as well as non-different from the world and individual souls.]

[Now, non-dualists raise their objection to this interpretation.]

ननु च 'तत्त्वमसि श्वेतकेतो' (छा॰ उ॰ ६/८/७), 'तस्य तावदेव चिरम्' (छा॰ उ॰ ६/१४/२) इत्यैक्यज्ञानमेव परमपुरुषार्थलक्षणमोक्षसाधनमिति गम्यते । नैतदेवम् । 'पृथगात्मानं प्रेरितारं च मत्वा जुष्टस्ततस्तेनामृतत्वमेति' (श्वे॰ उ॰ १/६) इत्यात्मानं प्रेरितारं चान्तर्यामिणं पृथग्मत्वा ततः पृथक्त्वज्ञानाद्वैतोस्तेन परमात्मना जुष्टोऽमृतत्वमेतीति साक्षादमृतत्वप्राप्तिसाधनमात्मनो नियन्तुश्च पृथग्भावज्ञानमेवेत्यवगम्यते ॥

The non-dualist might object here and say, "But the Upanishad states: "You are that, Shvetaketu" (Chhandogya Upanishad 6/8/7) and "There is delay for him (who knows the unity of the individual self and Supreme Being only until he becomes free from the body." (Chhandogya Upanishad 6/14/2). These passages imply that only the knowledge of unity between the individual self and Supreme Being is the means to attain release from bondage, which is the supreme goal of life."

We answer: "It is not so. The passage in Shvetashvatara Upanishad 1/12 says, "Only by knowing that Inner Self within, directing the individual self, is different from the individual self, one attains immortality after gaining his grace". This is the meaning of the passage: Knowing the individual self and its inner controller Supreme as different, and after thus knowing the Supreme Being as distinct from him, one serves him and with his grace becomes immortal. Thus, it becomes clear that the direct means of attaining immortality is knowledge of the difference between the individual self and the Inner Ruler who controls and directs it.

[Ramanuja says that Shvetashvatara Upanishad directly shows the knowing Supreme Being, as its inner soul, though distinctly different from itself, a soul attains immortality. Hence, it is to be taken as a reference here and not the verses of Chhandogya Upanishad.]

[The non-dualists give their reasons for not taking the reference of Shvetashvatara Upanishad here.]

ऐक्यवाक्यविरोधादेतदपरमार्थसगुणब्रह्मप्राप्तिविषयमित्यभ्युपगन्तव्यमिति चेत् । पृथक्त्वज्ञान-स्यैव साक्षादमृतत्वप्राप्तिसाधनत्वश्रवणाद्विपरीतं कस्मान्न भवति । एतदुक्तं भवति । द्वयोर्तुल्य -योर्विरोधे सत्यविरोधेन तयोर्विषयो विवेचनीय इति । कथमविरोध इति चेत् । अन्तर्यामिरूपेणा -वस्थितस्य परस्य ब्रह्मणः शरीरतया प्रकारत्वाज्जीवात्मनस्तत्प्रकारं ब्रह्मैव त्वमिति शब्देनाभि-धीयते । तथैव ज्ञातव्यमिति तस्य वाक्यस्य विषयः । एवंभूताज्जीवात्तदात्मतयावस्थितस्य परमात्मनो निखिलदोषरहिततया सत्यसंकल्पत्वादनवधिकातिशयासंख्येयकल्याणगुणगणा-कर्तृत्वेन च यः पृथग्भावः सोऽनुसंधेय इत्यस्य वाक्यस्य विषय इत्ययमर्थः पूर्वमसकृदुक्तः ।

The non-dualists might say, "This text in Shvetashvatara Upanishad should be considered as referring to the attainment of the Supreme Being with attributes, which is not the ultimate goal.

We ask: "Why should not the reverse be true, namely, that this knowledge of difference is the means of attaining immortality, since the Shvetashvatara text explicitly states it to be so, whereas the Chhandogya passage ('you are that') has no such explicit statement (to the contrary)? That is when there is (apparent) conflict between two (texts) of equal validity, their real import should be carefully studied without ignoring (either of them).

The non-dualists might ask "How could there be no conflict between the two texts in your interpretation?"

We answer: The meaning of the Chhandogya text is, "Since the individual self is the body of the Supreme Self, who is within him as his inner ruler and director, the word "you" means "Supreme Being who has that (individual self) as His mode". The sentence 'you are that' should be understood in this way. The meaning of the

Shvetashvatara text is that the difference between the individual self who is the body and the Supreme Self who abides in him as his soul, who is free from all defects and imperfections, and who is the abode of wonderful and innumerable auspicious qualities should be borne in mind (for liberation). This meaning of the sentence has also been repeatedly explained.

[The statement of Chhandogya Upanishad depicts the Supreme Being as the material cause of everything so an individual soul is His body.]

[On the other hand, Shvetashvatar Upanishad highlights the distinctive features of the Supreme Being in comparison to living and non-living entities.]

'भोक्ता भोग्यं प्रेरितारं च मत्वा' (श्वे॰ उ॰ १/१२) इति भोग्यरूपस्य वस्तुनोऽचेतनत्वं परमार्थत्वं सततं विकारास्पदत्वमित्यादयः स्वभावाः, भोक्तुर्जीवात्मनश्चामलापरिच्छिन्नज्ञानानन्द स्वभाव-स्यैवानादिकर्मरूपाविद्याकृतनानाविधज्ञानसंकोचविकासौ भोग्यभूताचिद्वस्तुसंसर्गश्च परमात्मो-पासनान्मोक्षश्चेत्यादयः स्वभावाः, एवंभूतभोक्तृभोग्ययोरन्तर्यामि रूपेणावस्थानं स्वरूपेण चापरिमितगुणौघाश्रयत्वेनावस्थानमिति परस्य ब्रह्मस्त्रिविधावस्थानं ज्ञातव्यमित्यर्थः ॥

Shvetashvatara Upanishad 1/12 mentions three entities - The experiencing subject (the sentient individual self), the object of experience (insentient nature), and the Ruler who directs all, etc. A thing that is the object of experience is of this nature: it is non-sentient: it exists always for others; it is subject to changes or modifications and so on. The individual self, who is the experiencing subject, is of the following nature. It is essentially of the nature of infinite and pure knowledge and bliss; but owing to ignorance which is due to beginningless action, its knowledge is subject to contraction and expansion. It becomes connected with non-sentient matter due to it, which is the object of experience or enjoyment. It is capable of obtaining release from bondage by devout adoration of the Supreme Being. The Supreme Being exists in the individual self and also in non-sentient things as their Inner Ruler. Apart from this, He also exists in His essential nature, as the abode of countless attributes. Thus, the meaning of the Shvetashvatara text is that the Supreme Being exists in three forms.

[It says that distinctive knowledge of the Supreme Being and thereafter his service leads one to liberation. Earlier, it was not known, since the knowledge of the individual soul was contracted under the influence of his actions. In this state, he remains indulged in the insentient nature and considers himself as a body. When he knows his distinction from his body, and then the Supreme Being, he serves the Supreme Being for his liberation.]

[Ramanuja now points out that his interpretation is in accordance with that of earlier revered Gurus Brahmanandi (Vakyakara) and Dramidacharya (the interpreter). According to them, Chhandogya Upanishad depicts the attainment of the Supreme Being with attributes.]

तत्त्वमसीति सद्विद्यायामुपास्यं ब्रह्म सगुणं सगुणब्रह्मप्राप्तिश्च फलमित्यभियुक्तैः पूर्वाचार्यैर्व्या-
ख्यातम् । यथोक्तं वाक्यकारेण – 'युक्तं तद्गुणकोपासनादिति' । व्याख्यातं च द्रमिडाचार्येण –
'विद्याविकल्पं वदता यद्यपि सच्चितो न निर्भुग्नदैवतं गुणगणं मनसानुधावेत्तथाप्यन्तर्गुणामेव
देवतां भजत इति तत्रापि सगुणैव देवता प्राप्यते' इति । सच्चित्तः सद्विद्यानिष्ठः । न निर्भुग्नदैवतं
गुणगणं मनसानुधावेतपहतपाप्मत्वादिकल्याणगुणगणं दैवताद्विभक्तं यद्यपि दहरविद्यानिष्ठ इव
सच्चितो न स्मरेत् । तथाप्यन्तर्गुणामेव देवतां भजते देवतास्वरूपानुबन्धित्वात्सकलकल्याण-
गुणगणस्य केनचिद्परदेवतासाधारणेन निखिलजगत्कारणत्वादिना गुणेनोपास्यमानापि देवता
वस्तुतः स्वरूपानुबन्धि सर्वकल्याणगुणगणविशिष्टैवोपास्यते । अतः सगुणमेव ब्रह्म तत्रापि
प्राप्यमिति सद्विद्यादहरविद्ययोर्विकल्प इत्यर्थः ॥

(Moreover) the wise gurus of ancient times have logically explained that the sentence, "You are that", present within the context of Sad-Vidaya (knowledge of reality), is about the worship of the Supreme

Being with attributes. Its result is the attainment of the Supreme Being with attributes. For instance, the Vakyakara says, "It is in accordance with reason that the goal is the attainment of Supreme Being with attributes (since the worship) according to Sad-Vidya is of Supreme Being with attributes." Dramidacharya has also commented upon it while pointing out the optional nature of the knowledge related to the Supreme Being (between Dahara Vidya (knowledge of inner conscious space) and SadVidya): "The seeker meditating on 'sat' (reality) does not meditate on the other attributes of the Deity as apart from the Deity. He meditates on the Deity as inclusive of attributes and the Deity attained is also possessed of attributes."

'The seeker meditating on "sat" means one who is devoted to the meditation prescribed and elaborated in the section of Chhandogya Upanishad known as Sad-Vidya. 'Does not meditate on the other attributes of the Deity as apart from the Deity' means that the devotee of the meditation on 'sat' does not dwell on the other auspicious qualities of the Supreme Being like 'freedom from sin' etc. apart from the Deity. It is similar to the case of the devotee of the meditation on dahara' (i.e., subtle ethereal space in the heart), he does meditate on the attributes of the Deity such as truth (sat), consciousness, etc. Since all the glorious attributes of the Supreme Being are inherent in its substantive nature and even when only some inherent and unique attributes, like being the cause of the world, are taken up for meditation along with the Deity, in reality, the Deity is meditated upon qualified by all the auspicious qualities which, as a matter of fact, are connected with its essential nature. Therefore, even in Sad-Vidya the goal is only the attainment of Supreme Being with attributes. Hence one can choose either Sad-Vidya or Dahara Vidya to attain the Supreme Being with attributes (as their result is the same).

[If one meditates on the Supreme Being consisting of certain attributes, he will attain the Supreme Being with those attributes and not an attributeless reality as pointed out by the non-dualists. Since it is not possible to meditate on all attributes of the Supreme Being at once, a seeker chooses those attributes of the Supreme Being for which he has some special liking. However, the end result is going to the same Supreme Being in various types of such worship of his intrinsic attributes, who consists of all such auspicious qualities collectively.]

[Now, non-dualists raise another doubt in the viewpoint of Ramanuja.]

ननु च सर्वस्य जन्तोः परमात्मान्तर्यामी तन्नियाम्यं च सर्वमेवेत्युक्तम् । एवं च सति विधिनिषेधशास्त्राणामधिकारी न दृश्यते । यः स्वबुद्ध्यैव प्रवृत्तिनिवृत्तिशक्तः स एवं कुर्यान्न कुर्यादिति विधिनिषेधयोग्यः । न चैष दृश्यते । सर्वस्मिन् प्रवृत्तिजाते सर्वस्य प्रेरकः परमात्मा कारयितेति तस्य सर्वनियमनं प्रतिपादितम् । तथा च श्रूयते – 'एष एव साधु कर्म कारयति ते यमेभ्यो लोकेभ्य उन्निनीषति । एष एवासाधु कर्म कारयति तं यमधो निनीषतीति ।' (कौ० उ० ३/९) साध्वसाधुकर्मकारयितृत्वान्नैर्घृण्यं च ॥

Here, another objection might be raised: "You have said that the Supreme Self is the Inner Ruler who directs all creatures. If it is so, there appears no person to whom scriptural injunctions and prohibitions (such as "Do this" and "This should not be done") could apply. Only a person who is capable of acting or refraining from action in accordance with his intellect can be subject to the injunctions and prohibitions such as "Do this" and "This should not be done". According to you, there is no such person (since everyone is directed and controlled by the Supreme Self). Since the Supreme Being is the inspirer and director in all actions, you have admitted His power of control over all. It is also said in the Upanishad: "He, whom this Supreme Being desires to raise to a higher position, him the Supreme Being directs to do good deeds. He, whom the

Supreme Being desires to cast down, him the Supreme Being directs to do evil deeds". (Kaushitaki Upanishad 3/9). Further in making them do good and evil deeds, it appears as if the Supreme Being is heartless (and partial).

[Here the contention is - If the Supreme Being controls the actions of all individual souls, there is no use of scriptural injunctions and prohibitions.]

[Ramanuja clarifies his position on this contention.]

अत्रोच्यते सर्वेषामेव चेतनानां चिच्छक्तियोगः प्रवृत्तिशक्तियोग इत्यादि सर्वं प्रवृत्तिनिवृत्तिपरिकरं सामान्येन संविधाय तन्निर्वहणाय तदाधारो भूत्वान्तः प्रविश्यानुमन्तृतया च नियमनं कुर्वञ्शेषि- त्वेनावस्थितः परमात्मैतदाहितशक्तिः सन्प्रवृत्तिनिवृत्त्यादि स्वयमेव कुरुते । एवं कुर्वाणमीक्ष- माणः परमात्मोदासीन आस्ते । अतः सर्वमुपपन्नम् । साध्वसाधुकर्मणोः कारयितृत्वं तु व्यवस्थितविषयं न सर्वसाधारणम् । यस्तु सर्वं स्वयमेवातिमात्रमानुकूल्ये प्रवृत्तस्तं प्रति प्रीतः स्वयमेव भगवान् कल्याणबुद्धियोगदानं कुर्वन् कल्याणे प्रवर्तयति । यः पुनरतिमात्रे प्रातिकूल्ये प्रवृत्तस्तस्य क्रूरां बुद्धिं ददन् स्वयमेव क्रूरेष्वेव कर्मसु प्रेरयति भगवान् ।

The answer to this objection is as follows: The Lord endows all sentient beings, in general, with the power of intelligence, the power of initiating action, and all other such things as are necessary for the performance as well as the non-performance of actions. He becomes their support and basis to enable them to carry out their purposes so He enters into them and controls them by giving His assent to their will. In all this, the Lord remains a basis (support) for the individual self, who thus endowed with these powers, acts or refrains from action in accordance with his own will (independently of the Lord). In these situations, the Supreme Being witnesses the individual self doing these things and remains indifferent (or neutral). Therefore, everything is just. Directing some to do good deeds and some to do evil deeds is not a general rule but according to the context. If a person has already begun, of his own accord, to do things that are extremely pleasing to the Lord, the Lord becomes pleased with his love, and endows him further with wisdom, and inspires him to further deeds of merit. If, on the other hand, a person has already begun to do extremely evil deeds, the Lord strengthens him in his evil nature and makes him do, of his own accord, only cruel deeds thereafter.

[Just as a king or government controls its subject, the Supreme Being also controls the individual souls. However, some do not follow the rules and indulge in unlawful or immoral activities; these fellows are punished in accordance with their crimes. There is nothing unjust or cruel in it because if they are not stopped from doing their crimes, they will keep doing them increasingly and trouble other innocuous living beings.]

[Ramanuja supports his interpretation with the verses of Gita.]

यथोक्तं भगवता – 'तेषां सततयुक्तानां भजतां प्रीतिपूर्वकम् । ददामि बुद्धियोगं तं येन मामुपयान्ति ते ॥ तेषामेवानुकम्पार्थमहमज्ञानजं तमः । नाशयाम्यात्मभावस्थो ज्ञानदीपेन भास्वता ॥' (गीता १०/१०-११), तानहं द्विषतः क्रूरान् संसारेषु नराधमान् । क्षिपाम्यजस्रम-शुभानासुरीष्वेव योनिषु ॥ (गीता १६/१९)' इति ॥

The Lord says: "Those, who are constantly devoted to me and worship me with love, I give them the mental wisdom of realizing me through which they attain me. (Gita 10/10)

"To enable them to attain my grace, I, dwelling in their hearts, reveal my attributes within their minds to destroy their darkness, arising out of their ignorance, by the shining lamp of wisdom." (Gita 10/11)

"Those, who, owing to their cruel nature hate me - I cast these wicked sinners into the cycle of births and deaths and that too only in inauspicious wicked forms of life." (Gita 16/19)

[Here, one should understand that punishment given by the Supreme Being is also for the improvement of the embodied soul, just as a loving mother punishes her kids. So, it is also a form of his grace towards his children, when other benevolent ways to improve the embodied souls fail. And, if an individual soul decides to mend his ways after going through the pain, he receives his grace like a close friend as other righteous embodied souls are receiving it.]

[Having answered the queries of opposition, Ramanuja discusses the supreme welfare of an individual soul. When the Supreme Being is the grandest well-wisher of all, an embodied soul wants to attain him. He might ask about the means to attain him.]

सोऽयं परब्रह्मभूतः पुरुषोत्तमो निरतिशयपुण्यसंचयक्षीणाशेषजन्मोपचितपापराशेः परमपुरुष-चरणारविन्दशरणागतिजनिततदभिमुख्यस्य सदाचार्योपदेशोपबृंहितशास्त्राधिगत तत्त्वयाथा-त्म्यावबोधपूर्वकाहरहरूपचीयमानशमदमतपःशौचक्षमार्जवभयाभयस्थानविवेकदयाहिंसाद्यात्म-गुणोपेतस्य वर्णाश्रमोचितपरमपुरुषाराधनवेषनित्यनैमित्तिककर्मोपसंहृतिनिषिद्धपरिहारनिष्ठस्य परमपुरुषचरणारविन्दयुगलन्यस्तात्मात्मीयस्य तद्भक्तिकारितानवरतस्तुतिस्मृतिनमस्कृतिवन्दन-यतनकीर्तनगुणश्रवणवचनध्यानार्चनप्रणामादिप्रीतपरमकारुणिकपुरुषोत्तमप्रसादविध्वस्तस्वा-न्तध्वान्तस्यानन्यप्रयोजनानवरतनिरतिशयप्रियविशदतमप्रत्यक्षतापन्नानुध्यानरूपभक्त्येकल-भ्यः ।

Now, this Supreme Being, who is the most excellent among the souls, is to be attained. The way to attain Him is as follows - He is attainable by one who has accumulated the greatest virtues, who has won the Lord's grace by seeking refuge at the lotus-like feet, due to which his sins, bundled up during all previous births are destroyed. Then, he gains real knowledge of the truths and their real significance as mentioned in the Scriptures and clearly explained by great gurus who themselves are devoted to the Supreme Being. Then, one makes a steady effort to develop the qualities of the soul such as control of the mind, control of the senses, the practice of austerities and penances, purity of body, patience, straight-forwardness or integrity, the distinctive knowledge of what to fear (namely, offense to the Lord and His devotees and the like) and what not to fear (the conviction that the Lord is his Saviour), compassion (towards those afflicted with suffering), non-violence, etc. in his day to day activities. He never ceases to perform the prescribed compulsory as well as occasional rites and duties in accordance with his caste and stage of life, as forms of worship of the Supreme Person and desists from those actions that are forbidden for someone who has surrendered himself and whatever belongs to him at the lotus feet of the Supreme Being. He, on account of his devotion, is ever engaged in the praise of the Lord, in remembrance of Him, in adoration of Him, in obeisance to Him, in efforts (to render service to Him), in reciting His holy names, in listening to His qualities, in explaining His qualities to others, on meditating Him, in performing his worship and in prostration before Him. The Supreme Person, who is overflowing with compassion, is pleased by such love and showers his grace on the aspirant, which destroys all his inner darkness. Then, one develops supreme devotion towards the Lords which seeks no other reward, which is characterized by boundless love, which is an absolute delight in itself, constant and continuous. Then, this intense devotion takes the form of meditation, which, by its vividness, becomes as direct as the sense perception. Through such intense devotion, the Supreme Lord is attained.

[It can baffle one's mind that being such a small creature how can I ever attain the Lord of the universe? However, intense love towards him is the simplest way to attain him. How can one achieve this emotion of intense love towards him? It comes gradually by serving him, acting according to him as enshrined in the scriptures, thinking about him in various ways, being grateful to him, etc. And, through this intense devotion towards him, a soul attains its supreme, greatest, infallible, and ultimate goal.]

[Ramanuja shows that his views are in total accordance with that of his Guru, and other sacred texts.]

तदुक्तं परमगुरुभिर्भगवद्यामुनाचार्यपादैः – 'उभयपरिकर्मितस्वान्तस्यैकान्तिकात्यन्तिक भक्तियोगलभ्य' (आ० सि०) इति । ज्ञानयोगकर्मयोगसंस्कृतान्तःकरणस्येत्यर्थः । तथा च श्रुतिः – 'विद्यां चाविद्यां च यस्तद्वेदोभयं सह । अविद्यया मृत्युं तीर्त्वा विद्ययामृतमश्नुते ॥' (ई० उ० ११) इति । अत्राविद्याशब्देन विद्येतरत्वाद्वर्णाश्रमाचारादि पूर्वोक्तं कर्मोच्यते विद्याशब्देन च भक्तिरूपापन्नं ध्यानमुच्यते । यथोक्तम् – 'इजाय सोऽपि सुबहून्यज्ञाञ्ज्ञानव्यपाश्रयः । ब्रह्म-विद्यामधिष्ठाय तर्तुं मृत्युमविद्यया ॥' (वि० पु० ६/६/१२) इति । 'तमेवं विद्वानमृत इह भवति नान्यः पन्था अयनाय विद्यते ।' (तै० आ० ३/१२/१७), 'य एनं विदुरमृतास्ते भवन्ति ।' (तै० ना० १/११), 'ब्रह्मविदाप्नोति परम् ।' (तै० उ० १/१/३), 'सो यो ह वै तत्परं ब्रह्म वेद ब्रह्मैव भवति' (मु० उ० ३/२/९) इत्यादि । वेदनशब्देन ध्यानमेवाभिहितम् । निदिध्यासितव्य इत्यादिना ऐकार्थ्यात् ।

The great spiritual teacher, Lord Yamunacharya has likewise said, "He can be attained (only) by him whose mind has been purified by the practice of the two paths (viz., action and knowledge) and whose devotion is boundless and is exclusively directed towards the Lord. This ceaseless devotion is an end in itself." (Atma Siddhi) The practice of the double paths means the culturing of inner sense organs (mind, etc.) by following the path of action and knowledge.

The Upanishad also says: "He, who knows both knowledge and ignorance, overcomes his sins by ignorance (actions) and attains immortality by knowledge." (Isha Upanishad 11). Here, the word ignorance means that which is other than knowledge, namely, action or the performance of rites and duties ordained for each caste and stage of life. The word knowledge means meditation which has reached the form of devotion.

Use of the word ignorance in the sense of actions like fire-sacrifices (Yajna) may be seen from the following sloka: "He, too, performed many fire-sacrifices (Yajna) in order to cross (overcome) his sins by ignorance i. e. action, in order to possess the knowledge of Supreme Being." (Vishnu Purana 6/6/2)

Another Upanishas says "He, who meditates on Him, attains immortality (salvation). There is no other way to attain him." (Taittiriya Aranyaka 3/12/17)

"Those, who know him, become immortal." (Taittiriya Narayana Upanishad 1/11)

"The person, who knows the Supreme Being, attains the ultimate". (Taittiriya Upanishad 1/1/3)

"He, who meditates on Supreme Being, becomes Supreme Being (i. e. resembles Supreme Being)." (Mundaka Upanishad 3/2/9)

In all these sentences, the word 'vedana' or knowledge (vid - to know) really means 'meditation', to maintain the same meaning of the texts such as "should be meditated upon (nididhyasitavya)".

[Everywhere knowing the Supreme Being is said to be the cause of immortality or the highest achievement. And, this attainment comes through thinking about him all the time. Then, this thinking becomes intense or meditative. When continued further, it becomes illuminating and then blissful.]

[Ramanuja highlights the distinct power of this intense devotion or refuge in Supreme Being again, due to its fundamental importance.]

तदेव ध्यानं पुनरपि विशिनष्टि – 'नायमात्मा प्रवचनेन लभ्यो न मेधया न बहुधा श्रुतेन । यमेवैष वृणुते तेन लभ्यस्तस्यैष आत्मा विवृणुते तनूं स्वाम्' (मु० उ० ३/२/३) इति । भक्तिरूपापन्ना- नुध्यानेनैव लभ्यते न केवल, वेदनामात्रेण न मेधयेति केवलस्य निषिद्धत्वात् ॥

The following Upanishad further describes this meditation meditation of the Supreme Being: "The (Supreme) self cannot be attained by speaking about it, neither by intelligence nor by much hearing. By him, who seeks to know it only, it can be attained. To him, it reveals its true nature." – (Mundaka Upanishad 3/2/3, also Katha Upanishad 1/2/22)

Not by mere meditation but by constant and continuous meditation that is transformed into devotion can one attain the Supreme Being. Mere meditation cannot do it because it is negated in the phrase, 'not by the exercise of intellect.'

[Having said that the Supreme Being is attainable through intense devotion, the Upanishads also negate all other means to attain him. Meditation, without devotion, cannot lead us to him. This confirms that intense devotion is the only way.]

[Thus, when one performs all his actions, with a sense of devotion towards the Supreme Being in his mind (rather heart), it becomes a means to attain him.]

एतदुक्तं भवति - योऽयं मुमुक्षुर्वेदान्तविहितवेदनरूपध्यानादिनिष्ठो यदा तस्य तस्मिन्नेवानुध्याने निरवधिकातिशया प्रीतिर्जायते तदैव तेन लभ्यते परः पुरुष इति । यथोक्तं भगवता – 'पुरुषः स परः पार्थ भक्त्या लभ्यस्त्वनन्यया ।' (गीता ८/२२), 'भक्त्या त्वनन्यया शक्योऽहमेवंविधोऽर्जुन । ज्ञातुं द्रष्टुं च तत्त्वेन प्रवेष्टुं च परन्तप ॥' (गीता ११/५४), 'भक्त्या मामभिजानाति यावान् यश्चास्मि तत्त्वतः । ततो मां तत्त्वतो ज्ञात्वा विशते तदनन्तरम् ॥' (गीता १८/५५) इति ।
तदनन्तरं तत एव भक्तितो विशत इत्यर्थः । भक्तिरपि निरतिशयप्रियानन्यप्रयोजनसकलेतरवैतृ- ष्ण्यावहज्ञानविशेष एवेति । तद्युक्त एव तेन परेणात्मना वरणीयो भवतीति तेन लभ्यत इति श्रुत्यर्थः ।

It comes to mean this: Only when a person desirous of release from bondage performs meditation, etc. as ordained in Vedanta, and when this continuous meditation turns into boundless love to the Lord, then through that love does he become capable of attaining the Lord.

Lord Krishna has also stated the same: " O son of Kunti, Arjun, that Supreme Being (reality) in which all living beings reside, that which pervades all, is attainable only by exclusive devotion. ("Exclusive" means that the devotion is only to Him and to no other deity.) (Gita 8/22)

"O Arjun, the tormentor of foes! Seeing me in this way, knowing by real nature and abiding in me is possible only through the exclusive devotion." (Gita 11/54)

"Through the supreme devotion, he gets to know what and who I am, then, after knowing my essence, he merges into me without delay." (Gita 18/55)

The meaning is this: After that, without a delay, owing to that devotion, he enters into the Supreme Being. Devotion is a special form of knowledge that is characterized by unsurpassed love, in which there is no expectation of any reward other than itself and which eliminates the desire for all other things. Only when a person has this kind of devotion, does he become capable of being chosen by the Lord (for His Grace), and through that grace he attains the Lord. This is the meaning of the Upanishad verse cited above.

[One starts his journey of transformation with normal devotion towards the Supreme Being. Gradually, it becomes intense. In this stage of intense devotion, he experiences or knows the Supreme Being directly. After this experience of the Supreme Being, his devotion culminates in its supreme form. Then, this supreme or ultimate devotion alone leads him to the Supreme Being. So, it is said that the Supreme Being is attainable solely through devotion.]

[Now, Ramanuja summarizes how anyone can attain Supreme Being.]

एवंविधपरभक्तिरूपज्ञानविशेषस्योत्पादकः पूर्वोक्ताहरहरुपचीयमानज्ञानपूर्वककर्मानुगृहीत-
भक्तियोग एव । यथोक्तं भगवता पराशरेण – ‘वर्णाश्रमाचारवता पुरुषेण परः पुमान् ।
विष्णुराराध्यते पन्था नान्यस्तत्तोषकारकः ॥’ (वि० पु० ३/८/९) इति । निखिलजगदुद्धारणाया
-वनितलेऽवतीर्णः परब्रह्मभूतः पुरुषोत्तमः स्वयमेवैतदुक्तवान् – ‘स्वकर्मनिरतः सिद्धिं यथा
विन्दति तच्छृणु ॥ यतः प्रवृत्तिर्भूतानां येन सर्वमिदं ततम् । स्वकर्मणा तमभ्यर्च्य सिद्धिं विन्दति
मानवः ॥’ (गीता १८/४५-४६) इति । यथोदितक्रमपरिणतभक्त्येकलभ्य एव ॥

This kind of supreme devotion, which is a special form of knowledge, arises only from following the path of devotion. This path of devotion results from following the path of action, which involves the day-by-day performance of rites and duties (in absolute detachment in the spirit of service to the Lord), it results in the knowledge of the essential nature of the soul. So says Lord Parashara:

"A person, who performs the duties and rites according to his caste and stage of his life, worships the Supreme Person. There is no other way of pleasing Him". (Vishnu Purana 3/8/6)

The most exalted among the soul, the Supreme Person who incarnated in this world for the redemption of the whole world, has stated this Himself: "Listen to me. I will tell you how a person who is earnestly engaged in the performance of his duties attains salvation. The great Lord, whose power makes everyone function, and who pervades this entire world - worshiping him by doing one's inherent duty, a person attains perfection (salvation)." (Gita 18/45-46)

It means: That he can be attained only by devotion which has gradually developed in strength, in accordance with what has been said before.

[One can start with his current situation by following his duties and then cultivating love towards the Supreme Being in the manner described above. This will lead him to the Supreme Being as he has himself said it in Gita.]

[Why should one follow the viewpoint of Ramanuja and not others?]

बोधायनटङ्कद्रमिडगुहदेवकपर्दिभारुचिप्रभृत्यविगीतशिष्टपरिगृहीतपुरातनवेदवेदान्तव्याख्यान
सुव्यक्तार्थश्रुतिनिकरनिर्दिशितोऽयं पन्थाः । अनेन चार्वाकशाक्याउलूक्याक्षपादक्षपणककपिल-
पतञ्जलिमतानुसारिणो वेदबाह्यावेदावलम्बिकुदृष्टिभिः सह निरस्ताः ।

This is the path indicated in all the Upanishads whose meaning has been made clear by ancient commentaries on the Veda and the Vedanta and approved, without exception, by holy persons such as Bodhayana, Tanka, Dramida, Guhadeva, Kapardi, and Bharuchi. By this (exposition of right doctrine), Charvakas, Buddhists, the followers of Kanada, Gautama, Jains, and the followers of Kapila and Patanjali, who are all unbelievers in the Veda, have been refuted, along with those who hold incorrect views, while believing in the authority of the Veda.

[The viewpoint of Ramanuja is in total accordance with great sages of the past and does not inhibit the correct meaning of the Vedas in any way. On the other hand, some others, though they appear to follow the Vedas, do not follow its essence in completeness.]

[Why do others, who appear to follow the Vedas, err in their viewpoints?]

वेदावलम्बिनामपि यथावस्थितवस्तुविपर्ययस्तादृशां बाह्यसाम्यं मनुनैवोक्तम् – 'यो वेदबाह्याः
स्मृतयो याश्च काश्च कुदृष्टयः । सर्वास्ता निष्फलाः प्रेत्य तमोनिष्ठा हि ताः स्मृताः ॥' (म॰ स्मृ॰
१२/९५) इति । रजस्तमोभ्यामस्पृष्टमुत्तमं सत्त्वमेव येषां स्वाभाविको गुणस्तेषामेव वैदिकी
रुचिर्वेदार्थयाथात्म्यावबोधश्चेत्यर्थः ॥

Even among those who believe in the authority of the Veda, those whose vision is blind to the knowledge of the true nature of things are considered by Manu on the same footing as those who do not acknowledge the authority of the Veda. "Those smritis (memory-based texts) which do not acknowledge the authority of the Veda and those again that are perverse in their vision - all these are of no avail after death; for they are associated with darkness (tamas)". (Manu Smriti 12/95)

This is the meaning: Only those texts whose essential nature is true sattva (endowed with righteousness) untainted by any trace of rajas (activity, anxiety) and tamas (darkness), can interpret the Veda in the right spirit and have an understanding of their real significance.

[When a person is not established in the purest form of Sattva (righteousness), he can err in his viewpoint.]

[What is the basis of this claim?]

यथोक्तं मात्स्ये – 'संकीर्णाः सात्त्विकाश्चैव राजसास्तामसास्तथा ।' (म० पु०) इति । केचिद्ब्रह्मकल्पाः संकीर्णाः केचित्सत्त्वप्रायाः केचिद्रजःप्राया केचित्तमःप्राया इति कल्पविभाग-मुक्त्वा सत्त्वरजस्तमोमयानां तत्त्वानां माहात्म्यवर्णनं च तत्तत्कल्पप्रोक्तपुराणेषु सत्त्वादिगुण-मयेन ब्रह्मणा क्रियत इति चोक्तम् – 'यस्मिन् कल्पे तु यत्प्रोक्तं पुराणं ब्रह्मणा पुरा । तस्य तस्य तु माहात्म्यं तत्स्वरूपेण वर्ण्यते ॥' (म० पु०) इति । विशेषतश्चोक्तम् – 'अग्नेः शिवस्य माहात्म्यं तामसेषु प्रकीर्त्यते । राजसेषु च माहात्म्यमधिकं ब्रह्मणो विदुः ॥ सात्त्विकेषु च कल्पेषु माहात्म्यमधिकं हरेः । तेष्वेव योगसंसिद्धा गमिष्यन्ति परां गतिम् ॥ संकीर्णेषु सरस्वत्याः ... ॥' (म० पु०) इत्यादि ।

It has also been said in the Matsya Purana: "Some epochs (kalpas, cosmic periods equal to a day of Brahma) are mixed, some are sattvika, and some again are rajasa, while others are tamasa."

It points out the differences among the epochs by saying that some among Brahma's epochs are mixed, some are predominantly sattvic, and some are predominantly rajasic, while others are predominantly tamasic. After this classification of epochs, it describes the characteristics of elements (and their presiding deities) endowed with Sattva, Rajas, and Tamas. Then it says that the creation of puranas, belonging to the respective epoch, is according to the predominant attribute like Sattva present in it because their composer Brahma is also likewise influenced by those attributes. It is also said there - "Whatever Purana was said in a particular previous epoch by Brahma, it describes the greatness of only the deity having predominance in that epoch." - Matsya Puranam

This principle is more specifically laid down in the following verse: "The greatness of fire-god (Agni) and Shiva is extolled in puranas which are tamasic; the greatness of Brahma is highly described in puranas which are rajasic and in puranas which are sattvic, the greatness of Hari is seen prominently. Only those who follow the path prescribed in these sattvika (righteous) Puranas reach the Supreme Goal. The Puranas, belonging to a mixed epoch, describe the greatness of Saraswati and of the forefathers and so on.

[Even Lord Brahma is not immune to the nature of the epoch, in which he is delivering the Puranas to the sages. If an epoch is mixed with Rajas and Tamas, the viewpoints established in that time would also become slightly contaminated.]

[All living and non-living entities are under the influence of the three attributes of nature – Sattva, Rajas, and Tamas. They leave their imprint on everyone.]

एतदुक्तं भवति - आदिक्षेत्रज्ञत्वाद्ब्रह्मणस्तस्यापि केषुचिदहस्सु सत्त्वमुद्रिकं केषुचिद्रजः केषुचित्तमः । यथोक्तं भगवता – 'न तदस्ति पृथिव्यां वा दिवि देवेषु वा पुनः । सत्त्वं प्रकृतिजैर्मुक्तं यदेभिः स्यात्त्रिभिर्गुणैः ॥' (गीता १८/४०) इति । 'यो ब्रह्माणं विदधाति पूर्वं यो वै वेदांश्च प्रहिणोति तस्मा' (श्वे० उ० ६/१८) इति श्रुतेः । ब्रह्मणोऽपि सृज्यत्वेन शास्त्रवश्यत्वेन च क्षेत्रज्ञत्वं गम्यते । सत्त्वप्रायेष्वहस्सु तदितरेषु यानि पुराणानि ब्रह्मणा प्रोक्तानि तेषां परस्परविरोधे सति सात्त्विकाहःप्रोक्तमेव पुराणं यथार्थं तद्विरोध्यन्यदयथार्थमिति पुराणनिर्णया- यैवेदं सत्त्वनिष्ठेन ब्रह्मणाभिहितमिति विज्ञायत इति ।

This is what it means: Though Brahma is the first among created beings, in him too, on certain days (of his), sattva is predominant, in others rajas and others still, tamas. Lord Krishna has also said this: "Neither among the beings on the earth nor again among the gods in heaven is there any created being free from these three qualities of matter (viz. sattva, rajas and tamas)." (Gita 18/40)

The Upanishad says: "He who first created Brahma and He, who conveyed the Vedas to him, (He is Supreme Being)". (Shvetashvatara Upanishad 6/18)

From this, it may be inferred that Brahma is also a created being, and he, too, is subject to the authority of the scriptures, like any other individual self. If there is a conflict (of statements) between the Puranas dictated by him on the days, which were sattvic and those, which were dictated by him on other days, only that Purana which was dictated on the sattvic days is authoritative; those which conflict with it are not. The superior validity of a particular Purana has to be determined after considering whether or not it was dictated by Brahma on his sattvic days because only on a sattvic day, Brahma can know the reality correctly.

[One has to decide the superiority of a Purana over others according to the mental state of its preacher. If we see a conflict among various puranas, we need to give priority to those that are classified as Sattvika, e.g. Vishnu Purana, Bhagavata Purana, etc.]

[It is due to the intrinsic nature of these attributes that error of judgment can come into the great persons as well.]

सत्त्वादीनां कार्यं च भगवतैवोक्तम् – 'सत्त्वात्संजायते ज्ञानं रजसो लोभ एव च । प्रमादमोहौ तमसो भवतोऽज्ञानमेव च ॥' (गीता १४/१७), 'प्रवृत्तिं च निवृत्तिं च कार्याकार्ये भयाभये । बन्धं मोक्षं च या वेत्ति बुद्धिः सा पार्थ सात्त्विकी ॥ यथा धर्ममधर्मं च कार्यं चाकार्यमेव च । अयथावत्प्रजानाति बुद्धिः सा पार्थ राजसी ॥ अधर्मं धर्ममिति या मन्यते तमसावृता । सर्वार्थान्

विपरीतांश्च बुद्धिः सा पार्थ तामसी ॥' (गीता १८/३०-३२) इति । सर्वान् पुराणार्थान् ब्रह्मणः
सकाशादधिगम्यैव सर्वाणि पुराणानि पुराणकाराश्चक्रुः । यथोक्तम् - 'कथयामि यथा पूर्वं
दक्षाद्यैर्मुनिसत्तमैः । पृष्टः प्रोवाच भगवानब्जयोनिः पितामहः ॥' (वि० पु० १/२/८) इति ॥

The effects of sattva and the other qualities are stated as follows by
Lord Krishna Himself: "Sattva (righteousness) leads to knowledge
(real nature of the soul) and Rajas definitely leads to greed (for the
pleasures of this life and of heaven) and Tamas to delusion and
ignorance also." (Gita 14/17)

"O son of Kunti, Arjun! The intellect, which knows the differences
between the actions (that leads to the pleasures of this world) as
well as their renunciation (that leads to salvation), what is to be
done and what should not be done, fear and fearlessness, bondage
and salvation - is called righteous (Sattviki)." (Gita 18/30)

"O son of Kunti, Arjun! The intellect by which a person does not
properly know righteousness and unrighteousness, what is to be
done and what should not be done, that intellect is Rajasika or
passionate in nature." (Gita 18/31)

"O son of Kunti, Arjun! Surrounded by the darkness of ignorance,
the intellect that considers wrong to be right, and similarly
perverted view as the correct one in other matters, that intellect is
Tamasika or ignorant." (Gita 18/32)

The authors of the Puranas learned what was said in the respective
Puranas from Brahma himself and then composed the Puranas. This
may be seen (in the following verse): "I will tell you, as Lord Brahma,
born in the lotus, previously told on being asked by the great sages
like Daksha (what is said in the Puranas)." (Vishnu Purana 1/2/8)

[Thus, while establishing his viewpoint, Ramanuja has also explained
the opposite viewpoints and the reasons for their error.]

Deduction of Narayana as the Supreme Being

[The critics might still say that even if there is a difference in various other scriptures regarding the Supreme Being, there should be unanimity about him in the Vedas since Vedas are not composed by humans. However, we see that sometimes Shiva (or Rudra) is also referred to as Supreme Being.]

अपौरुषेयेषु वेदवाक्येषु परस्परविरुद्धेषु कथमिति चेत् । तात्पर्यनिश्चयादविरोधः पूर्वमेवोक्तः । यदपि चेदेवं विरुद्धवदृश्यते – 'प्राणं मनसि सह कारणैर्नादान्ते परमात्मनि संप्रतिष्ठाय ध्यायीतव्यं प्रध्यायीतव्यं सर्वमिदं । ब्रह्मविष्णुरुद्रास्ते सर्वे संप्रसूयन्ते, न कारणं' (अथर्वशिख० उ० २/१४-१६), '...कारणं तु ध्येयः । ... सर्वैश्वर्यसंपन्नः सर्वेश्वरः शंभुराकाशमध्ये ध्येयः ।' (अथर्वशिख० उ० ३/१७), 'यस्मात्परं नापरमस्ति किंचिद्यस्मान्नाणीयो न ज्यायोऽस्ति कश्चित् वृक्ष इव स्तब्धो दिवि तिष्ठत्येकस्तेनेदं पूर्णं पुरुषेण सर्वम् । ततो यदुत्तरतरं तदरूपमनामयं य एतद्विदुरमृतास्ते भवन्ति, अथेतरे दुःखमेवापियन्ति । सर्वाननशिरोग्रीवः सर्वभूतगुहाशयः । सर्वव्यापी च भगवांस्तस्मात्सर्वगतः शिवः ॥' (श्वे० उ० ३/९-११), 'यदा तमस्तन्न दिवा न रात्रिर्न सन्न चासच्छिव एव केवलः । तदक्षरं तत्सवितुर्वरेण्यं प्रज्ञा च तस्मात्प्रसृता पुराणी ॥' (श्वे० उ० ४/१८) इत्यादि नारायणः परं ब्रह्मेति च पूर्वमेव प्रतिपादितं, तेनास्य कथमविरोधः ॥

If you ask how the decision should be arrived at in cases where there is mutual conflict among the passages in the Vedas, which are not of human authorship. We have already said that the conflict is resolved by careful consideration of the previous and afterward texts and then determining their right meaning.

Here are some passages in the Upanishads which appear to be conflicting:

(1) "Fix vital airs (prana), mind, and the senses on the highest self, present at the end of nada (sound), one should meditate and meditate again on the controlling Lord, who is the cause of all." (Atharva Shikha Upanishad 2/14)

(2) "Brahma, Vishnu, Rudra, and Indra are all created beings. So, they are not the ultimate causes. What is to be meditated on is the

(ultimate) cause. Only Shambhu (Shiva), who possesses all supreme powers and who is the Lord of all, is fit to be meditated upon in the midst of the space (within the heart)". (Atharva Shikha Upanishad 2/15-16)

(3) "There is none superior to Him; neither is he inferior to anyone else. There is nothing smaller or greater than Him. He, who stands alone and unshaken like a tree in the heavens, by him is this entire (universe) filled. That Being is far beyond this world, is formless, and free from misery. They who know Him become immortal. But all others have indeed to suffer misery alone. That (Being) has its faces everywhere, its heads everywhere, and its necks everywhere. It lives in the cave of the heart of all creatures. It pervades all things. It is the Lord who is called Shiva." (Shvetashvatara Upanishad 3/9-11)

(4) "When there was darkness (tamas) everywhere, there was no such (division) as day and as night; there was neither existence (sat) nor non-existence (asat), only Shiva existed then. He is the imperishable, radiant, and auspicious reality, which is worthy of adoration. It is from Him during creation that the consciousness of (living) beings attains expansion." (Shvetashvatara Upanishad 4/18)

You have already pointed out that Narayana is the Supreme Being. How, then, you could say this does not conflict with the passages cited above, where Shiva is stated to be the Supreme Being?

[Here, the opposition has cited various references which declare Shiva as Supreme Being.]

[Ramanuja resolves their doubt in the next few paragraphs.]

अत्यल्पमेतत् – ‘वेदवित्प्रवरप्रोक्तवाक्यन्यायोपबृंहिताः । वेदाः साङ्गा हरिं प्राहुर्जगज्जन्मादि-कारणम् ॥’ ‘जन्माद्यस्य यतः:’ (ब्र॰ सू॰ १/१/२), ‘यतो वा इमानि भूतानि जायन्ते, येन जातानि जीवन्ति, यत्प्रयन्त्यभिसंविशन्ति, तद्विजिज्ञानस्व तद्ब्रह्म’ (तै॰ उ॰ ३/२) इति

जगज्जन्मादिकारणं ब्रह्मेत्यवगम्यते । तच्च जगत्सृष्टिप्रलयप्रकरणेष्ववगन्तव्यम् । 'सदेव
सोम्येदमग्र आसीदेकमेवाद्वितीयम्' (छा॰ उ॰ ६/२/१) इति जगदुपादानताजगन्निमित्तता-
जगदन्तर्यामितादिमुखेन परमकारणं सच्छब्देन प्रतिपादितं ब्रह्मेत्यवगतम् । अयमेवार्थः - 'ब्रह्म
वा इदमेकमेवाग्र आसीत्' (बृ॰ उ॰ ३/४/११) इति शाखान्तरे ब्रह्मशब्देन प्रतिपादितः । अनेन
सच्छब्देनाभिहितं ब्रह्मेत्यवगतम् । अयमेवार्थस्तथा शाखान्तर 'आत्मा वा इदमेक एवाग्र आसी-
न्नान्यत्किंचन मिषत्' (ऐ॰ उ॰ १/१) इति सद्ब्रह्मशब्दाभ्यामात्मैवाभिहित इत्यवगम्यते । तथा
च शाखान्तर 'एको ह वै नारायण आसीन्न ब्रह्म नेशानो नेमे द्यावापृथिवी न नक्षत्राणि' (महो॰
१/१) इति सद्ब्रह्मात्मादिपरमकारणवादिभिः शब्दैर्नारायण एवाभिधीयत इति निश्चीयते ॥

It is a very trivial issue. The Vedas, along with their supplementary treatises, as elaborated by the principles of interpretation by their best knowers declare that Hari (Narayana) is the cause of the origin, dissolution, etc. of the universe. Vyasa says: "From whom the origin, sustenance, etc. of the universe proceed is Supreme Being." (Brahma Sutra 1/1/2), "That from which all these beings are born, in which they continue to live, and into which they all merge, is Supreme Being" (Taittriya Upanishad 3/2)

From these statements, it is evident that the Supreme Being is the cause of the creation, etc. of the world. Moreover, this has to be understood only from the sections dealing with the creation of the world. "This (world) existed, my dear, as existence (Sat) at the beginning, single and without a second." (Chhandogya Upanishad 6/2/1) From this text, it is learned that the material and the instrumental cause of the world, the Inner Ruler of all, and the final cause is denoted by the word 'existence' (Sat). Another branch of the Upanishad says: "In the beginning, Supreme Being alone existed." (Brihat Aranyaka Upanishad 3/4/11) Here, the final cause is referred to by the word 'Supreme Being'. So it is clear that what is referred to by the word existence (Sat) is the Supreme Being only. In another branch, the same meaning is conveyed: "In the beginning, the soul alone existed and nothing else." (Aitreya Upanishad 1/1) Here, the final cause is referred to by the word soul. This brings out that the soul itself was described in the other two sections as existence and the Supreme Being. Similarly, in another branch, it is said: "Only Narayana existed (then), neither Brahma nor Ishana (Shiva), nor the sky nor the earth". (Mahopanishad 1/1) Here, the final cause is referred to by the word 'Narayana'. From this, it may be determined that 'Narayana' itself was described in other sections by words like existence, Supreme Being, soul, etc. expressive of the final cause of all.

[Ramanuja shows that the Supreme Being is endowed with extraordinary attributes, such as creation, maintenance, and dissolution of the world, he is the material and instrumental cause also. He is also referred to as truth, reality, existence, soul, etc. Mahopanishad specifically says that Narayana alone was present in the beginning, and not Shiva or Brahma. It is the same as saying that in the beginning, truth or reality alone was present. This shows that Narayana is the Supreme Being and no one else. When we refer to the Supreme Being by words truth, reality, existence, etc., it is his general reference to highlight a specific aspect of him. However, when we refer to the Supreme Being by the word Narayana, it is his distinguished or special reference.]

[He, further, cites those passages which are solely related to the description of the Supreme Being, and names him as Narayana.]

'यमन्तः समुद्रे कवयो वयन्ति' (तै० ना० उ० १/३) इत्यादि । 'नैनमूर्ध्वं न तिर्यञ्चं न मध्ये परिजग्रभत् । न तस्येशे कश्चन तस्य नाम महद्यशः ॥ न संदृशे तिष्ठति रूपमस्य न चक्षुषा पश्यति कश्चनैनम्, हृदा मनीषा मनसाऽभिक्लृप्तो य एवं विदुरमृतास्ते भवन्ति' (तै० ना० उ० १/१०-११) इति सर्वस्मात्परत्वमस्य प्रतिपाद्य, 'न तस्येशे कश्चन' (तै० ना० उ० १/१०) इति तस्मात्परं किमपि न विद्यत इति च प्रतिषिध्य, 'अद्भ्यः सम्भूतो हिरण्यगर्भ इत्यष्टौ' (तै० ना० उ० ३/१२) इति तेनैकवाक्यतां गमयति । तच्च महापुरुषप्रकरणं – 'ह्रीश्च ते लक्ष्मीश्च पत्न्यौ' (तै० ना० उ० ३/१३) इति च नारायण एवेति द्योतयति ॥

A passage begins with – "The seers see him within the ocean of their heart." (Taittiriya Narayana Upanishad 1/3) and ends with "No one grasps him from above, none grasps him horizontally, none in the center. No one rules over Him. His glory, indeed, is greatly magnanimous (as the creator and protector of the world). His form is not within the scope of vision, and no one can see Him with his eye. He can be realized only in the heart by a mind fully immersed in resolute devotion. Those who see Him become immortal." (Taittiriya Narayana Upanishad 1/10-11) This passage brings out that the Supreme Being is beyond all else. It also denies the existence of anything superior to Him by saying 'none rules over Him". Then, through eight hymns beginning with "the golden egg (Hiranyagarbha or Brahma) arose from the divine waters (Supreme Being)" (Taittiriya Narayana Upanishad 3/12), this passage conveys the same meaning. This context is related to the Supreme Being. It praises Supreme Being by the sentence, "Hrih (i.e.) Bhumi) and Lakshmi are His consorts." (Taittiriya Narayana Upanishad 3/13) So it is Narayana, this context is referring to.

['Lying on the ocean' and 'being the Spouse of Lakshmi' are marks from which it may be inferred that the deity referred to is Narayana.]

[Now, Ramanuja explains the previous references.]

अयमर्थो नारायणानुवाके प्रपञ्चितः - 'सहस्रशीर्ष देवम्' (तै० ना० उ० ११/१) इत्यारभ्य 'स ब्रह्म स शिवः सेन्द्रः सोऽक्षरः परमः स्वराट्' (तै० ना० उ० ११/१२) इति । सर्वशाखासु परतत्त्वप्रतिपादनपरानक्षरशिवशंभुपरब्रह्मपरज्योतिःपरतत्त्वपरायणपरमात्मादिसर्वशब्दांस्तत्त-द्गुणयोगेन नारायण एव प्रयुज्य तद्व्यतिरिक्तस्य समस्तस्य तदाधारतां तन्नियाम्यतां तच्छेषतां तदात्मकतां च प्रतिपाद्य ब्रह्मशिवयोरपीन्द्रादिसमानाकारतया तद्विभूतित्वं च प्रतिपादितम् । इदं च वाक्यं केवलपरतत्त्वप्रतिपादनैकपरमन्यत्किंचिदप्यत्र न विधीयते ॥

This idea is explicitly stated in the Narayana Anuvaka: It commences with "He is the God with a thousand heads" (Taittiriya Narayana Upanishad 11/1) and ends with "He is Brahma, He is Shiva, He is Indra, He is the freed soul (Akshara); He is the Supreme Ruler with absolute sway". (Taittiriya Narayana Upanishad 11/12)

This section employs those words for Narayana which, in all the branches of the Vedas, denote the Supreme Reality and his extraordinary qualities; words like 'the freed soul', 'Shiva', 'Shambhu', "The Supreme Being", "The Supreme Light', "The Supreme Truth or Reality", "The Supreme Goal', and the 'Supreme Being' denote here Narayana only, endowed with the respective qualities. It further points out that all other things are dependent on Him, are pervaded by Him, are supported by Him, are controlled by Him, exist for Him to serve His purposes, and have Him as their soul. It also shows how Brahma and Shiva are in the same category as Indra and other deities and are therefore among His glories (special manifestations or subserving officers). This sentence in the section is solely intended to determine the nature of the Supreme Reality as it does not describe anything else apart from this.

[This section establishes Narayana as the Supreme Being by listing his several unique and extraordinary properties. Whenever we see the mention of any of these unique properties like the cause of all causes, basis of everything, controller of all, creator, destroyer of the world, etc., we should interpret it as the reference of Narayana. These properties are exclusive to him and there is none who is equal or superior to him. Here we also see that Narayana is referred to as Shiva, Brahma, etc. also because he is the soul of all.]

[Employing his special status as the soul of all, other Upanishads prescribe his worship as the inner soul, cause of all causes, giver of liberation, etc.]

अस्मिन् वाक्ये प्रतिपादितस्य सर्वस्मात्परत्वेनावस्थितस्य ब्रह्मणो वाक्यान्तरेषु 'ब्रह्मविदाप्नोति
परम्,' (तै० उ० १/१) इत्यादिष्वूपासनादि विधीयते । अतः 'प्राणं मनसि सह करणैः' (अथर्व-
शिख० उ० २) इत्यादि वाक्यं सर्वकारणे परमात्मनि करणप्राणादि सर्व विकारजातमुपसंहृत्य
तमेव परमात्मानं सर्वस्येशानं ध्यायीतेति परब्रह्मभूतनारायणस्यैव ध्यानं विदधाति ॥

The adoration of the Supreme Being, who is declared in this
passage as being above all else, is mentioned in other passages as
well. "He who meditates on Supreme Being attains the Supreme".
(Taittiriya Upanishad 1/1) This sentence prescribes meditation on
the Supreme Being. Therefore, "one should meditate on the
Supreme Being, who is the cause of everything, by withdrawing the
senses, vital breaths, and the mind and fixing them on Him".
(Atharva Shikha Upanishad 2) It says to meditate on the Supreme
Being, who is the Lord of all. Thus, it prescribes meditation on
Narayana, who is the Supreme Being.

[Till here, we have established the consistency of those descriptions
which directly or indirectly show Narayana as Supreme Being.]

[Now, Ramanuja interprets how the word 'Shambhu', commonly
used for Lord Shiva, is used here to denote Narayana because he is
the inner soul of all.]

'पतिं विश्वस्य' (तै० ना० उ० ११/३) इति 'न तस्येशे कश्चन' (तै० ना० उ० १/१०) इति च
तस्यैव सर्वस्येशानता प्रतिपादिता । अत एव 'सर्वैश्वर्यसंपन्नः सर्वेश्वरः शंभुराकाशमध्ये ध्येयः'
(अथर्वशिख० २) इति नारायणस्यैव परमकारणस्य शंभुशब्दवाच्यस्य ध्यानं विधीयते । 'कश्च
ध्येयः' (अथर्वशिख० १) इत्यारभ्य 'कारणं तु ध्येय' (अथर्वशिख० २) इति कार्यस्याध्येयता-
पूर्वककारणैकध्येयतापरत्वाद्वाक्यस्य । तस्यैव नारायणस्य परमकारणता शंभुशब्दवाच्यता च
परमकारणप्रतिपादनैकपरे नारायणानुवाक एव प्रतिपन्नेति तद्विरोधर्थान्तरपरिकल्पनं
कारणस्यैव ध्येयत्वेन विधिवाक्ये न युज्यते ॥

The word 'Ishana' applies to Narayana (and not to Shiva) because
the Upanishads say "He is the Lord of the Universe" (Taittiriya

Narayana Upanishad 11/3) and "There is no ruler over Him". (Taittiriya Narayana Upanishad 1/10) The passage "Shambhu is the overlord of all, to him belong all diving opulence, he should be meditated in the middle of the sky (inner space)." (Atharva Shikha Upanishad 2) also prescribes the meditation on Narayana, who is the ultimate cause and so for him the word 'Shambhu' is used. This passage begins with the question "On whom should one meditate?" (Atharva Shikha Upanishad 1) and ends with "The cause should be meditated on." (Atharva Shikha Upanishad 2) It lays down first that the effect or what is produced should not be meditated and only the cause is fit to be meditated on. Since Narayana Anuvaka deals solely with the question of determining the ultimate cause, it declares Narayana as the ultimate cause and also denotes Him by the word 'Shambhu' so both of them denote the same reality. Therefore, to give it any other interpretation besides this is against reason because it will conflict with the prescription in the text that the only cause should be meditated upon.

[The entire section of Atharva Shikha Upanishad makes sense if the word Shambhu means Narayana here. Since it earlier says to meditate on the cause of all causes, and then it refers to him by the word Shambhu. It means that the word Shambhu is used for Narayana because he alone is the cause of all causes.]

[Now, Ramanuja explains how the word 'Shiva' denotes Narayana.]

यदपि 'ततो यदुत्तरम्' (श्वे उ॰ ३/१०) इत्यत्र पुरुषादन्यस्य परतरत्वं प्रतीयत इत्यभ्यधायि तदपि – 'यस्मात्परं नापरमस्ति किंचिद्यस्मान्नाणीयो न ज्यायोऽस्ति कश्चित्' (श्वे उ॰ ३/९) यस्मादपरं यस्मादन्यत्किंचिदपि परं नास्ति केनापि प्रकारेण पुरुषव्यतिरिक्तस्य परत्वं नास्ती- त्यर्थः । अणीयस्त्वं सूक्ष्मत्वम् । ज्यायस्त्वं सर्वेश्वरत्वम् । सर्वव्यापित्वात्सर्वेश्वरत्वादस्यैतद्व्यति- रिक्तस्य कस्याप्यणीयस्त्वं ज्यायस्त्वं च नास्तीत्यर्थः । यस्मान्नाणीयो न ज्यायोऽस्ति कश्चिदिति पुरुषादन्यस्य कस्यापि ज्यायस्त्वं निषिद्धमिति तस्मादन्यस्य परत्वं न युज्यत इति प्रत्युक्तम् ॥

It might appear from the sentence, "That which is superior to Him" (Shvetashvatara Upanishad 3/10) that there is some reality higher than the Supreme Being. However, this possibility is ruled out by the following sentence. "There is none superior to Him; neither is he inferior to anyone else. There is nothing smaller or greater than Him." (Shvetashvatara Upanishad 3/9), which says there is none superior to the Supreme Being in any possible way. The passage means - "The word smaller implies subtleness, greater implies "Lordship over all". Since He pervades all and is the Lord of all, nothing else is subtler or greater than Him. The phrase "there is nothing more subtle or greater than Him" also denies the superiority of any one else other than the Supreme Being. So, this consideration rules out the supremacy of any other deity.

[The references used in Shvetashvatara Upanishad describe the extraordinary attributes of the Supreme Being, which are unique to him. So, it means that the context refers to Supreme Being.]

[Ramanuja explains the meaning of the referenced verses to make it clear.]

कस्तर्ह्यस्य वाक्यस्यार्थः । अस्य प्रकरणस्योपक्रमे 'तमेव विदित्वातिमृत्युमेति नान्यः पन्था विद्यतेऽयनाय' (श्वे॰ उ॰ ३/८) इति पुरुषवेदनस्यामृतत्वहेतुतां तद्व्यतिरिक्तस्यापथतां च प्रतिज्ञाय 'यस्मात्परं नापरमस्ति किंचित्तेनेदं पूर्णं पुरुषेण सर्वम्' (श्वे॰ उ॰ ३/९) इत्येतदन्तेन सर्वस्मात्परत्वं प्रतिपादितम् । यतः पुरुषतत्त्वमेवोत्तरतरं ततो यदुत्तरतरं पुरुषतत्त्वं तदेवारूपम-नामयं 'य एतद्विदुरमृतास्ते भवन्ति, अथेतरे दुःखमेवापियन्ति' (श्वे॰ उ॰ ३/१०) इति पुरुषवेदन-स्यामृतत्वहेतुत्वं तदितरस्यापथत्वं प्रतिज्ञातं सहेतुकमुपसंहृतम् । अन्यथोपक्रमगतप्रतिज्ञाभ्यां विरुध्यते । पुरुषस्यैव शुद्धिगुणयोगेन शिवशब्दाभिप्रायत्वं, 'शाश्वतं शिवमच्युतम्' (तै॰ ना॰ उ॰ ११/३) इत्यादिना ज्ञातमेव । पुरुष एव शिवशब्दाभिधेय इत्यनन्तरमेव वदति - 'महान् प्रभुर्वै पुरुषः सत्त्वस्यैष प्रवर्तकः' (श्वे॰ उ॰ ३/१२) इति । उक्तेनैव न्यायेन 'न सन्न चासच्छिव एव केवलः' (श्वे॰ उ॰ ४/१८) इत्यादि सर्वं नेयम् ॥

If you ask what the meaning of this passage is, the answer is as follows: At the beginning of this section, it is said, "Only by meditating on Him does a person attain immortality. There exists no other way". (Shvetashvatara Upanishad 3/8) This shows that the meditation on the Supreme Being is the cause of immortality and that the meditation of anyone other than Him is in no way at all. Then, follows the sentence - "There is nothing else superior to Him or different than Him." (Shvetashvatara Upanishad 3/9) and ends with "From Him, this all is pervaded". This declares that the Supreme Being is above everyone else. Since the Supreme Being alone is superior to all other individual selves, it is called the final reality, even after the individual souls. "Those, who know this formless and faultless reality, become immortal. Others only attain sorrow." (Shvetashvatara Upanishad 3/10) By this sentence, knowing of the Supreme Being is said to be the cause of immortality and that of others not being the proper way, which were stated earlier as propositions, are now concluded with reasons. If it is interpreted otherwise, the conclusion would be in conflict with the two statements stated at the beginning. Since this Supreme Being is free from all taint of impurity, He is fit to be called Shiva. It is known also from the words "the eternal, the pure". It is only the Supreme Being that is referred to by the word Shiva, which is evident from what is later said: "He is the great Lord, the Lord (of all) who inspires us with goodness". (Shvetashvatara Upanishad 3/12)

By the same argument (as is followed here), all statements like "There was neither existence nor non-existence, only Shiva existed" (Shvetashvatara Upanishad 4/18), should be interpreted. In all such statements the word 'Shiva' refers to Narayana.

[Again, the inner consistency of the context in Shvetashvatara Upanishad and its coordination (solidarity) with other Upanishads can only be maintained if the word 'Shiva' refers to Narayana.]

[Now, Ramanuja explains the use of the word 'Maheshwara', which is also used for Lord Shiva, is for Narayana. Similarly, the word 'Om' is also used for Narayana.]

किंच 'न तस्येशे कश्चन' (तै० ना० उ० १/१०) इति निरस्तसमाभ्यधिकसंभावनस्य पुरुषस्य 'अणोरणीयान्' (तै० ना० उ० १०/११) इत्यस्मिन्ननुवाके वेदाद्यन्तरूपतया वेदबीजभूतप्रणव-स्य प्रकृतिभूताकारवाच्यतया महेश्वरत्वं प्रतिपाद्य दहरपुण्डरीकमध्यस्थाकाशान्तर्वर्तितयोपास्य-त्वमुक्तम् । अयमर्थः - सर्वस्य वेदजातस्य प्रकृतिः प्रणव उक्तः । प्रणवस्य च प्रकृतिरकारः । प्रणवविकारो वेदः स्वप्रकृतिभूते प्रणवे लीनः । प्रणवोऽप्यकारविकारभूतः स्वप्रकृतावकारे लीनः । तस्य प्रणवप्रकृतिभूतस्याकारस्य यः परो वाच्यः स एव महेश्वर इति सर्ववाचकजातप्रकृति-भूताकारवाच्यः सर्ववाच्यजातप्रकृतिभूतनारायणो यः स महेश्वर इत्यर्थः । यथोक्तं भगवता – 'अहं कृत्स्नस्य जगतः प्रभवः प्रलयस्तथा । मत्तः परतरं नान्यत्किंचिदस्ति धनंजय ॥' (गीता ७/६-७), 'अक्षराणामकारोऽस्मि' (गीता १०/३३) इति । अ इति ब्रह्मेति च श्रुतेः । अकारो वै सर्वा वागिति च । वाचकजातस्याकारप्रकृतित्वं वाच्यजातस्य ब्रह्मप्रकृतित्वं च सुस्पष्टम् । अतो ब्रह्मणोऽकारवाच्यताप्रतिपादनादकारवाच्यो नारायण एव महेश्वर इति सिद्धम् ॥

Further, in the section which begins with "In the boundless conscious water" (Taittiriya Narayana Upanishad 1/10) the Supreme Being is described as one who is without an equal or a superior by the phrase "No one rules over Him" (Taittiriya Narayana Upanishad 10/11). The same Supreme Being is described in the section beginning with "He is subtler than the atom" and is called great Lord (Maheshwara) who is signified by the syllable 'a' which is the origin of the sound 'om' (Pranava), which, in turn, is the origin of the Veda, being both the beginning and the end thereof. The section then prescribes the meditation of the Supreme Being as existing within the (inner) space of the lotus-like heart. This is the meaning: Of all the Vedas, the sound 'om' (Pranava) is called the origin. Of Pranava, too, the origin is the syllable 'a'. Since the Veda originates from 'om', it merges in it during dissolution. Similarly, 'om' also merges in its origin (cause), the syllable 'a' during dissolution. He, who is beyond the syllable 'a, which is the origin of 'om', is called the great Lord (Maheshwara). Since, Narayana is said as beyond the syllable 'a', which is the origin of all words that are expressive and who is also the origin of all things, therefore, he is denoted as the great Lord (Maheshwara) here.

Lord Krishna has said the same: "I am the origin and its dissolution of the whole universe. O Arjun, there is nothing else that is above me". Gita 7/6-7 and "Of all syllables, I am the syllable 'a'." Gita 10/33

Narayana is that which is denoted by the syllable 'a', for the Upanishad says "'a' is the Supreme Being". All words have the syllable 'a', as their origin, for it is said "All speech is the syllable 'a'". It is evident that all things expressed by words have 'a' as their origin. Since the syllable 'a' denotes Narayana, it follows that Narayana is the great Lord (Maheshwara) referred to here and not Shiva.

[A careful observation of the section in which the word "Maheshwara' is used shows that the section was related to the Supreme Being. Hence, Narayana is the intended meaning of the word 'Maheshwara' and not Shiva. Similarly, 'Om' is said to be the beginning and end of everything so it also refers to Narayana.]

[There might be several such instances which can cause confusion in a seeker's mind so Ramanuja addresses them all by a general rule, outlined by Vyasa in Brahma Sutra.]

तस्यैव 'सहस्रशीर्षं देवम्' (तै० ना० उ० १/११) इति केवलपरतत्त्वविशेषप्रतिपादनपरेण नारायणानुवाकेन सर्वस्मात्परत्वं प्रपञ्चितम् । अनेनानन्यपरेण प्रतिपादितमेव परतत्त्वमन्यपरेषु सर्ववाक्येषु केनापि शब्देन प्रतीयमानं तदेवेत्यवगम्य इति । 'शास्त्रदृष्ट्या तूपदेशो वामदेववत्' (ब्र० सू० १/१/३१) इति सूत्रकारेण निर्णीतम् । तदेतत्परं ब्रह्म क्वचिद्ब्रह्मशिवादिशब्दादव-गतमिति केवलब्रह्मशिवयोर्न परत्वप्रसङ्गः । अस्मिन्ननन्यपरेऽनुवाके तयोरिन्द्रादितुल्यतया तद्विभूतित्वप्रतिपादनात् । क्वचिदाकाशप्राणादिशब्देन परं ब्रह्माभिहितमिति भूताकाशप्राणादे-र्यथा न परत्वम् ॥

Narayana Anuvaka, whose sole purpose is to determine the Supreme Reality, explicitly declares Narayana as the Supreme Being, who is superior to all, using terms such as "thousand-headed God" (Taittiriya Narayana Upanishad 1/11). From this, we can conclude that in other sections, those who describe the Supreme Reality as someone else, refer to Narayana alone in the ultimate sense. This is decided by Vyasa in Brahma Sutra 1/1/31 which says: "This instruction (regarding the worship of Indra as Supreme Self) is based on insight into the Scriptures, as in the case of Vamadeva".

On the ground that sometimes the Supreme Being is signified by the words Brahma, Shiva, etc., it would not follow that Brahma and Shiva are Supreme Realities, for, in this section which has no other purpose than treating the Supreme Being, Brahma and Shiva are placed among the glories of the Supreme Being, on the same footing as Indra and others.

From the fact that sometimes words like space, and Prana (vital airs) are employed in the Upanishads to denote the Supreme Being, it would not be right to say that Prana (the vital breath) and sky (space), etc. are the Supreme Reality.

[In Koushitaki Upanishad, a seeker asks Indra, the Lord of Heavenly deities, to instruct him about the most beneficial goal (or liberation). To it, Indra says, "Worship me, Indra, the slayer of Vritra (demon)'. Vyasa discusses the meaning of this sutra and concludes that the object of meditation or worship is not Indra but the Inner Self of Indra, namely, the Supreme Being. So, Indra's teaching is that the Inner Self within him should be meditated on. While prescribing his worship, he had in mind the scriptures, which say that the Supreme Being is the Inner Self of all. The illustrious sage Vamadeva, who attained enlightenment in the womb of his mother, experienced that he became the sun, Manu, etc. As Vamadeva experienced his identity with the sun, Manu, etc, Indra, thinking of his identity with his innermost soul or Supreme Being, was also instructing the seeker in a similar manner. Elsewhere too, use of the words like Brahma and Shiva means the Inner Self of Brahma and Shiva, namely, Narayana.]

[Now, Ramanuja explains the word 'sky' is sometimes used in the sense of a conscious sky, which also means Supreme Being or Narayana.]

यत्पुनरिदमाशङ्कितम् 'अथ यदिदमस्मिन् ब्रह्मपुरे दहरं पुण्डरीकं वेश्म दहरोऽस्मिन्नन्तरा-
काशस्तस्मिन् यदन्तस्तदन्वेष्टव्यं तद्वा व विजिज्ञासितव्यम्' (छा० उ० ८/१/१) इत्यत्राकाश
शब्देन जगदुपादानकारणं प्रतिपाद्य तदन्तर्वर्तिनः कस्यचित्तत्त्वविशेषस्यान्वेष्टव्यता प्रतिपाद्यते ।
अस्याकाशस्य नामरूपयोर्निर्वोढृत्वश्रवणात्पुरुषसूक्ते पुरुषस्य नामरूपयोः कर्तृत्वदर्शनाच्चाका-
शपर्यायभूतात्पुरुषादन्यस्यान्वेष्टव्यतयोपास्यत्वं प्रतीयत इत्यनधीतवेदानामदृष्टशास्त्राणामिदं
चोद्यम् ॥

Now for another objection: Chhandogya Upanishad 8/1/1 says: "In this city of Supreme Being (viz., the body of the worshipper) there is a small abode like the lotus (viz., the heart); inside (that abode) there is an infinitely small sky (space). What is within that space should be sought. That is to be known". The word sky here denotes (Supreme Being), the material cause of the world, and we are asked to seek (and know) something that is within that sky (for purposes of meditation). This sky is said to evolve the names and forms in the world. In the Purusha Sukta, the Supreme Being is said to be the dispenser of names and forms. So, it appears that meditation is not on the Supreme Being but something else, synonymous with the (physical) sky.

This objection can be raised only by those who have not studied the Veda (properly) and who have not met the seers who have studied (realized) the scriptures.

[Since the physical sky (or space) cannot be the material cause of the world, it is not the intended meaning of the word 'sky' here. Moreover, the sky cannot be a dispenser of name and form.]

[What does the word 'sky' refer to?]

यतस्तत्र श्रुतिरेवास्य परिहारमाह । वाक्यकारश्च । 'दहरोऽस्मिन्नन्तराकाश: किं तदत्र विद्यते यदन्वेष्टव्यं यद्वा व विजिज्ञासितव्यम्' (छा० उ० ८/१/२) इति चोदिते 'यावान् वा अयमाकाशस्तावानेषोऽन्तर्हृदय आकाश' (छा० उ० ८/१/३) इत्यादिनास्याकाशशब्दवाच्यस्य परमपुरुषस्यानवधिकमहत्त्वं सकलजगदाधारत्वं च प्रतिपाद्य, 'तस्मिन् कामा: समाहिता' (छा० उ० ८/१/५) इति कामशब्देनापहतपाप्मत्वादिसत्यसंकल्पपर्यन्तगुणाष्टकं निहितमिति परमपुरुषवत्परमपुरुषगुणाष्टकस्यापि पृथिविजिज्ञासितव्यताप्रतिपादयिषया तस्मिन् यदन्तस्तद -न्वेष्टव्यमित्युक्तमिति श्रुत्यैव सर्व परिहृतम् ॥

The Upanishad, itself, gives the answer to this objection. So also its commentator the Vakyakara answers it. The Upanishad raises the question, "What is there within that small sky that should be searched and known?" (Chhandogya Upanishad 8/1/2) and answers thus "This space, which is within the heart, is as immense as the physical or material sky" (Chhandogya Upanishad 8/1/3), thereby it indicates Supreme Being by the word (inner) sky, who is of boundless splendor and is the cause and the support of the world. Then, the Upanishad proceeds to state: "In Him, all auspicious qualities are established eternally." (Chhandogya Upanishad 8/1/5) This self is untainted by evil, has no old age, nor death, no sorrow, no hunger, nor thirst: it has all objects of desire and its will is irresistible. Thus, the eight qualities, which are the characteristics of the Supreme Being, beginning with freedom from evil and ending with irresistible will are placed in it (the inner sky). So, as for the Supreme Being, the eight qualities of the Supreme Person (within the sky are to be meditated on, and separately known. Therefore, the Upanishad itself has refuted this objection.

[The word 'sky' refers to the inner space of the heart. But, this inner space has the same attributes that are unique to the Supreme Being. Therefore, the word sky refers to the Supreme Being.]

[The Upanishad itself makes it clear by saying this inner space is the place of creation, maintenance, and dissolution of the world.]

एतदुक्तं भवति - किं तदत्र विद्यते यदनेष्टव्यमित्यस्य चोद्यस्य तस्मिन् सर्वस्य जगतः सष्टृत्वमाधारत्वं नियन्तृत्वं शेषित्वमपहतपाप्मत्वादयो गुणाश्च विद्यन्त इति परिहार इति । तथा च वाक्यकारवचनम् – 'तस्मिन् यदन्तरिति कामव्यपदेशः' इति । काम्यन्त इति कामाः । अपहतपाप्मत्वादयो गुणा इत्यर्थः । एतदुक्तं भवति - यदेतद्द्वराकाशशब्दाभिधेयं निखिलजगदु -दयवैभवलयलीलं परं ब्रह्म तस्मिन् यदन्तर्निहितमनवधिकातिशयमपहतपाप्मत्वादिगुणाष्टकं तदुभयमप्यन्वेष्टव्यं विजिज्ञासितव्यमिति । यथाह – 'अथ य इहात्मानमनुविद्य व्रजन्त्येतांश्च सत्यान् कामांस्तेषां सर्वेषु लोकेषु कामचारो भवन्ति' (छा० उ० ८/१/६) इति ॥

It comes to mean this: "What is there within it that is to be sought? To this question, the answer is: "In Him (viz., the sky) qualities like being the creator and support of the world, the quality of being its controller, the quality of being one for whom the world exists, freedom from evil, etc. This is the refutation of the view of those who think it is a physical sky being referred to here. The Vakyakara, too, says: By "What is that within" the desires are referred to. These desires are those auspicious attributes that are desired, e.g. freedom from evil, etc. It means this: That Supreme Being, which is referred to here as 'small inner space' and whose play unfolds as creation, maintenance, and dissolution of the whole universe, and the supremely wonderful eight qualities like freedom from evil, etc. which are within it, both of these are to be sought and known. The Upanishad says again, "Those who depart (from this world) after knowing this soul (Supreme Being) and also its qualities, attain freedom as they desire in all the worlds." (Chhandogya Upanishad 8/1/6)

[Since knowing the Supreme Being alone can result in liberation or unhindered freedom, which is mentioned as the result of knowing this inner space in the Upanishad, it implies this inner space is identical to the Supreme Being.]

[Now, another doubt regarding the birth of Supreme Being as Vishnu and other incarnations is raised.]

यः पुनः कारणस्यैव ध्येयताप्रतिपादनपरे वाक्ये विष्णोरनन्यपरवाक्यप्रतिपादितपरतत्त्वभूतस्य कार्यमध्ये निवेशः स स्वकार्यभूततत्त्वसंख्यापूरणं कुर्वतः स्वलीलया जगदुपकाराय स्वेच्छावतार इत्यवगन्तव्यः । यथा लीलया देवसंख्यापूर्णं कुर्वत उपेन्द्रत्वं परस्यैव, यथा च सूर्यवंशोद्भवराज-संख्यापूर्णं कुर्वतः परस्यैव ब्रह्मणो दाशरथिरूपेण स्वेच्छावतारः, यथा च सोमवंशसंख्यापूरणं कुर्वतो भगवतो भूभारावतारणाय स्वेच्छया वसुदेवगृहेऽवतारः ॥

Again, it might be asked: "How is it that, in a sentence which says that only the (ultimate) cause is to be meditated upon, indulged in finding the ultimate reality alone, determines Vishnu as the Supreme Reality but places him among created beings?" (The answer to this question is as follows) "We have to understand that Vishnu (Supreme Being), who is placed here alongside Brahma and Rudra, by way of sport and by His own will, for the benefit of the world, to complete the number of the fundamental deities, who were His own creations, incarnated himself as Vishnu. This is just like the Supreme Being incarnating as Upendra (younger brother of Indra, Vamana), by way of sport, to complete the number of the gods. It is also like the Supreme Being incarnating, by His own will, as the son of Dasaratha to complete the number of kings born of the solar race. And, it is like the Lord incarnating in the house of Vasudeva by His own will to relieve the burden on the earth, while completing the number of the kings of the lunar race.

[The births or incarnations of the Supreme Being are for the welfare of the world by his own unfailing wish. He does not take birth under the influence of his actions like other individual souls. Hence, there is no inconsistency in it.]

[Now, Ramanuja explains how Atharva Shikha Upanishad itself shows that Supreme Being is different from Shiva.]

सृष्टिप्रलयप्रकरणेषु नारायण एव परमकारणतया प्रतिपाद्यत इति पूर्वमेवोक्तम् । यत्पुनरथर्व-
शिरसि रुद्रेण स्वसर्वैश्वर्यं प्रपञ्चितं 'तत्सोऽन्तरादन्तरं प्राविशत्' इति परमात्मप्रवेशादुक्तमिति
श्रुत्यैव व्यक्तम् । 'शास्त्रदृष्ट्या तूपदेशो वामदेववत्' (ब्र० सू० १/१/३१) इति सूत्रकारेणैवंवा-
दिनामर्थः प्रतिपादितः ॥

It has already been said that, in all contexts dealing with creation and dissolution, Narayana alone is stated to be the ultimate cause. It may be objected again that, in the Atharva Shiras, Shiva describes himself as possessed of supreme lordship. The Upanishad itself replies to this objection by saying: "He has entered into all and into all the quarters." (The word 'He' in this sentence refers to the Supreme Being and not to Shiva). Therefore, it was said so by Shiva on the ground that the Supreme Being had entered into Him. Vyasa himself has explained the meaning of this and other such passages by saying, " This instruction (is based) on insight into the Scriptures, as in the case of Vamadeva" (Brahma Sutra 1/1/31).

[Therefore, in all cases of confusion, where a word is used to denote another deity and is also said to possess supreme authority, we should interpret it as referring to Narayana, who is the inner soul of all.]

[Ramanuja shows the prevalence of such uses by citing Vishnu Purana.]

यथोक्तं प्रह्लादेनापि – 'सर्वगत्वादनन्तरस्य स एवाहमवस्थितः । मत्तः सर्वमहं सर्वं मयि सर्वं
सनातने ॥' (वि० पु० १/१९/८५) इत्यादि । अत्र सर्वगत्वादनन्तस्येति हेतुरुक्तः । स्वशरीरभूत-

स्य सर्वस्य चिदचिद्वस्तुन आत्मत्वेन सर्वगः परमात्मेति सर्वे शब्दाः सर्वशरीरं परमात्मानमेवाभि-
दधतीत्युक्तम् । अतोऽहमिति शब्दः स्वात्मप्रकारप्रकारिणं परमात्मानमेवाचष्टे ।

It has also been stated similarly by Prahlada: "Since infinite
Narayana pervades everywhere, I am Him; from me (arises) all; I am
all; everything is in me who am eternal." (Vishnu Purana 1/19/85)

Here the reason for pervading everything is that Narayana is
infinite. The Supreme Being pervades all because He is the soul of
everything, sentient and non-sentient, which forms His body.
Therefore, all words (like Shiva and the rest) denote only the
Supreme Being. Hence the word 'I' in Prahlada's speech refers only
to the Supreme Being, who has all souls as His modes.

[Here, the great devotee Prahalad is also referring to Supreme
Being by the word 'I'.]

[Ramanuja explains when a devotee sees the Supreme Being as his
inmost soul, he refers to Him as I.]

अत इदमुच्यते - 'आत्मेत्येव तु गृह्णीयात्सर्वस्य तन्निष्पत्तेः' इत्यादिनाहंग्रहणोपासनं वाक्य-
कारेण कार्यावस्थः कारणावस्थश्च स्थूलसूक्ष्मचिदचिद्वस्तुशरीरः परमात्मैवेति सर्वस्य तन्निष्पत्ते-
रित्युक्तम् । 'आत्मेति तूपगच्छन्ति ग्राहयन्ति च' (ब्र॰ सू॰ ४/१/३) इति सूत्रकारेण च ।

The Vakyakara (Brahmanandi), therefore says, "It is said in such
statements as Supreme Being should be meditated on as the soul (of
all) since it is the cause of all". It is only the Supreme Self that
stands as the effect and as the cause and has for His body, sentient
and non-sentient things, both in their gross and in their subtle
state. So the Vakyakara says 'It is the cause of all.' Vyasa also says:
"Supreme Being should be meditated on as the soul; (it is) in this
way that (previous worshippers) have meditated, the scriptures too
give the same instruction. (Brahma Sutra 4/1/3)

[When one worships the Supreme Being as his soul, he experiences him as the ultimate cause of everything, including himself. This is how Vyasa and Brahmanandi interpret it.]

[In Mahabharata, during an interaction between Brahma and Shiva, Brahma himself has said to Shiva that Narayana or Vishnu is the soul of all, and both of us also originated from him.]

महाभारते च ब्रह्मरुद्रसंवादे ब्रह्मा रुद्रं प्रत्याह – 'ममान्तरात्मा तव च ये चान्ये देहिसंज्ञिताः ।' (म० भा० शा० ३५१/४) इति । रुद्रस्य ब्रह्मणश्चान्येषां च देहिनां परमेश्वरो नारायणोऽन्तरा-त्मतयावस्थित इति । तथा तत्रैव – 'विष्णुरात्मा भगवतो भवस्यामिततेजसः । तस्माद्धनुज्यर्या-संस्पर्शे स विषेहे महेश्वरः ॥' (म० भा० क० २६/३४) इति । तत्रैव – 'एतौ द्वौ विबुधश्रेष्ठौ प्रसादक्रोधजौ स्मृतौ । तदादर्शितपन्थानौ सृष्टिसंहारकारकौ ॥' (म० भा० शा० ३४१/१९) इति । अन्तरात्मतयावस्थितनारायणदर्शितपथौ ब्रह्मरुद्रौसृष्टिसंहारकार्यकरावित्यर्थः ॥

In the Mahabharata also, in the dialogue between Brahma and Rudra, Brahma says to Rudra: (He) is the inner self of you, of me, and of all embodied beings". (Mahabharata Shanti Parva 351/4) It means Narayana, the Supreme Ruler, is the Inner Self of Rudra, Brahma, and other embodied beings. In the same (treatise) occurs (the following): "Vishnu is the soul of Lord Shiva, who possesses immeasurable splendor". (Mahabharata Karna Parva 26/34)

In the same text occurs the following: "These two (Brahma and Rudra) deities, greatest of gods, are stated to be produced from the graciousness and wrath respectively of Vishnu, act as the agents of creation and destruction following the path pointed out by Him (Narayana)" (Mahabharata Shanti Parva 341/19). It means that Brahma and Rudra carry out the work of creation and destruction, as shown by Narayana, who resides within them as their inner self.

[Shanti Parva or the 'section of Peace' in Mahabharata, to be more specific, its subsection Moskha Dharma, or 'Righteousness leading to Liberation' is dedicated to matters related to liberation and the ultimate cause of the world. It also establishes that Narayana (Krishna) is the supreme cause during the interaction of Shiva and Brahma themselves. Thus, it concludes the discussion, which proves that Narayana is the ultimate cause.]

Narayana is Material and Instrumental Cause

[Some others say that the Supreme Being is the material cause and Shiva is the instrumental cause of the world. Ramanuja discards their assumption and shows that the Supreme Being is the material as well as the instrumental cause.]

निमित्तोपादानयोस्तु भेदं वदन्तो वेदबाह्या एव स्युः । 'जन्माद्यस्य यतः' (ब्र० सू० १/१/२), 'प्रकृतिश्च प्रतिज्ञादृष्टान्तानुपरोधात्' (ब्र० सू० १/४/२३) इत्यादि वेदवित्प्रणीतसूत्रविरोधात् । 'सदेव सोम्येदमग्र आसीदेकमेवाद्वितीयम्' (छा० उ० ६/२/१), 'तदैक्षत बहु स्यां प्रजायेय' (छा० उ० ६/२/३), 'ब्रह्मवनं ब्रह्म स वृक्ष आसीद्यतो द्यावापृथिवी निष्टतक्षुः ब्रह्माध्यतिष्ठद्भुवनानि धारयन्' (तै० सं० २/८/७/९), 'सर्वे निमेषा जज्ञिरे विद्युतः पुरुषादधि' (तै० ना० उ० १/८), 'न तस्येशे कश्चन तस्य नाम महद्यशः' (तै० ना० उ० १/१०), 'नेह नानास्ति किंचन' (बृ० उ० ६/४/११), 'सर्वस्य वशी सर्वस्येशानः' (बृ० उ० ६/४/२२), 'पुरुष एवेदं सर्वं यद्भूतं यच्च भव्यमुतामृतत्त्वस्येशानः' (तै० आ० ३/१२/२), 'नान्यः पन्था अयनाय विद्यते' (तै० आ० ३/१२/१७) इत्यादि सर्वश्रुतिविरोधाच्च ॥

Those who maintain that the instrumental cause of the world is different from its material cause should be looked upon as outside the purview of the Vedas (for their view is against the Vedas). Their view is also against that of the Sutras composed by that (great) authority on the Vedas, Vyasa, who says - "That from which arise the origin, etc., of this world, is Supreme Being." (Brahma Sutra 1/1/2) and "Supreme Being is also the material cause since this is not in conflict with the proposition and the illustrations". (Brahma Sutra 1/4/23)

It is also against a large number of Upanishads (e. g.) (1) "This, my dear, existed at the beginning as reality and without a second" (Chhandogya Upanishad 6/2/1) (2) "It resolved that it should become manifold" (Chhandogya Upanishad 6/2/3), (3) "Supreme Being is the forest and Supreme Being is the tree from which the earth and the sky come into being. Supreme Being presides and supports the worlds." (Taittiriya Sanhita 2/8/7/9), (3) "All the moments (of time) originated from the Supreme Being, whose splendour is like that of lightning" (Taittiriya Narayana Upanishad 1/8), (4) "No one rules over Him, his fame is great "(Taittiriya Narayana Upanishad 1/10), (5) There is nothing many here, (Brihat Aranyaka Upanishad 6/4/11) (6) "He has everything under His control and is the ruler of all" (Brihat Aranyaka Upanishad 6/4/22), (7) The Supreme Being alone is all this, both the past and the present and He is the Lord of immortality (Taittiriya Aranyaka 3/12/2), (8) (9) "There is no other way to immortality but to attain Him" (Taittiriya Aranyaka 3/12/17).

[Brahma Sutra says if we accept material and instrumental causes to be different, it will break the proposition that by knowing one reality, one knows it all. The example of clay and the pots also say the same thing. Various Upanishads also assert the same view. Since, in the beginning, reality alone was present, without anything else, it is both the material and instrumental cause from which this world originated.]

[Other texts like Mahabharata, etc. also accept Narayana as the only supreme cause.]

इतिहासपुराणेषु च सृष्टिस्थितिप्रलयप्रकरणयोरिदमेव परतत्त्वमित्यवगम्यते । यथा महाभारते - 'कुतः सृष्टिमिदं सर्वं जगत्स्थावरजङ्गमम् । प्रलये च कमभ्येति तन् तो ब्रूहि पितामह ॥' (म० भा० शा० १८१/१) इति पृष्टो, 'नारायणो जगन्मूर्तिरनन्तात्मा सनातन ।' (म० भा० शा० १८१/११) इत्यादि च वदति । 'ऋषयः पितरो देवा महाभूतानि धातवः । जङ्गमाजङ्गमं चेदं जगन्नारायणोद्भवम् ॥' (म० भा० अनुशा० १३/१३८) इति च ।

Likewise, in the Ithihasas (History-texts) and Puranas, while describing creation and dissolution, this Supreme Being or Narayana (alone), is indicated to be the highest reality. In the Mahabharata occurs the following verse: "Who created all this, O Grandfather Bhishma, both the moving and the non-moving? Whom do they go to at the time of dissolution? Tell me this." (Mahabharata Shanti Parva 181/1) He answers - "Narayana has the (whole) world as His body; He is the inner self of all; He is eternal". (Mahabharata Shanti Parva 181/11) And, it is also said later - "The sages, the forefathers, the gods, the great elements, the minerals, this world consisting of moving and non-moving things, all had their origin from Narayana". (Mahabharata Anushasana Parva 13/138)

[The last verse is a part of the famed Vishnu Sahastranama or a thousand names of Vishnu. These verses also say that Narayana has created everything from himself.]

[Vishnu Purana, widely acclaimed by everyone, also describes Narayana or Vishnu as the ultimate cause of the entire world, whether material or instrumental.]

प्राच्योदीच्यदाक्षिणात्यपाश्चात्यसर्वशिष्टैः सर्वधर्मसर्वतत्त्वव्यवस्थायामिदमेव पर्याप्तमित्यविगान-
परिगृहीतं वैष्णवं च पुराणं ‘जन्माद्यस्य यत’ इति जगज्जन्मादिकारणं ब्रह्मेत्यवगम्यते ।
तज्जन्मादिकारणं किमिति प्रश्नपूर्वकं ‘विष्णोः सकाशाद्भूतम्’ (वि० पु० १/१/३१) इत्यादिना
ब्रह्मस्वरूपविशेषप्रतिपादनैकपरतया प्रवृत्तमिति सर्वसंमतम् । तथा तत्रैव - ‘प्रकृतिर्या ख्याता
व्यक्ताव्यक्तस्वरूपिणी । पुरुषश्चप्युभावेतौ लीयेते परमात्मनि ॥ परमात्मा च सर्वेषामाधारः
परमेश्वरः । विष्णुनामा स वेदेषु वेदान्तेषु च गीयते ॥‘ (वि० पु० ६/४/३९-४०) इति । सर्ववेद-
वेदान्तेषु सर्वैः शब्दैः परमकारणतयायमेव गीयत इत्यर्थः ।

The Vishnu Purana, which is accepted unanimously by all learned men in the east, north, south, and west as being adequate, by itself, to determine the nature of all righteousness (duty, dharma) and of all reality raises the question, "What is the cause of the origin, etc. of the world?" and answers it by saying "(All this) arose from Vishnu". (Vishnu Purana 1/1/31) From such passages as this, it is agreed by all that this Purana exists solely for the purpose of pointing out the specific form of the Supreme Being (viz., Vishnu).

So also in the concluding section of this treatise, it is said:-

"Nature, both in its manifested state during creation and in its unmanifested state during dissolution, and also all the individual selves, merge in me, the Supreme Self". (This means that the Supreme Self is the ultimate cause of the world). The Supreme Self is the support of all and is the Supreme Ruler. In the Vedas and the Vedantas (the Upanishad), it is celebrated by the name of Vishnu". It means that He alone is sung in the verses of all the Vedas and Vedanta by all words as the ultimate cause." (Vishnu Purana 6/4/39-40)

[Since everything, including nature, arises and dissolves in Vishnu, he is the ultimate cause of all.]

[Ramanuja, now, explains why we should consider Vishnu Purana authoritative in this matter.]

यथा सर्वासु श्रुतिषु केवलपरब्रह्मस्वरूपविशेषप्रतिपादनायैव प्रवृत्तो नारायणानुवाकस्तथेदं वैष्णवं च पुराणम् – 'सोऽहमिच्छामि धर्मज्ञ श्रोतुं त्वत्तो यथा जगत् । बभूव भूयश्च यथा महाभाग भविष्यति ॥ यन्मयं च जगद्ब्रह्मन्यतश्चैतच्चराचरम् । लीनमासीद्यथा यत्र लयमेष्यति यत्र च ॥' (वि० पु० १/१/४-५) इति परं ब्रह्म किमिति प्रक्रम्य – 'विष्णोः सकाशादुद्भूतं जगत्तत्रैव च स्थितम् । स्थितिसंयमकर्तासौ जगतोऽस्य जगच्च सः ॥' (वि० पु० १/१/३१), 'परः पराणां परमः परमात्मात्मसंस्थितः । रूपवर्णादिनिर्देशविशेषणविवर्जितः ॥ अपक्षय-विनाशाभ्यां परिणामर्द्धिजन्मभिः । वर्जितः शक्यते वक्तुं यः सदस्तीति केवलम् ॥ सर्वत्रासौ समस्तं च वसत्यत्रेति वै यतः । ततः स वासुदेवेति विद्वद्भिः परिपठ्यते ॥ तद्ब्रह्म परं नित्यमज-मक्षयमव्ययम् । एकस्वरूपं च सदा हेयाभावाच्च निर्मलम् ॥ तदेव सर्वमेवैतद्व्यक्ताव्यक्त-स्वरूपवत् । तथा पुरुषरूपेण कालरूपेण च स्थितम् ॥' (वि० पु० १/२/१०-१४)

Just as the Narayana Anuvaka, among all the Upanishads, aims solely to determine the specific form of the Supreme Being, so also this Vishnu Purana is devoted to that particular end. It opens with the questions: "From you, O, knower of righteousness (dharma), I desire to learn whence this world arose, how it arose, whence it will arise again, and how it will arise; illustrious sir, tell me by whom it is pervaded and in whom this world of moving and non-moving things lay merged before and in which it will become absorbed again". (Vishnu Purana 1/1/4-5) Thus, it essentially asks, "What or who Supreme Being is?" It, then, proceeds to describe the specific nature of this Supreme Being: "The world was produced from Vishnu; it exists in him; he is the cause of its continuance and cessation; he is the world." (Vishnu Purana 1/1/31)

"He is greater than the greatest; He is the Supreme Soul. He is self-existent; He is without the specifications of the qualities like form, color, etc. He is not subject to decay and death, to modification, to growth, and to birth. He can only be described as the ever-existent. He dwells everywhere and in everything. Therefore, the wise call Him Vasudeva. He is the Supreme Being, eternal, unborn, unchanging, and undecaying. He is always of the same nature; He is pure because there is no imperfection in Him. He is all this nature which is the manifest (gross, visible) and the unmanifest (subtle, invisible). And, he also exists in the form of the individual selves and time." (Vishnu Purana 1/2/10-14)

[Vishnu Purana clearly describes that Supreme Being consists of infinite auspicious qualities and at the same time, he is devoid of everything that is inauspicious. It is from this Purana that Ramanuja has taken the fundamental building block of his philosophy.]

[Earlier paragraph lists the verses present in the initial part of Vishnu Purana. Now, Ramanuja shows that the concluding verses also describe the Supreme Being in a similar manner.]

'स सर्वभूतप्रकृतिं विकारान् गुणादिदोषांश्च मुने व्यतीतः । अतीतसर्वावरणोऽखिलात्मा तेनास्तृतं यद्भुवनान्तराले ॥ समस्तकल्याणगुणात्मकोऽसौ स्वशक्तिलेशोद्धृतभूतवर्गः । इच्छा-गृहीताभिमतोरुदेहः संसाधिताशेषजगद्धितोऽसौ ॥ तेजोबलैश्वर्यमहावबोधसुवीर्यशक्त्यादि-गुणैकराशिः । परः पराणां सकला न यत्र क्लेशादयः सन्ति परावरेशे ॥ स ईश्वरो व्यष्टिसमष्टि-रूपोऽव्यक्तस्वरूपः प्रकटस्वरूपः । सर्वेश्वरः सर्वदृक्सर्ववेत्ता समस्तशक्तिः परमेश्वराख्यः ॥

संज्ञायते येन तदस्तदोषं शुद्धं परं निर्मलमेकरूपम् । संदृश्यते वाप्यधिगम्यते वा तज्ज्ञानम-
ज्ञानमतोऽन्यदुक्तम् ॥' (वि० पु० ६/५/८३-८७) इति परब्रह्मस्वरूपविशेषनिर्णयायैव प्रवृत्तम् ॥

"He is beyond the modifications of nature, which is the cause of all
the elements. He is beyond attributes (viz. sattva, rajas, and tamas)
and blemishes of nature. He is beyond all obscuration of ignorance.
He is the soul of all, O Sage because whatever exists in this world is
pervaded by Him. His essential nature consists of all auspicious
qualities. By only a small fraction of His might, He supports all kinds
of beings. By His independent will and pleasure, He assumes
wonderful forms to promote the well-being of the whole world. He
is the unique abode of qualities like splendor, strength, wisdom,
valor, and might. He is the greater than the greatest. Not even one
of the imperfections like pain, etc. exists in Him, for He is the ruler
of the great and the small. He is the Lord of the individual selves in
their individual state and in their collective, causal state; He is also
the Lord of nature in its manifested (visible) and unmanifested
(invisible) state. He is the Lord; He witnesses all. He knows all; he
consists of all powers that can only exist in the Supreme Being. That
knowledge by which this Supreme Being is attained, known, or
understood as free from the taint (peculiar to nature), pure (without
the action which binds the individual self), and ever defect-free is
(by an action like the released souls), supreme, and always the same
- that knowledge alone is real knowledge; the rest is called
ignorance". (Vishnu Purana 6/5/83-87)

In this way, the Vishnu Purana is interested only in determining the
distinctive form of the Supreme Being.

[Thus, from Vishnu Purana, we conclusively know that the Supreme
Being is not attributeless, rather, he consists of infinitely many
auspicious qualities. It is devoid of all afflictions. During dissolution
everything, living being and insentient matter, reside in him in a
subtle manner. In this state, there is no distinction between their
names and forms. During creation, they again sprout forth from the

Supreme Being in a visible (gross) form. And this cycle of creation and dissolution goes on like this.]

[What should one do if other Puranas describe the Supreme Being in a different manner?]

अन्यानि सर्वाणि पुराणान्येतदविरोधेन नेयानि । अन्यपरत्वं च तत्तदारम्भप्रकारैरवगम्यते । सर्वात्मना विरुद्धांशस्तामसत्वादनादरणीयः ॥

Therefore, all other Puranas are to be interpreted so as not to conflict with it. That they are interested in other subjects (than the Supreme Being) may be seen even in the manner they begin. That in them, which is entirely opposed to the Supreme Being (as described in the Vishnu Purana), is due to ignorance and, therefore, we should disregard it.

[One should try to reconcile the description of other Puranas with that of Vishnu Purana. If it is not possible then that specific portion should be discarded.]

[Now, opposition raises their doubt that in Vishnu Purana itself at various places we see that Brahma, Vishnu, and Shiva are described to be equal. How would you establish Vishnu as Supreme among them?]

नन्वस्मिन्नपि, 'सृष्टिस्थित्यन्तकरणीं ब्रह्मविष्णुशिवात्मिकाम् । स संज्ञा याति भगवानेक जनार्दनः ॥' (वि० पु० १/२/६७) इति त्रिमूर्तिसाम्यं प्रतीयते । नैतदेवम् । एक एव जनार्दन इति जनार्दनस्यैव ब्रह्मशिवादिकृत्स्नप्रपञ्चतादात्म्यं विधीयते । जगच्च स इति पूर्वोक्तमेव विवृणोति – 'स्रष्टा सृजति चात्मानं विष्णुः पाल्यं च पाति च । उपसंह्रियते चान्ते संहर्ता च स्वयं प्रभुः ॥' (वि० पु० १/२/६८) इति च स्रष्टृत्वेनावस्थितं ब्रह्माणं सृज्यं च संहर्तारं संहार्यं च युगपन्निर्दिश्य सर्वस्य विष्णुतादात्म्योपदेशात्सृज्यसंहार्यभूताद्वस्तुनः स्रष्टृसंहर्तृर्जनार्दनविभूतित्वेन विशेषो दृश्यते । जनार्दनविष्णुशब्दयोः पर्यायत्वेन ब्रह्मविष्णुशिवात्मिकामिति विभूतिम् । अत एव स्वेच्छया लीलार्थं विभूत्यन्तर्भाव उच्यते । यथेदमनन्तरमेवोच्यते – 'पृथिव्यापस्तथा तेजो वायुराकाश एव च । सर्वेन्द्रियान्तःकरणं पुरुषाख्यं हि यज्जगत् ॥ स एव सर्वभूतात्मा विश्वरूपो

यतोऽव्ययः । सर्गादिकं ततोऽस्यैव भूतस्थमुपकारकम् ॥ स एव सृज्यः स च सर्वकर्ता स एव
पात्यत्ति च पाल्यते च । ब्रह्माद्यवस्थाभिरशेषमूर्तिर्विष्णुर्वरिष्ठो वरदो वरेण्यः ॥' (वि० पु०
१/२/६९-७१) इति ॥

But it might still be said, even in this (Purana), the equality of the
trinity (Brahma, Vishnu, and Shiva) is apparent as in the following:
"Lord Janardana alone takes the names of Brahma, Vishnu, and
Shiva, while engaged in the (respective) work of creating,
maintaining and destroying". (Vishnu Purana 1/2/67)

We answer: It is not true. "Janardana alone" means that Janardana is
stated in this context to be identical to Brahma, Vishnu, Shiva, and
the rest of the world. What was stated succinctly before in "He is
this entire world" is elaborated next.

"He is the creator of the world, and He also creates Himself as
Vishnu and functions as its maintainer and protector. He destroys it
in Himself at the end (in dissolution) so He is himself the destroyer,
as he is the Lord (of all)." (Vishnu Purana 1/2/68)

Here by indicating Brahma in his capacity as creator and the object
of creation, and likewise Shiva as the destroyer and the destroyed
at the same time, Vishnu is said to be the soul of everything.
Therefore, the creator and destroyer as well as created and
destroyed entities are the glories (special manifestations) of
Janardana. The former appears to be special in comparison to the
latter. Since the words, Janardana and Vishnu are synonymous,
Brahma, Vishnu, and Shiva all are the manifestations of Janardana.
Here, Vishnu is counted among his manifestations as His own sport
and at His own pleasure; the possessor of these glories becomes
himself one of the glories. This idea is set forth immediately
afterward:-

"Earth, water, and likewise, fire, air and sky, all the senses, the mind,
and the individual selves, which constitute the world, are only His
forms. Though He is unchanging, He is the soul of all beings and has

the universe as His body. Therefore, the creation, etc. of all beings is by him to help everyone. He alone is the created, and He alone is the creator; He protects and destroys and is the protected at the same time. Vishnu, who has everything as His form, assumes the states of Brahma, etc., and grants us the objects we desire. He is the object of worship; He is the highest of all." (Vishnu Purana 1/2/69-71)

[Thus, if we look at the context in totality, it is clear that Vishnu alone is the supreme cause. Since Brahma and Shiva are his special manifestations, they are also mentioned here alongside him. Through them, he creates and destroys the world, i.e. they are not independent in their functions.]

[Now, one can doubt if Vishnu has become this all then all defects will come to him. How would you resolve it?]

अत्र सामानाधिकरण्यनिर्दिष्टं हेयमिश्रप्रपञ्चतादात्म्यं निरवद्यस्य निर्विकारस्य समस्तकल्याण-गुणात्मकस्य ब्रह्मणः कथमुपपद्यत इत्याशङ्क्य – 'स एव सर्वभूतात्मा विश्वरूपो यतोऽव्यय' (वि० पु० १/२/७०) इति स्वयमेवोपपादयति । स एव सर्वेश्वरः परब्रह्मभूतो विष्णुरेव सर्वं जगदिति प्रतिज्ञाय, 'सर्वभूतात्मा विश्वरूपो यतोऽव्यय' (वि० पु० १/२/७०) इति हेतुरुक्तः । सर्वभूतानामयमात्मा विश्वशरीरो यतोऽव्यय इत्यर्थः । वक्ष्यति च – 'तत्सर्वं वै हरेस्तनुः' (वि० पु० १/२२/३८) इति । एतदुक्तं भवति । अस्याव्ययस्यापि परस्य ब्रह्मणो विष्णोर्विश्वशरीरतया तादात्म्यविरुद्धमित्यात्मशरीरयोश्च स्वभावा व्यवस्थिता एव ।

Here, the Purana raises the question of whether it is proper to affirm the identity between the world consisting of imperfections and mixed qualities and the Supreme Being who possesses all auspicious qualities and is not subject to any imperfections or changes. If we accept the Supreme Being as the common basis of all as mentioned in 'he is the entire world', these imperfections will come to him. Then, it answers this itself next with the words: "Though unchanging, He alone is the soul of all beings and has the universe as His body". (Vishnu Purana 1/2/70) The claim is "This Vishnu, alone, is the Ruler of all and the Supreme Being has become the whole world" and the reason is given in: "Though unchanging, He is the soul of all beings and has the universe as His body." Later, it will be said, "All that exists is the body of Vishnu" (Vishnu Purana 1/22/38). It means this: Though this Supreme Being Vishnu is unchanging, it can be called the universe as it is His body. This identification of Him with the world is not against reason since the nature of the soul and the body are, of course, different.

[We can understand this apparent anomaly by the example of the body and the soul. Though the body undergoes many changes, the underlying soul does not change. In a similar manner, none of the defects of this world affect the Supreme Being even in the slightest manner.]

[Some might ask if the Supreme Being incarnate as a human, etc., he will also come under bondage like others. How will you resolve it?]

एवंभूतस्य सर्वेश्वरस्य विष्णोः प्रपञ्चान्तर्भूतनियाम्यकोटिनिविष्टब्रह्मादिदेवतिर्यङ्मनुष्येषु तत्त-त्समाश्रयणीयत्वाय स्वेच्छावतारः पूर्वोक्तः । तदेतद्ब्रह्मादीनां भावनात्रयान्वयेन कर्मवश्यत्वं भगवतः परब्रह्मभूतस्य वासुदेवस्य निखिलजगदुपकाराय स्वेच्छया स्वेनैव रूपेण देवादिष्ववतार इति च षष्ठेंऽशे शुभाश्रयप्रकरणे सुव्यक्तमुक्तम् । अस्य देवादिरूपेणावतारेष्वपि न प्राकृतो देह इति महाभारते – 'न भूतसंघसंस्थानो देहोऽस्य परमात्मनः ।' (म० भा० शा०) इति प्रतिपादितः ।

It has already been stated that Vishnu, who is the Supreme Lord of all, incarnates as Vishnu again, at His own pleasure. This incarnation occurs so that the gods like Brahma, etc., humans, animals, etc., those who are under His control in the world, may seek refuge under Him. In the sixth chapter of the Vishnu Purana, while speaking of a sacred object for meditation, it is clearly stated that Brahma and others are under the sway of action, therefore, Lord Vasudeva, who is the Supreme Being, takes an incarnation among the deities, of His own accord and in His essential nature, for the good of the whole world. Mahabharata explains that even in these incarnations as gods and the rest, His body is not constituted of matter. "The body of this Supreme Being is not built up of the five elements (earth, water, etc., which are evolutes of nature)." (Mahabharata Shanti Parva)

[Like ordinary individual souls, the Supreme Being does not take birth under the influence of ignorance or his previous action. His incarnations are due to his infallible will and for the welfare of others. Therefore, his body is also not composed of five elements like others. It is simply divine.]

[The Upanishads also mention his incarnations in various ways.]

श्रुतिभिश्च – 'अजायमानो बहुधा विजायते तस्य धीराः परिजानन्ति योनि' (तै० आ० ३/१२) इति । कर्मवश्यानां ब्रह्मादीनामनिच्छतामपि तत्तत्कर्मानुगुणप्रकृतिपरिणामरूपभूतसंघसंस्थान-विशेषदेवादिशरीरप्रवेशरूपं जन्मावर्जनीयम् । अयं तु सर्वेश्वरः सत्यसंकल्पो भगवानेवंभूत-शुभेतरजन्माकुर्वन्नपि स्वेच्छया स्वेनैव निरतिशयकल्याणरूपेण देवादिषु जगदुपकाराय बहुधा जायते, तस्यैतस्य शुभेतरजन्माकुर्वतोऽपि स्वकल्याणगुणानन्त्येन बहुधा योनिं बहुविधजन्म धीराधीरमतामग्रेसरा जानन्तीत्यर्थः ॥

The Upanishad also says "Though unborn, He is born in many forms. The foremost among the wise are aware of His birth". (Taittiriya Aranyaka 3/12) To Brahma and others, who are subject to the effects of their actions, birth, which is of the nature of entrance into the bodies of gods, humans, etc. that are special configurations of the fundamental elements that are themselves modifications of nature, is inescapable, according to their actions, though they may not desire it. On the other hand, this Lord, who is the Ruler of all and whose will is omnipotent, though He never performs any action which is other than pure, is born manifold, of His own accord and in His own wonderfully auspicious form among gods and the like for the well-being of the world. It means this - His manifold auspicious births and actions in accordance with His innumerable auspicious qualities, among many species, the foremost among the wise know.

[Those, who have purified their mind, and are exclusively devoted to Lord, directly experience his secret incarnations.]

[Now, Ramanuja shows that Brahma Sutra also conclusively asserts that the Supreme Being is the material as well as the instrumental cause of the world, and there is no authority higher than him.]

तदेतन्निखिलजगन्निमित्तोपादानभूतात् 'जन्माद्यस्य यतः' (ब्र० सू० १/१/२), 'प्रकृतिश्च प्रतिज्ञादृष्टान्तानुपरोधात्' (ब्र० सू० १/४/२३) इत्यादिसूत्रैः प्रतिपादितात्परस्माद्ब्रह्मणः परम-पुरुषादन्यस्य कस्यचित्परतरत्वं 'परमतः सेतून्मानसंबन्धभेदव्यपदेशेभ्यः' (ब्र० सू० ३/२/३०) इत्याशङ्क्य - 'सामान्यात्तु', 'बुद्ध्यर्थः' पादवत्', 'स्थानविशेषात्प्रकाशादिवत्', 'उपपत्तेश्च', 'तथान्यप्रतिषेधात्', 'अनेन सर्वगतत्वमायामादिशब्दादिभ्यः' (ब्र० सू० ३/२/३१-३६) इति सूत्रकारः स्वयमेव निराकरोति ॥

Vyasa has himself refuted the idea of there being a higher principle (being, element) than this Supreme Person who has been explained as the material and instrumental cause of the world in the following sutras: "From which the origin and the like (of this world) proceed, is Supreme Being." (Brahma Sutra 1/1/2) and "(Supreme Being is) also the material cause as it is not opposed to the proposition and the illustrations" (Brahma Sutra 1/4/23) and other such sutras. In Brahma Sutra 3/2/30 he raises the view of opposition again - "There must be another (reality) higher than this Supreme Person because he is said to be the bridge to the reality, his (finite) measurability, his connection with the final reality as a means to lead to it, and his difference from the reality". Then, he refutes the view of the opposition in the following Sutras: "he is mentioned as a bridge due to its resembling function in making people cross this world."(31); "(It is) for the purpose of contemplation that extent of Supreme Being said to have four parts, etc. This makes it possible for intellect to grasp it." (32); though the Supreme Being is infinite, it may be meditated on as finite, just as we see light, and sky from a small opening. (33); "For Narayana, it is possible to be the means as well as the end." (It can be the bridge as well as the destination.) (34); "Since the existence of other higher being is denied, there is nothing higher than the Supreme Being. (35); His all-pervasiveness is mentioned through various words denoting his extent. (Brahma Sutra 3/2/31-36)

[Brahma Sutra shows that everything emanates and dissolves in him so he is the material cause. It later emphasizes that the Supreme Being is not only the material cause but also the instrumental cause of the world; only then by knowing him every other thing can be known. In some Upanishads, the Supreme Being is said to be the bridge to reality, so some might suspect it might be a means to some other end. Brahma Sutra affirms that it is the means as well as the end and it is mentioned as a bridge to make it understandable to all. If one asks how we can know anything that is infinite. Vyasa answers that light from an opening gives us an idea about the light as well as its source. In a similar way, we can know the Supreme Being by investigating him within our hearts. If you say we do not see that means itself is the end in worldly matters. It again asserts that for Supreme Being it is very well possible because he is not like anything else. If someone raises a doubt can anything be greater than him? To it, Vyasa answers, Upanishad forbids the presence of anything superior to him. Moreover, the use of various words like all-pervasive, omniscient, almighty, etc. reveals that there is no one like him.]

[Now, Ramanuja shows the references from Manu Smriti.]

मानवे च शास्त्रे – 'प्रादुरासीत्तमोनुद:' (म० स्मृ० १/६), 'सिसृक्षुर्विविधाः प्रजाः । अप एव
ससर्जादौ तासु वीर्यमपासृजत् ॥' (म० स्मृ० १/८), 'तस्मिञ्जज्ञे स्वयं ब्रह्म' (म० स्मृ० १/९)
इति ब्रह्मणो जन्मश्रवणात्क्षेत्रज्ञत्वमेवावगम्यते । तथा च स्रष्टुः परमपुरुषस्य तद्विसृष्टस्य च
ब्रह्मणः, 'अयं तस्य ताः पूर्वं तेन नारायणः स्मृतः ।' (म० स्मृ० १/१०), 'तद्विसृष्टः स पुरुषो
लोके ब्रह्मेति कीर्त्यते ॥' (म० स्मृ० १/११) इति नामनिर्देशाच्च । तथा च वैष्णवे पुराणे हिरण्य-
गर्भादीनां भावनात्रयान्वयादशुद्धत्वेन शुभाश्रयत्वानर्हतोपपादनात्क्षेत्रज्ञत्वं निश्चीयते ॥

In Manu Smriti also, we find (1) "Then appeared He who controls
darkness" (1/6), (2) "Desirous of creating all kinds of beings, first He
created water and placed His energy in it"(1/8), (3) From that arose
Brahma" (1/9). In these passages, since we hear about Brahma's
birth, it is evident that Brahma is an embodied soul.

It also gives the names of the Supreme Person, who is the creator,
and of Brahma, who was created by Him, in the following verses -
"The waters were His previous abode. Therefore, He is called
Narayana." (1/10); "The person created by Him, is celebrated in the
world as Brahma." (1/11)

Similarly, one can determine from the Vishnu Purana that Brahma,
etc. are embodied souls. Therefore, they cannot be the sacred
objects of meditation owing to their association with the three
kinds of afflictions.

[The sections of Manu Smriti clearly show that Brahma, the creator,
like all other living and non-living entities, is also created by the
Supreme Being. The Supreme Being is termed Narayana, which
etymologically means "He is the abode (Ayana, refuge) of the
(conscious) waters (Narah, living beings) or who lives in the
individual souls as their ultimate refuge. Three kinds of afflictions,
which everyone is subject to, are – 1) due to himself (body and
mind), 2) due to others, and 3) due to natural forces. Since the
Supreme Being alone is above all of them, he is the sole object of
meditation or worship for seekers of liberation.]

Refutation of Prabhakar's Mimansa Philosophy

[The followers of Mimansa philosophy say that Vedas describe three things – injunctions (methods), glorified verses or explanations, and hymns of worship. Their primary intention is towards the performance of actions, and they consider injunctions their main source. Actions can give their results by themselves; they do not require the Supreme Being to give their results. Moreover, Vedas cannot substantiate an entity that already exists, e.g. Supreme Being. Ramanuja refutes these incorrect opinions in this section.]

यदपि कैश्चिदुक्तम् - सर्वस्य शब्दजातस्य विध्यर्थवादमन्त्ररूपस्य कार्याभिधायित्वेनैव प्रामाण्यं वर्णनीयम् । व्यवहारादन्यत्र शब्दस्य बोधकत्वशक्त्यवधारणासंभवाद्व्यवहारस्य च कार्यबुद्धि- मूलत्वात्कार्यरूप एव शब्दार्थ: । न परिनिष्पन्ने वस्तुनि शब्द: प्रमाणमिति ।

There are some thinkers (Prabhakaras), who hold that words (in the Vedas) which consist of injunctions (methods), explanatation, and hymns, are meaningful (or authoritative) only when they denote an action to be done. The words cannot convey a meaning when they are used in connection with anything other than an action to be performed. All speech and worldly matters are based on the idea of the action to be performed. Therefore, the significance of the Vedas is, in their opinion, concerned only with actions to be done and they are not valid sources of knowledge in regard to all existing entities (like Supreme Being).

[They do not accept the authority of the Vedas as evidence for the existence of the Supreme Being.]

[Ramanuja shows how words, of which the Vedas are composed, can signify an already existing entity.]

अत्रोच्यते । प्रवर्तकवाक्यव्यवहार एव शब्दानामर्थबोधकत्वशक्त्यवधारणं कर्तव्यमिति किमियं राजाज्ञा । सिद्धवस्तुषु शब्दस्य बोधकत्वशक्तिग्रहणमत्यन्तसुकरम् । तथा हि केनचिद्धुस्तचेष्टा-

दिनापवरके दण्ड: स्थित इति देवदत्ताय ज्ञापयेति प्रेषित: कश्चित्तज्ज्ञापने प्रवृत्तोऽपवरके दण्ड: स्थित इति शब्दं प्रयुङ्क्ते । मूकवद्धस्तचेष्टामिमां जानन् पार्श्वस्थोऽन्य: प्राग्व्युत्पन्नोऽपि तस्यार्थस्य बोधनायापवरके दण्ड: स्थित इत्यस्य शब्दस्य प्रयोगदर्शनादस्यार्थस्यायं शब्दो बोधक इति जानातीति किमत्र दुष्करम् ।

Against this view, it may be said: Is it a king's command that the word can only signify the activities related to worldly matters as their meaning (and not the existing entities)? (There is none such). It is very easy to make one understand the signifying power of a word even in regard to already existing entities. For example, suppose a person (A) tells another person (B) by gestures to tell Devadatta, "The stick is in the room." Accordingly, the second person (B) proceeds to Devadatta and tells him, not by gesture but by using the words, "The stick is in the room." A fourth person (C) who stood there and observed the gestures employed by the first person (A) like a dumb man may not at first know their implied meaning. But, when he listens to the words of second person B to Devadatta, he understands the meaning of the gestures of the first person (A), and those gestures and likewise these words signify the presence of an already existing stick in the room. Where is the impossibility here as words easily signify the presence of an already existing stick?

[Ramanuja contradicts the assumption of the Mimansakas through a counter-example and shows that words can also signify an already existing entity.]

[The way children learn language through others is also an example of how words can signify the existing entities.]

तथा बालस्तातोऽयमियं मातायं मातुलोऽयं मनुष्योऽयं मृगश्चन्द्रोऽयमयं च सर्प इति मातापितृ-प्रभृतिभि: शब्दै: शनै: शनैरङ्गुल्या निर्देशने तत्र तत्र बहुश: शिक्षितस्तैरेव शब्दैस्तेष्वर्थेषु स्वात्म-नश्च बुद्ध्युत्पत्तिं दृष्ट्वा तेष्वर्थेषु तेषां शब्दानामङ्गुल्या निर्देशपूर्वक: प्रयोग: सम्बन्धान्तराभा-

वात्संकेतयितृपुरुषाज्ञानाच्च बोधकत्वनिबन्धन इति क्रमेण निश्चित्य पुनरप्यस्य शब्दस्यायमर्थ
इति पूर्ववृद्धैः शिक्षितः सर्वशब्दानामर्थमवगम्य स्वयमपि सर्वं वाक्यजातं प्रयुङ्क्ते । एवमेव
सर्वपदानां स्वार्थाभिधायित्वं संघातविशेषणां च यथावस्थितसंसर्गविशेषवाचित्वं च जानातीति
कार्यार्थैव व्युत्पत्तिरित्यादिनिर्बन्धो निर्निर्बन्धनः । अतः परिष्पन्नः वस्तुनि शब्दस्यबोधकत्व-
शक्त्य वधारणात्सर्वाणि वेदान्तवाक्यानि सकलजगत्कारणं सर्वकल्याणगुणाकरमुक्तलक्षणं
ब्रह्म बोधयन्त्येव ॥

For example, a child is told again and again by parents and elders with words accompanied by fingers pointing to the respective objects at the same time, "This is father", "This is mother', "This is uncle", "This is a man," "This is a beast", "This is the moon", "This is a serpent". Being taught in this way many times, the child knows their meanings as arising within him from those very words. Then, he uses these words accompanied by the gesture of his finger to indicate the corresponding objects. Later, he knows that there is no other association between a word and the gestures used to point at the object; he concludes the meaning of the words as told to him by his elders. Thus, he learns the meanings of all words told by the elders and uses them himself in the sentences. In the same way, he learns the meaning of all words, their specific associations, and connections. Therefore, the insistence that the knowledge of the meaning of words arises only in connection with things to be done is without reason. Hence, it is clear that the words can signify the known entities (both in ordinary speech and in the Vedas). It, therefore, follows that all the Vedic passages do give (us) knowledge of the Supreme Being, who is the cause of the entire world, who is the abode of all auspicious qualities and other attributes as mentioned earlier.

[Through this example, Ramanuja has shown that words can signify any already existing object without any difficulty. When someone learns a new language, it is through the association of words with the existing objects.]

[Now, Ramanuja further says that even if he agrees to the contention of the Mimansakas that words signify actions, it won't change anything.]

अपि च कार्यार्थ एव व्युत्पत्तिरस्तु । वेदान्तवाक्यान्यप्युपासनविषयककार्याधिकृतविशेषणभूत-फलत्वेन दुःखासंभिन्नदेशविशेषरूपस्वर्गादिवद्रात्रिसत्रप्रतिष्ठानादिवदपगोरणशतयातनासाध्य-साधनभाववच्च कार्योपयोगितयैव सर्वं बोधयन्ति ।

Further, let us admit for the moment that words are meaningful only in regard to an action to be done; even then, the statements of Vedanta text may also be shown to give actionable knowledge related to worship (meditation) as they prescribe an action to be done. In connection to worship, they tell about the action to be done, the knowledge of the person who meditates, and the results of the worship, which is an attribute of his worship. It is in the same way that you admit that explanations give valid knowledge of certain actions even when the instructions do not mention them. For instance, (1) the instruction says, "The person desirous of heaven should perform the Jyotishtoma sacrifice". It does not tell us what heaven is like or the attributes of heaven. An explanation says "Where there is no heat, no cold, and no grief is heaven". You admit this attribute of heaven as valid knowledge even though it does not occur in the instruction. Again (2) there is an instruction which enjoins: "The night session (sacrifices to be performed at night) should be done". It is not stated in the instructions what the reward would be. But an explanation following it says, "Those who perform these night sacrifices become well-established in life". You admit that this passage, though only an explanation, gives us valid knowledge about the reward resulting from the performance. Furthermore, (3) there is a prohibitory injunction to the following effect: "Therefore, one shall not threaten a Brahmin with assault". It does not state any penalty. Only an explanation says: "He who threatens shall be fined a hundred gold coins". This explanation is admitted by you as affording true knowledge. As in these (three) cases, explanatory passages in Vedanta do give true knowledge of the Supreme Being, the attainment of which is the reward of the meditation enjoined in the instruction ("Supreme Being should be meditated upon"), of the attributes of Supreme Being, of the person who meditates, and other such things. All of this information is related to the instruction.

[Here, Ramanuja points out three instances where a Mimansaka would also agree, to make sense of the instructions, they need to associate them with other explanatory passages of the Vedas.]

[Now, Ramanuja applies the same principle to Vedanta texts.]

तथाहि – 'ब्रह्मविदाप्नोति परम्' (तै० उ० १/१) इत्यत्र ब्रह्मोपासनविषयकार्याधिकृतविशेषण-भूतफलत्वेन ब्रह्मप्राप्तिः श्रूयते परप्राप्तिकामो ब्रह्म विद्यादित्यत्र प्राप्यतया प्रतीयमानं ब्रह्मस्वरूपं तद्विशेषणं च सर्वं कार्योपयोगितयैव सिद्धं भवति । तदन्तर्गतमेव जगत्स्रष्टृत्वं संहर्तृत्वमाधारत्वमन्तरात्मत्वमित्याद्युक्तमनुक्तं च सर्वमिति न किंचिदनुपपन्नम् ॥

To explain: In the text, 'One who knows Supreme Being attains the Highest (Taittiriya Upanishad 1)' the attainment of Supreme Being is promised as the reward, accruing to one who fulfills the injunction to meditate on him. It means that one desirous of the Highest must seek to know the Supreme Being. Supreme Being is presented here as that which is to be attained. Its existential nature and characteristics are all described, in addition to the action of meditation. The truths related to the existential nature and characteristics of the Supreme Being are that he is the creator of the world, the destroyer of it, the support of the world, the inner soul of it, and all the other truths, both previously mentioned and unmentioned. There is nothing in this that is against reason. Thus, even if we assume the requirement of subsidiary actions to the injunction prescribing meditation, all the existential propositions of the Vedanta, retain their validity and significance.

[Thus, there is no inconsistency even if one interprets the Vedanta texts following the method of Mimansakas.]

[Now, Ramanuja shows that an earlier Guru Dramida also accepts that explanatory passages supplement the instructions.]

एवं च सति मन्त्रार्थवादगता ह्याविरुद्धा अपूर्वाश्वार्थाः सर्वे विधिशेषतयैव सिद्धा भवन्ति । यथोक्तं द्रमिडभाष्ये – 'ऋणं हि वै जायत इति श्रुतेः' इत्युपक्रम्य 'यद्यप्यवदानस्तुतिपरं वाक्यं तथापि नासता स्तुतिरुपपद्यते' इति । एतदुक्तं भवति सर्वो ह्यर्थवादभागो देवताराधनभूत-यागादेः साङ्गस्याराध्यदेवतायाश्चादृष्टरूपान् गुणान् सहस्रशो वदन् सहस्रशः कर्मणि प्राशस्त्य-बुद्धिमुत्पादयति । तेषामसद्भावे प्राशस्त्यबुद्धिरेव न स्यादिति कर्मणि प्राशस्त्यबुद्ध्यर्थं गुण-सद्भावमेव बोधयतीति । अनयैव दिशा सर्वे मन्त्रार्थवादावगता अर्थाः सिद्धाः ॥

Therefore, the contents of texts, whether they are hymns or explanations, get established as a subsidiary to injunctions provided they are not opposed to other sources of valid knowledge and cannot be established by them. The commentary of Dramida concurs with this standpoint: Commencing with reference to the Upanishad, "The debt is born', it states, "This sentence is in praise of sacrificial offering (charity); however, this praise would be meaningless if it is not true." The meaning of the comment is this: All the (laudatory) explanations of the Vedas praise the virtues of the sacrifices, along with their complementary rites, as the acts of worship offered to gods. They also praise those virtues of the concerned gods, which cannot otherwise be known, in a thousand ways. The purpose of such praise is to create the idea of the worthiness in the prescribed religious action. If the virtues extolled do not actually exist, the idea of the worthiness of the said action will not ensue. So the explanatory passages, if they have to succeed in creating the idea of the worthiness of the actions prescribed, must, of necessity, affirm and teach the reality of the virtues praised. Along the same line of reasoning, the truth of all hymns and laudatory explanations gets proved.

[Thus, all types of statements of the Vedas have their relevance and purpose. We cannot assume that only their injunctions are meaningful.]

[Now, Ramanuja asks Mimansakas about the definition of action.]

अपि च कार्यवाक्यार्थवादिभिः किमिदं कार्यत्वं नामेति वक्तव्यम् । कृतिभावभाविता कृत्युद्देश्यता चेति चेत् । किमिदं कृत्युद्देश्यत्वम् । यदधिकृत्य कृतिर्वर्तते तत्कृत्युद्देश्यत्वमिति चेत् । पुरुषव्यापाररूपायाः कृतेः कोऽयमधिकारो नाम । यत्प्राप्तीच्छया कृतिमुत्पादयति पुरुषः तत्कृत्युद्देश्यत्वमिति चेद्धन्त तर्हीष्टत्वमेव कृत्युद्देश्यत्वम् ।

Further, those who hold that the meanings of words are related only to an action to be done should define what they mean by action. If you say that an action leads to an accomplishment after aiming at it, then, we ask what that action, which aims for this accomplishment, is as the action is something a person does. You might say that wishing to attain an accomplishment, a person performs the action, so it is what one aims at. Then, it means 'to be aimed at by an act' means precisely 'to be desired'.

[Thus, action means doing something for a desired end.]

[How can a desire arise in us?]

अथैवं मनुषे इष्टस्यैव रूपद्वयमस्ति । इच्छाविषयतया स्थितिः पुरुषप्रेरकत्वं च । तत्र प्रेरकत्वा-कारः कृत्युद्देश्यत्वमिति सोऽयं स्वपक्षाभिनिवेशकारितो वृथाश्रमः । तथा हीच्छाविषयतया प्रतीतस्य स्वप्रयत्नोत्पत्तिमन्तरेणासिद्धिरेव प्रेरकत्वम् । तत एव प्रवृत्तेः । इच्छायां जातायामिष्ट-स्य स्वप्रयत्नोत्पत्तिमन्तरेणासिद्धिः प्रतीयते चेत्ततश्चिकीर्षा जायते ततः प्रवर्तते पुरुष इति

तत्त्वविदां प्रक्रिया । तस्मादिष्टस्य कृत्यधीनात्मलाभत्वातिरेकि कृत्युद्देश्यत्वं नाम किमपि न दृश्यते ।

Now agreeing on this, you might say, "There are two aspects of desire, one is the existence of the object of desire and the other is to inspire the person to act for it. It is this inspiring aspect that is the meaning of "being aimed at by an action." This effort (to amend the definition) is due to an obstinate insistence on your theory is all in vain. The power of inspiration is nothing but the absolute dependence on one's own effort to realize his object of desire. Only then a person makes an effort to attain it. When the desire for a thing (heaven, etc.) has arisen, and when the person realizes that the desired object cannot be secured without beginning his effort, the desire to act arises, and then the person acts. This is the order of sequence as understood by those who know the truth of these things. Therefore, there is no meaning in anything else being aimed at by an accomplishment, apart from the desired object being dependent for its attainment on one's efforts.

[When a person understands that to attain a desired object, he needs to make efforts, only then he can be motivated to act.]

[The Mimansaka raises another doubt.]

अथोच्यते - इष्टाहेतुश्च पुरुषानुकूलता । तत्पुरुषानुकूलत्वं कृत्युद्देश्यत्वमिति चेत् । नैवम् । पुरुषानुकूलं सुखमित्यनर्थान्तरम् । तथा पुरुषाननुकूलं दुःखपर्यायम् । अतः सुखव्यतिरिक्तस्य कस्यापि पुरुषानुकूलत्वं न संभवति । ननु च दुःखनिवृत्तेरपि सुखव्यतिरिक्तायाः पुरुषानुकूलता दृष्टा । नैतत् । आत्मानुकूलं सुखमात्मप्रतिकूलं दुःखमिति हि सुखदुःखयोर्विवेकः । तत्रात्मानु-कूलं सुखमिष्टं भवति । तत्प्रतिकूलं दुःखं चानिष्टम् । अतो दुःखसंयोगस्यासह्यतया तन्निवृत्तिर-पीष्टा भवति । तत एवेष्टतासाम्यादनुकूलताभ्रमः ।

The Mimamasaka might now say, "The reason for a thing being desired is its being agreeable to a person. So, that which is agreeable to a person is that which is aimed at by action". We dismiss this explanation. That which is agreeable to a person (is synonymous with pleasure and) means nothing else but pleasure. In the same way, that which is disagreeable to a person is synonymous with pain. There is nothing else than pleasure that can be said to be agreeable to a person. You might object to it and reply, "The removal of pain, which is other than pleasure, is seen to be agreeable to a person". We refute this statement as follows: "Whatever is agreeable to one's self is pleasure and whatever is disagreeable to one's self is pain. This is the differentiation between pleasure and pain. Between them, pleasure which is agreeable to one's self becomes an object of desire, and pain which is disagreeable to one's self becomes undesirable. Since contact with pain is unbearable, relief from it, too, becomes an object of desire. Since it becomes an object of desire, in the same way as pleasure, relief from pain is wrongly conceived as pleasure (though it is not the same as pleasure).

[Here, Ramanuja shows that the removal of pain is not the same as pleasure.]

[He further explains how relief from pain is not the same as pleasure.]

तथा हि - प्रकृतिसंसृष्टस्य संसारिणः पुरुषस्यानुकूलसंयोगः प्रतिकूलसंयोगः स्वरूपेणावस्थिति-रिति च तिस्रोऽवस्थाः । तत्र प्रतिकूलसंबन्धनिवृत्तिश्चानुकूलसंबन्धनिवृत्तिश्च स्वरूपेणावस्थिति-रेव । तस्मात्प्रतिकूलसंयोगे वर्तमाने तन्निवृत्तिरूपा स्वरूपेणावस्थितिरपीष्टा भवति । तत्रेष्टता-साम्यादनुकूलताभ्रमः । अतः सुखरूपत्वादनुकूलतायाः नियोगस्यानुकूलतां वदन्तं प्रामाणिकाः परिहसन्ति । ॥

Moreover, for a man, who is still in the stream of births and deaths, owing to contact with nature, there are three possible states: contact with what is agreeable, contact with what is disagreeable, and being in his own essential nature (with neither pleasure nor pain). The absence of contact with pleasure and absence of contact with pain is the third state in which one remains in his essential nature. Therefore, when contact with disagreeable occurs, relief from it, which is this third state of being in one's essential nature, becomes desirable. Since, there is a similarity between pleasure and this relief from pain in both of them being desirable, relief from pain is illusorily mistaken for pleasure. The wise, who go by the valid evidence, ridicule them who consider the relief from pain as the same as pleasure due to their desirability.

[Since both relief from pain and pleasure are desirable to us, some of us mistakenly assume them to be the same.]

[Now, Ramanuja shows the right way to interpret the statements of the Vedas and says that actions in themselves are not meaningful.]

इष्टस्यार्थविशेषस्य निर्वर्तकतयैव हि नियोगस्य नियोगत्वं स्थिरत्वमपूर्वत्वं च प्रतीयते । स्वर्गकामो यजेतेत्यत्र कार्यस्य क्रियातिरिक्ता स्वर्गकामपदसमभिव्याहारेण स्वर्गसाधनत्व-निश्चयादेव भवन्ति । न च वाच्यं यजेतेत्यत्र प्रथमं नियोगः स्वप्रधानतयैव प्रतीयते स्वर्गकामपद-समभिव्याहारात्स्विसिद्धये स्वर्गसिद्ध्यनुकूलता च नियोगस्येति । यजेतेति हि धात्वर्थस्य पुरुष-प्रयत्नसाध्यता प्रतीयते । स्वर्गकामपदसमभिव्याहारादेव धात्वर्थातिरेकिणो नियोगत्वं स्थिरत्वम् -पूर्वत्वं चेत्यादि । तच्च स्वर्गसाधनत्वप्रतीतिनिबन्धनम् समभिव्याहृतस्वर्गकामपदार्थान्वययोग्यं स्वर्गसाधनमेव कार्यं लिङादयोऽभिदधतीति लोकव्युत्पत्तिरपि तिरस्कृता ।

Bringing about the accomplishment of the desired object, which is enduring (long-lasting) and transcendent (non-worldly), seems to be the purpose of a command (instruction). In the instruction "He, who is desirous of heaven, shall perform the fire-sacrifice", 'perform the fire-sacrifice' is determined as the means to attain heaven, due to the presence of the phrase 'desirous of heaven' in between. It cannot be the meaning of the actionable phrase 'perform the fire-sacrifice' by itself. You cannot say that the phrase 'perform the fire-sacrifice' first independently suggests, as a matter of primary importance, to perform sacrifice, and afterward due to its association with the words 'desirous of heaven' says that it is conducive to the attainment of heaven.

The verb 'perform' suggests only "what can be accomplished by a person's effort". It is only by its being read in association with "He who is desirous of heaven", that you could infer what is not conveyed by the verb 'perform' and what is other than that denoted by the verb, namely "the thing to do", its enduring quality, and being a new transcendent entity. Performance of fire-worship is the means to heaven is suggested by the appearance of the phrase 'He who is desirous of heaven' after it and the imperative form of the verb 'perform'. It is the usual way to be accepted in ordinary interactions to comprehend a sentence, and the Mimamsakas have ignored it in their explanation.

[Thus, one should not just interpret a word, used in a sentence, in isolation. Other parts of the sentence can also influence its intended meaning.]

[Ramanuja gives an example to support his point of view.]

एतदुक्तं भवति – समभिव्यव्हृतपदान्तरवाच्यार्थान्वययोग्यमेवेतरपदप्रतिपाद्यमित्यन्विताभिधायि -पदसंघातरूपवाक्यश्रवणसमनन्तरमेव प्रतीयते । तच्च स्वर्गसाधनरूपम् । अतः क्रियावदन्या -र्थतापि विरोधादेव परित्यक्तेति । अत एव गङ्गायां घोष इत्यादौ घोषप्रतिवासयोग्यार्थोपस्था- पनपरत्वं गङ्गापदस्याश्रीयते । प्रथमं गङ्गापदेन गङ्गार्थः स्मृत इति गङ्गापदार्थस्य पेयत्वं न वाक्यार्थान्वयीभवति । एवमत्र अपि यजेतेत्येतावन्मात्रश्रवणे कार्यमनन्यार्थं स्मृतमिति वाक्या- र्थान्वयसमये कार्यस्यानन्यार्थता नावतिष्ठते ।

It means this: When a number of words are employed in a sentence, the meaning of a particular word can be taken to be only that which would be coherent with the meanings of other words uttered along with it. Moreover, the meaning of the word in question can be determined only after hearing the full sentence consisting of a number of words that express meaning in connection with one another (and not independently). Thus, the phrase 'performance of fire-sacrifice' in the sentence implies this action as 'the means of attaining heaven. But, if Mimamsakas give primary importance to just the meaning of the word 'perform' independently, without considering the meanings of the other words in the sentence, the meaning of the word 'perform' might also become incongruous with the meanings of the other words and, therefore, it will have to be discarded.

For example, in sentences like "On the Ganga (river), there is the village of the herdsmen," the word 'Ganga' appears to refer to a place capable of being dwelt in, with reference to the village of the herdsmen. At first, it is true that the term 'Ganga' (independently) means the river Ganga. But, there cannot be a village on the river Ganga; therefore, this meaning is not congruent with the other words of the sentence. Hence, we have to give up the meaning of Ganga as "the flow of river Ganga" and take the word to mean "on the bank of the Ganga." Similarly, here also, it is not proper to say that the word 'perform' independently suggests its meaning, without looking at the words that follow it in the sentence. When we determine the meaning of the sentence, after considering the sequence of the words in the sentences, its meaning might not stand right.

[Thus, words are to be interpreted according to the context, in association with other parts of the statement.]

[Now, Ramanuja refutes the contention that an action has to be agreeable.]

कार्याभिधायिपदश्रवणवेलायां प्रथमं कार्यमनन्यार्थं प्रतीतमित्येतदपि न संगच्छते । व्युत्पत्ति-
काले गवानयनादिक्रियाया दुःखरूपाया इष्टविशेषसाधनतयैव कार्यताप्रतीतेः । अतो नियोगस्य

पुरुषानुकूलत्वं सर्वलोकविरुद्धं नियोगस्य सुखरूपपुरुषानुकूलतां वदतः स्वानुभवविरोधश्च ।
करीर्या वृष्टिकामो यजेत्येत्यादिषु सिद्धेऽपि नियोगे वृष्ट्यादिसिद्धिनिमित्तस्य वृष्टिव्यतिरेकेण
नियोगस्यानुकूलता नानुभूयते । यद्यप्यस्मिञ्जन्मनि वृष्ट्यादिसिद्धेरनियमस्तथाप्यनियमादेव
नियोगसिद्धिरवश्याश्रयणीया । तस्मिन्ननुकूलतापर्यायसुखानुभूतिर्न दृश्यते । एवमुक्तरीत्या
कृतिसाध्येष्टत्वातिरेकि कृत्युद्देश्यत्वं न दृश्यते ॥

Your assumption that hearing an actionable word (e.g. perform fire-
sacrifice), immediately and independently of other words, suggests
'an action to be done', is itself not true. After determining the
meaning, activities like bringing the cow, etc. which appear
troublesome, become desirable only as a means of attaining some
specific pleasure (afterward). Therefore, to say that an instruction is
agreeable to a person by itself is opposed to all ordinary experience.
It is even against the experience of the person who maintains that
an instruction is of the nature of pleasure because it is agreeable.

In the case of instructions like "He, who is desirous of rain, shall
fire-sacrifice with bamboo shoots", it is not experienced as
agreeable in itself as apart from being the cause of the rain after the
sacrifice is over. The Mimamsaka might reply, "It is not experienced
as agreeable in this life, for the effect, namely, rain may occur either
in this life or in a later life." Since there is uncertainty regarding the
time of rain (as the result of the sacrifice), the Mimamsakas have
necessarily to assume that the effect of the sacrifice has already
been generated in this life. But, this effect is not experienced now
as agreeable or, in other words, pleasant. Thus, from these
arguments, it is evident that there is no such thing as "that which is
aimed at by the action" other than the desired object.

[Thus, if the end results are pleasant, a person can engage in
actions that are not agreeable to him at first. And, if a favorable end
result to our actions is not generated in this life, Mimansak has to
assume its certain effect in later lives; otherwise, the performance
of actions would be useless.]

[Now, Mimansaka gives another definition to the object of the action.]

कृतिं प्रति शेषित्वं कृत्युद्देश्यत्वमिति चेत् । किमिदं शेषित्वं किं च शेषत्वमिति वक्तव्यम् । कार्यं प्रति संबन्धी शेषः । तत्प्रतिसंबन्धित्वं शेषित्वमिति चेत् । एवं तर्हि कार्यत्वमेव शेषत्वमित्युक्तं भवति । कार्यत्वमेव विचार्यते । परोद्देशप्रवृत्तकृतिव्याप्त्यर्हत्वं शेषत्वमिति चेत् । कोऽयं परोद्देशो नामेति । अयमेव हि विचार्यते । उद्देश्यत्वं नामेप्सितत्वसाध्यत्वमिति चेत् । किमिदमी-प्सितत्वम् । कृतिप्रयोजनत्वमिति चेत्पुरुषस्य कृत्यारम्भप्रयोजनमेव हि कृतिप्रयोजनम् । स चेच्छाविषयः कृत्यधीनात्मलाभ इति पूर्वोक्त एव । अयमेव हि सर्वत्र शेषशेषिभावः । परगताति-शयाधानेच्छोपादेयत्वमेव यस्य स्वरूपं स शेषः । परः शेषी । फलोत्पत्तीच्छया यागादेस्तत्प्रयत्न-स्य चोपादेयत्वं यागादिसिद्ध्रीच्छयान्यत्सर्वमुपादेयम् ॥

The Mimamsaka might now attempt another definition of "that which is aimed at by an action" and say, "It is to which other things are subsidiary. We ask, "What is the definition of the main and subsidiary?" When two terms are associated with each other due to a common action, they are mutually associated; (for instance, 'father' and 'son' are mutually associated terms due to their relation). Hence, the Mimamsaka might reply: "Action is mutually associated with 'that which it is aimed at' and the main aim is likewise associated with the action. Here, action is defined as 'that which it is aimed at'. If now Mimamsaka defines the subsidiary as one which exists invariably along with the action which has started with something else for its aim", we ask, "What is this something else for its aim?" It is just this aim that was required to be defined. It may be said "aiming to accomplish a desire" is other than the aim. We ask again, "What is this thing that is desired?" The Minamsaka might reply, "The benefit to be derived from the action which stimulates a person at the beginning to do the effort and this is the object desired (namely heaven) which can be attained only by the action. This we have already stated. Everywhere the relationship between the subsidiary and the principal (main) is as follows: That whose whole existence, by its very nature, serves to promote the interests of another is the subsidiary and the other is the main. Sacrifices and the effort to perform them subserve solely the desire to attain the result. Owing to the desire to complete the sacrifices properly, the rest is subservient.

[Thus, Ramanuja shows that the viewpoint of Mimansaka converges with what he has already stated that actions are a means to an end, due to the desirability of the end result. He also defines the terms primary and secondary as per the scriptures.]

[Therefore, actions, themselves, do not have primary importance; rather, it is their end result for which they are done. So, their end result is their primary purpose, and actions themselves are secondary.]

एवं गर्भदासादीनामपि पुरुषविशेषातिशयाधानोपादेयत्वमेव स्वरूपम् । एवमीश्वरगतातिशया- धानेच्छयोपादेयत्वमेव चेतनाचेतनात्मकस्य नित्यस्यानित्यस्य च सर्वस्य वस्तुनः स्वरूपमिति सर्वमीश्वरशेषत्वमेव सर्वस्य चेश्वरः शेषीति 'सर्वस्य वशी सर्वस्येशानः', 'पतिं विश्वस्य' इत्याद्युक्तम् । कृतिसाध्यं प्रधानं यत्तत्कार्यमभिधीयत इत्ययमर्थः श्रद्धानेष्वेव शोभते ॥

Those, who are born slaves to others, exist solely (and primarily) to promote the highest interests of others, and are, therefore, subsidiary. Similarly, the essential nature of all things, sentient and non-sentient, eternal and non-eternal, is to subserve the highest purposes of the Supreme Being, so they are subsidiary, and He is the principal. The Upanishads, therefore, say, "He has all things under His control", "He rules over all", "the Lord of the universe", and so on. Therefore, only the attainment of heaven can be called principal and not action, for it is only the former that is the ultimate and supreme benefit derived from the action. The Mimamsaka's definition of "what is attainable through effort is primary, and action is its accomplishment" can convince only those having implicit and unquestioning (i.e. unreasonable) faith in Mimamsa doctrine.

[Supreme Being is the primary end of all actions, and making efforts to attain him are all secondary, so actions are secondary. Thus, this assumption of Mimansakas that action reigns supreme is contradicted.]

[Now, Ramanuja shows that the interpretation of Mimansakas is also incorrect according to the rules of grammar.]

अपि च, 'स्वर्गकामो यजेत' (आ० श्रौतसूत्र १०/२/१) इत्यादिषु लकारवाच्यकर्तृविशेषसमर्पण -पराणां स्वर्गकामादिपदानां नियोज्यविशेषसमर्पणपरत्वं शब्दानुशासनविरुद्धं केनावगम्यते । साध्यस्वर्गविशिष्टस्य स्वर्गसाधने कर्तृत्वान्वयो न घटत इति चेत् । नियोज्यत्वान्वयोऽपि न घटत इति हि स्वर्गसाधनत्वनिश्चयः । स तु शास्त्रसिद्धे कर्तृत्वान्वये स्वर्गसाधनत्वनिश्चयः क्रियते । यथा 'भोक्तुकामो देवदत्तगृहं गच्छेत्' इत्युक्ते भोजनकामस्य देवदत्तगृहगमने कर्तृत्वश्रवणादेव प्रागज्ञातमपि भोजनसाधनत्वं देवदत्तगृहगमनस्यावगम्यते । एवमत्रापि भवति ।

Further, in instances like "the man desirous of heaven shall perform the sacrifice" (Apastamba Shrauta Sutra 10/2/1), the imperative tense form 'perform' suggests an agent (doer) in general, and "The man desirous of heaven" makes it refer to a special kind of agent with a desire to attain the heaven, and this is the explanation of grammarians. How can a Mimamsaka infer it otherwise? Mimamsaka might reply, "How a man, who is desirous to attain heaven, can act when he does not know the performance of the sacrifice as a means to attain it?"

We ask the Mimamsaka in return, "How can then one even be asked to perform fire worship?" It is only as a means of attaining heaven that one can be instructed. The performance of fire worship as the means of attaining heaven is concluded by the scriptures; only after knowing it, can one decide to perform it. When a statement is made such as "He, who desires to eat, should go to the house of

Devadatta," since we hear of the activity of going to Devadatta's house on the part of one desiring to eat, we infer, though it was unknown before, that going to Devadatta's house is a means of attaining the desired end (eating food). Similarly, one should understand in the instance of fire-worship as a means to attain the heaven."

[Through instructions, one knows about the required actions to attain his desired end.]

[According to Ramanuja, Mimansakas are imagining an extra (unnecessary) result of the actions.]

न क्रियान्तरं प्रति कर्तृतया श्रुतस्य क्रियान्तरे कर्तृत्वकल्पनं युक्तम्; यजेतेति हि यागकर्तृतया श्रुतस्य बुद्धौ कर्तृत्वकल्पनं क्रियते । बुद्धे: कर्तृत्वकल्पनमेव हि नियोज्यत्वम् । यथोक्तं – 'नियोज्य सर्वकार्यं य: स्वकीयत्वेन बुध्यते' इति । यष्टृत्वानुगुणं तद्बुद्धोद्धृत्वमिति चेत् । देवदत्त: पचेदिति पाके कर्तृतया श्रुतस्य देवदत्तस्य पाकार्थगमनं पाकानुगुणमिति गमने कर्तृत्वकल्पनं न युज्यते ॥

It is not proper on the part of the Mimamsaka to attribute, to a person described as a doer of one action, the doership of an entirely different action. The term 'perform the fire sacrifice' describes the person as the (prospective) doer of the sacrifice who accepts this act, in his intellect, to be performed. The mental act of understanding in his intellect makes him the subject of instruction. It has been said that the subject of an instruction is one who considers the instruction pertaining to him. If you say this act of fire worship leads to this understanding, it is not right. For when it is said "Devadatta should cook (food)", he is stated to be the (prospective) doer of the cooking, and it is not proper to say that his act of going (to the kitchen, for example) is the reason of his cooking.

[After knowing the result of an action through scriptures, etc, a person intends to do it.]

[In those cases, where an action does not give an immediate result, Mimansaka has to assume its effect to make it meaningful. They call this effect 'apurva' or unseen, which did not exist before. It should remain until it gives the end result. Thus, they have to accept that actions, through this unseen, can give their results themselves. Ramanuja refutes this assumption.]

किं च लिङादिशब्दवाच्यं स्थायिरूपं किमित्यपूर्वमाश्रीयते । स्वर्गकामपदसमभिव्याहारानुपप-तेरिति चेत् । कात्रानुपपत्तिः । सिषाधयिषितस्वर्गो हि स्वर्गकामः । तस्य स्वर्गकामस्य कालान्तर -भाविस्वर्गसिद्धौ क्षणभङ्गिनी यागादिक्रिया न समर्थेति चेत् । अनाघ्रातवेदसिद्धान्तानामिय-मनुपपत्तिः । सर्वैः कर्मभिराराधितः परमेश्वरो भगवान्नारायणस्तत्तदिष्टं फलं ददातीति वेदविदो वदन्ति ।

Further, we ask, "Why do you postulate the existence of an enduring unseen entity (after the act is over)?" If their reply is, "The utterance of the words 'He who is desirous of heaven in conjunction with 'shall perform the sacrifice', would lose its meaning", we ask, "What is the difficulty that makes it lose its meaning?

Objection - "He who is desirous of heaven" means "He to whom the attainment of heaven is the end". Since heaven is to be attained at some future time, activity such as the performance of the sacrifice, which perishes immediately after it is over, cannot be its means.

Reply - This charge of unreasonableness can be made only by those who do not at all understand the true teaching of the Vedas. Those, who understand the Vedas, declare that Lord Narayana is the Supreme Ruler. He is worshipped by all sorts of actions. He rewards the desired results (of such activities to his worshippers).

[Ramanuja says it is needless to assume an apurva or unseen to give the remaining result of action when all scriptures tell that the Supreme Being gives the results of all our actions. This assumption of Mimansaka contradicts the statements of the Vedas, hence it should be discarded.]

[He shows the view of Dramidacharya to support his position.]

यथाहुर्वेदविदग्रेसरा द्रमिडाचार्याः – 'फलसंबिभत्सया हि कर्मभिरात्मानं पिप्रीषन्ति स प्रीतोऽलं फलायेति शास्त्रमर्यादा इति' । फलसंबन्धेच्छया कर्मभिर्यागदानहोमादिभिरिन्द्रियादिदेवता-मुखेन तत्तदन्तर्यामिरूपेणावस्थितमिन्द्रादिशब्दवाच्यं परमात्मानं भगवन्तं वासुदेवमारिराधयि-षन्ति, स हि कर्मभिराराधितस्तेषामिष्टानि फलानि प्रयच्छतीत्यर्थः ।

So says Dramidacharya, the foremost among the knowers of the Vedas, "It is certainly by the desire to attain the results that humans seek to please the Supreme Self by their actions. When He is pleased by their actions, He confers them the desired results". This is the teaching of the Scriptures." The meaning of this is as follows: "In order to attain the desired results, humans seek to worship Lord Vasudeva, the Supreme Self, who is expressed by words like Indra and others and who is within Indra and others as their inner self, by their actions such as sacrifices, charities, offerings made in the fire. He being so worshipped gives them the results they desire.

[When we please the Supreme Being with our actions, he gives us the desired result. Actions themselves cannot produce their results]

[Moreover, Upanishads directly assert that the Supreme Being is the giver of the results of our actions.]

तथा च श्रुति – 'इष्टापूर्तं बहुधा जातं जायमानं विश्वं बिभर्ति भुवनस्य नाभि' (तै॰ ना॰ उ॰ ४/६) इति । इष्टापूर्तमिति सकलश्रुतिस्मृतिचोदितं कर्मोच्यते । तद्विश्वं बिभर्ति इन्द्राग्निवरुणा-दिसर्वदेवतासंबन्धितया प्रतीयमानं तत्तदन्तरात्मतयावस्थितः परमपुरुषः स्वयमेव बिभर्ति

स्वयमेव स्वीकरोति । भुवनस्य नाभिः ब्रह्मक्षत्रादिसर्ववर्णपूर्णस्य भुवनस्य धारकः तैस्तैः
कर्मभिराराधितस्तत्तदिष्टफलप्रदानेन भुवनानां धारक इति नाभिरित्युक्तः । अग्निवायुप्रभृति-
देवतान्तरात्मतया तत्तच्छब्दाभिधेयोऽयमेवेत्याह – 'तदेवाग्निस्तद्वायुस्तत्सूर्यस्तदु चन्द्रमा' (तै०
ना० उ० १/७) इति ।

The Upanishad also says: "The Supreme Being, who is the center of
the Universe, maintains the world, which is the result of various
actions such as sacrifices and good deeds (like digging pools), either
done in the past or those that are being done in various ways."
(Taittiriya Narayana Upanishad 1/6) 'Sacrifices' and 'good deeds'
refer to all kinds of action prescribed in the Upanishads and the
Smritis (memory base texts). "Maintains the world" means
"Whatever actions are performed for all deities such as Indra, Agni
(fire-god), Varuna (water-god), etc. Supreme Being accepts them
himself as their inner self. "The center of the Universe" means "He
supports the world which consists of all castes such as the Brahmin,
Kshatriya, etc. He is called its center because He supports everyone
by granting their respective desires after they win His grace by
performing their actions as his worship. He is the person referred
to by such words as fire-god, wind-god, etc. on account of His
being their Inner Self is declared in the statement - "He alone is
fire-god, He is wind-god, He is the sun, He is the moon". (Taittiriya
Narayana Upanishad 1/7)

[The Upanishads state that the Supreme Being is the granter of our
actions; thus, they discard the view of Mimansaka.]

[Gita and Vishnu Purana also confirm the same.]

यथोक्तं भगवता – 'यो यो यां यां तनुं भक्तः श्रद्धयार्चितुमिच्छति । तस्य तस्याचलां श्रद्धां तामेव
विदधाम्यहम् ॥ स तस्य श्रद्धया युक्तस्तस्याराधनमीहते । लभते च ततः कामान्मयैव विहितान्हि
तान् ॥' (गीता ७/२१-२२) इति । यां यां तनुमितीन्द्रादिदेवताविशेषास्तत्तदन्तर्यामितयावस्थित-
स्य भगवतस्तनवः शरीराणीत्यर्थः । 'अहं हि सर्वयज्ञानां भोक्ता च प्रभुरेव च ।' (गीता ९/२४)

इत्यादि । प्रभुरेव चेति सर्वफलानां प्रदाता चेत्यर्थः । यथा च – 'यज्ञैस्त्वमिज्यसे नित्यं सर्वदेवमयाच्युत ।' (वि० पु० ५/२०/९७), 'यैः स्वधर्मपरैर्नाथ नरैरादाधितो भवान् । ते तरन्त्यखिलामेतां मायामात्मविमुक्तये ॥' (वि० पु० ५/३०/१६) इति ।

Lord Krishna also says - "Whatever divine form a devotee wishes to worship with reverence, I stabilize his faith in that deity as per his wish. Endowed with such faith, a person worships that deity with full devotion and receives his wishes fulfilled by that deity through me". (Gita 7/21-22) "Whatever divine form" means "particular deities such as Indra, etc. are, in fact, the bodies of Supreme Being who is within them as their Inner Self. And again in Gita 9/24, the Lord says: "I alone am the deity worshipped in all the sacrifices and, I am their master." Being their master means it is I who grants them all their desires.

Vishnu Purana also says: "O infallible one, you are the embodiment of all the gods; it is you being always worshipped in (all) sacrifices". (Vishnu Purana 5/20/97)

"O Lord, those who perform their respective duties and thus worship you, they transcend all this Maya and attain release from bondage". (Vishnu Purana 5/30/16)

[Thus, all texts certify the same fact.]

[Hence, we can conclude the same.]

सेतिहासपुराणेषु सर्वेष्वेव वेदेषु सर्वाणि कर्माणि सर्वेश्वराराधनरूपाणि, तैस्तैः कर्मभिराराधितः पुरुषोत्तमस्तत्तदिष्टं फलं ददातीति तत्र तत्र प्रपञ्चितम् ।

Thus, in all the Vedas, along with all the Itihasas (history texts) and Puranas, it is said that all acts are of the nature of the worship of the Lord. He, the Supreme Person, when worshipped through these actions, grants the desired objects. This truth is explained everywhere.

[Since the assumption of Mimansaka contradicts all Vedic texts, it is unacceptable.]

[Now, Ramanuja explains how the Supreme Being gives the results of all actions, even if one worships another deity and not him.]

एवं हि सर्वशक्तिं सर्वज्ञं सर्वेश्वरं भगवन्तमिन्द्रादिदेवतान्तर्यामिरूपेण यागदानहोमादिवेदोदित-
सर्वकर्मणां भोक्तारं सर्वफलानां प्रदातारं च सर्वाः श्रुतयो वदन्ति । 'चतुर्होतारो यत्र संपदं
गच्छन्ति देवैः' (तै॰ आ॰ ३/११) इत्याद्याः । चतुर्होतारो यज्ञाः, यत्र परमात्मनि देवेष्वन्तर्यामि-
रूपेणावस्थिते, देवैः संपदं गच्छन्ति देवैः संबन्धं गच्छन्ति यज्ञा इत्यर्थः । अन्तर्यामिरूपेणा-
वस्थितस्य परमात्मनः शरीरतयावस्थितानामिन्द्रादीनां यागादिसंबन्ध इत्युक्तं भवति । यथोक्तं
भगवता – 'भोक्तारं यज्ञतपसां सर्वलोकमहेश्वरम्' (गीता ५/२९) इति । तस्मादग्न्यादिदेवता-
न्तरात्मभूतपरमपुरुषाराधनरूपभूतानि सर्वाणि कर्माणि, स एव चाभिलषितफलप्रदातेति
किमत्रापूर्वेण व्युत्पत्तिपथदूरवर्तिना वाच्यतयाभ्युपगतेन कल्पितेन वा प्रयोजनम् ।

Similarly, all the Upanishads declare that the Supreme Being, who is worshipped by means of sacrifices, charity, and offerings made in the fire, receives them as the Inner Self of Indra and the other gods and he is also the giver of all objects desired. "Sacrifices become related to the gods through Him". (Taittiriya Aranyaka 3/11) "Through Him" means "Through Supreme Being who is within the gods as their inner self". "Sacrifices become related to the gods" means "Sacrifices become associated with the gods". It really means "Sacrifices become associated with gods like Indra, because they are the bodies to the Supreme Being, who is their inner Ruler.

Lord Krishna says, "He is the recipient of all sacrifices and austerities and that He is the Supreme Ruler of all the worlds". (Gita 5/29) It follows, therefore, that all actions are of the nature of the worship of the Supreme Person, who is the Inner self of Indra and the other gods, and that He alone is the giver of those objects that are desired. What, then, is the advantage of postulating an unseen effect (Apurva) of actions, which is far from the ordinary meaning of words, as being expressed by them?

[Since the Supreme Being is the inner soul of all, he gives the results of the actions as the self of the deity being worshipped through them.]

[Mimansaka now asks the reason for using the imperative tense in instructions.]

एवं च सति लिङादेः कोऽयमर्थः परिगृहीतो भवति । यज देवपूजायामिति देवताराधनभूत-
यागादेः प्रकृत्यर्थस्य कर्तृव्यापारसाध्यतां व्युत्पत्तिसिद्धां लिङादयोऽभिदधतीति न किंचिदनुपप-
न्नम् । कर्तृवाचिनां प्रत्ययानां प्रकृत्यर्थस्य कर्तृव्यापारसंबन्धप्रकारो हि वाच्यः । भूतवर्तमानादि-
कमन्ये वदन्ति । लिङादयस्तु कर्तृव्यापारसाध्यतां वदन्ति ॥

If it is asked, "What is the meaning to be taken from the imperative mode, etc. of the verbs (like sacrifice)?" We answer as follows: "The root of the word sacrifice ('yaja') means "to worship a deity" and refers to sacrifices, etc. which are of the nature of worship of a deity. The imperative mode, etc. expresses that the act signified by the root verb can be carried out by a doer". There is nothing unreasonable in this interpretation. According to the rules of grammar, the affixes, referring to the doer, point out the specific manner in which the action referred to by the root verb is related to the activity of the doer. The other affixes tell the tense to indicate past, present, or future. The imperative modes etc. indicate that the act denoted by the root verb is capable of being accomplished by the activity of the doer.

[Ramanuja says it only signifies that the action is doable by a person.]

[To understand its meaning in entirety, we need to look at other parts of the sentence.]

अपि च कामिनः कर्तव्यता कर्म विधाय कर्मणो देवताराधनरूपतां तद्द्वारा फलसंभवं च तत्तत्कर्मविधिवाक्यान्येव वदन्ति । 'वायव्यं श्वेतमालभत भूतिकामो वायुर्वै क्षेपिष्ठा देवता वायुमेव स्वेन भागधेयेनोपधावति स एवैनं भूतिं गमयति' (तै० सं० २/१/१/१) इत्यादीनि । नात्र फलसिद्ध्यनुपपत्तिः कापि दृश्यत इति फलसाधनत्वावगतिरौपादानिकीत्यपि न संगच्छति । विध्यपेक्षितं यागादेः फलसाधनत्वप्रकारं वाक्यशेष एव बोधयतीत्यर्थः ।

Further, the instructive sentences themselves, after prescribing the respective action to a person, who desires a particular object, state that the action is a form of worship of a deity and will bring out the desired end through that deity. For example, the text laying down a command says, "The man who desires to have prosperity, offer a white goat to wind-god, as a sacrifice." Then, there occurs the following sentence "Wind-god grants the desired end fastest". "So, he, who approaches wind-god with a suitable offering, will be rewarded by him with worldly prosperity." Here, there is nothing unreasonable in the statement that the desired end is attained through a god. Moreover, it is unreasonable to say that the means of accomplishing the desired end is inferred here. The sacrifice, etc. prescribed by the instructive sentence, are themselves the means to attain the end result; it is evident from the remaining part of the sentence.

[When we see the complete sentence, we know the desired end of the action.]

[Similar interpretation is to be done in case of prohibitions as well.]

'तस्माद्ब्राह्मणाय नापगुरेत्' (तै० सं० २/६/१०/१) इत्यत्रापगोरणनिषेधविधिपरवाक्यशेषे श्रूयमाणं निषेध्यस्यापगोरणस्य शतयातनासाधनत्वं निषेधविध्युपयोगीति हि स्वीक्रियते । अत्र पुनः कामिनः कर्तव्यतया विहितस्य यागादेः काम्यस्वर्गादिसाधनत्वप्रकारं वाक्यशेषावगतमना-

दृत्य किमित्युपादानेन यागादेः फलसाधनत्वं परिकल्प्यते । हिरण्यनिधिमपवरके निधाय याचते
कोद्रवादिलुब्धः कृपणं जनमिति श्रूयते तदेतद्युष्मासु दृश्यते ।

In the rule of prohibition: "Therefore, one shall not threaten a
person of Brahmana caste with (death-like) assault," though the
instruction does not state what would happen to one who so
threatens, still, we understand that the action of doing so is a
prohibited act. It is accepted to result in a hundred types of
punishment; this follows from the sentence coming after the
prohibitive text. We accept that prohibited action leads to a
hundred types of punishment, as it is useful in making the enjoining
prohibition meaningful.

While this is so, why should you ignore what is plainly understood
from the sentences closely following the instruction? To a person
desiring heaven, the performance of fire-sacrifice is mentioned, this
is evident from the later part of the sentence. Then, why do you
resort to an (indirect) inference (in the form of an unseen effect) to
state that the sacrifice will yield the desired end? There is a saying
to this effect; "Who will bury a treasure of gold in his own house
and go to beg of a miser for a handful of grains?" This saying holds
well in your case (Mimamsaka's).

[Ramanuja says that when sentences are directly revealing their
intent why should one resort to their indirect meanings.]

[In case of prohibition also, the result of actions is not given by the
unseen or 'Apurva' as Mimansakas say.]

शतयातनासाधनत्वमपि नादृष्टद्वारेण । चोदितान्यनुतिष्ठो विहितं कर्माकुर्वतो निन्दितानि च
कुर्वतः सर्वाणि सुखानि दुःखानि च परमपुरुषानुग्रहनिग्रहाभ्यामेव भवन्ति । 'एष
ह्येवानन्दयाति' (तै० उ० २/७/१), 'अथो सोऽभयं गतो भवति', 'अथ तस्य भयं भवति',
'भीषास्माद्वातः पवते भीषोदेति सूर्यो भीषास्मादग्निश्चन्द्रश्च मृत्युर्धावति पञ्चमः (तै०
२/७/२) इति ।', 'एतस्य वा अक्षरस्य प्रशासने गार्गि सूर्याचन्द्रमसौ विधृतौ तिष्ठतः', 'एतस्य वा

अक्षरस्य प्रशासने गार्गि ददतो मनुष्याः प्रशंसन्ति यजमानं देवा दर्वीं पितरोऽन्वायत्ता' (बृ० उ०
३/८/९) इत्याद्यनेकविधाः श्रुतयः सन्ति ।

Besides, a hundred types of punishment are also not the result of
any (intermediary) indirect effect (apurva) of actions. To the person,
who obeys the commands laid down (in the Scriptures), to the
person who does not follow them, and to the person who does what
is prohibited, all of them receive pleasure or pain as the case may
be, directly through the favor or disfavor of the Supreme Person. To
prove this, there are various Upanishads, such as these that follow:
"It is indeed He who confers bliss." (Taittiriya Upanishad 2/7/1);
"When a man is in constant and uninterrupted meditation of the
Supreme Being, he has no fears. (When there is an interruption in
the meditation), then does he become subject to fear?" "For fear of
Him does the wind blow; for fear of Him does the sun rise, for fear
of Him, do fire-god and Indra (perform their respective duties) and
the god of death who is the fifth among them runs for fear of Him.
(Taittiriya Upanishad 2/7/2); "It is by the orders of this
imperishable (Supreme Being), O Gargi, that the sun and the moon
remain stable. It is by the orders of the Supreme Being that humans,
who have received gifts, praise the giver, being obliged to him; the
gods praise those that perform sacrifices and the forefathers
(manes) those who perform post-death rituals." (Brihad Aranyaka
Upanished 3/8/9)

[Upanishads say that all living beings and natural forces function
under his control. It is how this world is held together. There is no
mention of 'unseen' or 'apurva' anywhere.]

[The great guru Dramida also says the same.]

यथोक्तं द्रमिडभाष्ये – 'तस्याज्ञया धावति वायुर्नद्यः स्रवन्ति तेन च कृतसीमानो जलाशयाः समदा इव मेषविसर्पितं कुर्वन्ति' इति । तत्संकल्पनिबन्धना ह्रीमे लोके न च्यवन्ते न स्फुटन्ते । स्वशासनानुवर्तिनां ज्ञात्वा कारुण्यात्स भगवान् वर्धयेत विद्वान् कर्मदक्ष इति च ॥

So the commentary of Dramida says: "By His orders, the wind sweeps along and the rivers flow; the oceans leap about like an excited sheep but within the bounds prescribed by Him". "These worlds, governed by His will, stand without falling or burst into pieces. He knows those who abide by his commands and rewards them in His compassion because He knows everything and is proficient in all the actions."

[His rule is binding over all; that is why no natural force crosses their limits.]

[If one does not follow the rules, it will generate fear in him.]

परमपुरुषयाथात्म्यज्ञानपूर्वकतदुपासनादिविहितकर्मानुष्ठायिनस्तत्प्रसादात्तत्प्राप्तिपर्यन्तानि सुखान्यभयं च यथाधिकारं भवन्ति । तज्ज्ञानपूर्वकं तदुपासनादिविहितं कर्माकुर्वतो निन्दितानि च कुर्वतस्तन्निग्रहादेव तदप्राप्तिपूर्वकापरिमितदुःखानि भयं च भवन्ति ।

It means, "To a person who understands the real truth concerning the nature of the Supreme Person and then performs the duties prescribed for him, as also His worship accompanied by knowledge, all pleasures extending up to the attainment of Him result by His grace and so also freedom from fear, each according to his efforts. To the man who does not meditate on Him with true knowledge of His nature and who does not perform the duties prescribed for Him and performs those that have been condemned as evil, immeasurable sufferings, including the nonattainment of Him, result from His frown and so also fear."

[If one functions as per the rules, it gives him freedom from fear.]

[In Gita, Lord Krishna has himself said to follow the prescribed rules.]

यथोक्तं भगवता – 'नियतं कुरु कर्म त्वं कर्म ज्यायो ह्यकर्मणः ।' (गीता ३/८) इत्यादिना कृत्स्नं कर्म ज्ञानपूर्वकमनुष्ठेयं विधाय – 'मयि सर्वाणि कर्माणि संन्यस्य' (गीता ३/३०) इति सर्वस्य कर्मणः स्वाराधनतामात्मनां स्वनियाम्यतां च प्रतिपाद्य – 'ये मे मतमिदं नित्यमनुतिष्ठन्ति मानवाः । श्रद्धावन्तोऽनसूयन्तो मुच्यन्ते तेऽपि कर्मभिः ॥ ये त्वेतदभ्यसूयन्तो नानुतिष्ठन्ति मे मतम् । सर्वज्ञानविमूढांस्तान् विद्धि नष्टानचेतसः ॥' (गीता ३/३१-३२) इति स्वाज्ञानुवर्तिनः प्रशस्य विपरीतान् विनिन्द्य पुनरपि स्वाज्ञानुपालनमकुर्वतामासुरप्रकृत्यन्तर्भावमभिधायाधमा गतिश्चोक्ता – 'तानहं द्विषतः क्रूरान् संसारेषु नराधमान् । क्षिपाम्यजस्रमशुभानासुरीष्वेव योनिषु ॥ आसुरीं योनिमापन्ना मूढा जन्मनि जन्मनि । मामप्राप्यैव कौन्तेय ततो यान्त्यधमां गतिम् ॥' (गीता १९-२०) इति । 'सर्वकर्माण्यपि सदा कुर्वाणो मद्व्यपाश्रयः । मत्प्रसादादवाप्नोति शाश्वतं पदमव्ययम् ॥' (गीता १८/५६) इति च स्वाज्ञानुवर्तिनां शाश्वतं पदं चोक्तम् । अश्रुतवेदान्तानां कर्मण्यश्रद्धा मा भूदिति देवताधिकरणेऽतिवादाः कृताः कर्ममात्रे यथा श्रद्धा स्यादिति, सर्वमेकशास्त्रमिति वेदविसिद्धान्तः ॥

Lord Krishna himself says: "Perform the duties as prescribed in the scriptures; for action is definitely superior to inaction. (Gita 3/8) Having laid down here that all action should be performed before knowledge, He says again: "Surrender all action unto me." (Gita 3/30) By this, He declares that all actions are of the nature of His worship and that all souls are subject to His control. He then proceeds to say: "Those, who follow my instructions with reverence, without finding any faults in it, they, too, are freed from their actions." (Gita 3/31) But, those who do not follow my instructions by finding faults in it, know them to be deluded in all types of knowledge and doomed to downfall. (Gita 3/32)

Thus, Lord Krishna praises those who abide by His commands and censures those who act contrary to His commands and states again that those who do not act according to His command are of a demonic nature and describe their destined fall.

"I cast those cruel haters and worst among humans into inauspicious demoniac bodies (wombs) again and again." (Gita 16/19)

"O son of Kunti, Arjun! Having obtained the demonic births, deluded birth after birth, without ever reaching me, they sink down to even lower states." (Gita 16/20)

He also points out that those who follow his commands attain eternal bliss - "He, who always performs all actions by taking total refuge in me, attains the eternal imperishable abode with my grace." (Gita 18/56)

In the sections discussing deities, some exaggerated statements are made regarding the self-sufficiency of religious actions. This is done so that those who have not studied Vedanta may not lose their faith in action and continue to perform actions. Those, who are well-versed in the Vedas, know that the two parts, related to action and knowledge, form a single scripture.

[In order to emphasize the importance of action and praise their performance, at some places it is stated that the results of the action come of itself. The real intention is not to deny the agency of the gods but to encourage the performance of actions. To ensure overall consistency in all scriptures, it is necessary to accept the Supreme Being as the granter of all results.]

Eternal Glories of Supreme Being

[According to Ramanuja, the Supreme Being consists of infinite auspicious qualities, and at the same time, he is devoid of any imperfections. In this section, he discusses these qualities of the Supreme Being, along with his consorts, associates, abode, etc. using the references from the scriptures.]

तस्यैतस्य परस्य ब्रह्मणो नारायणस्यापरिच्छेद्यज्ञानानन्दामलत्वस्वरूपवज्ज्ञानशक्तिबलैश्वर्यवीर्य-तेजःप्रभृत्यनवधिकातिशयासंख्येयकल्याणगुणवत्स्वसंकल्पप्रवर्त्यस्वेतरसमस्तचिदचिद्वस्तुजात वत्स्वाभिमतस्वानुरूपैकरूपदिव्यरूपतदुचितनिरतिशयकल्याणविविधानंतभूषणस्वशक्तिसद् शापरिमितानन्ताश्चर्यनानाविधायुधस्वाभिमतानुरूपस्वरूपगुणविभवैश्वर्यशीलाद्यनवधिकमहिमम हिसीस्वानुरूपकल्याणज्ञानक्रियाद्यपरिमेयगुणानन्तपरिजनपरिच्छेदस्वोचितनिखिलभोग्यभोगो पकरणाद्यनन्तमहाविभवावाङ्मनसगोचरस्वरूपस्वभावदिव्यस्थानादिनित्यतानिरवद्यतागोचरा-श्च सहस्रशः श्रुतयः सन्ति ।

In the same way, the Supreme Being, Narayana, has infinite knowledge, bliss, and purity as his attributes that define His essential nature. He has countless, perfect, unsurpassed, auspicious qualities such as wisdom, power, strength, lordship, might, and splendor. He controls and sustains, by his will, all other things, sentient and non-sentient. He has a celestial and unchanging form, which, besides being to his liking, conforms to His nature. He has countless ornaments of wonderful and varied beauty in keeping with His form. He also has innumerable and wonderful weapons suited to His might. He has a Spouse of unsurpassed glory, with a form pleasing to Him and conforming to His greatness and with beauty, greatness, sovereignty, and goodness suited to His nature. He has, moreover, a group of countless followers and attendants who possess boundless auspicious qualities like wisdom and the capacity for rendering service suited to Him. He has, further, countless objects and acompaniments of enjoyment suited to His nature, and to his greatness. He has a celestial abode that far transcends the power of speech and of mind to describe. There are thousands of passages in the Upanishads that state all of his qualities, thus stated, are eternal and perfect.

[Since it is not possible to discuss his infinite auspicious qualities, Ramanuja lists out those qualities that are more beneficial for a seeker to meditate on.]

[How does the Supreme Being look in his divine form? And, how can one see him?]

'वेदाहमेतं पुरुषं महान्तमादित्यवर्णं तमसः परस्तात् ।' (श्वे॰ उ॰ ३/८), 'य एषोऽन्तरादित्ये हिरण्मयः पुरुषः । तस्य यथा कप्यासं पुण्डरीकमेवमक्षिणी ।' (छा॰ उ॰ १/६/६), 'य एषोऽन्तर्हृदय आकाशस्तस्मिन्नयं पुरुषो मनोमयोऽमृतो हिरण्मयः ।' (तै॰ उ॰ १/६/१); मनोमय इति मनसैव विशुद्धेन गृह्यत इत्यर्थः । 'सर्वे निमेषा जज्ञिरे विद्युतः पुरुषादधि' (तै॰ ना॰ उ॰ ११/११); विद्युद्वर्णात्पुरुषादित्यर्थः ।

(Here are some of the statements which depict his greatness): "I know this Supreme Person whose complexion is radiant like the sun." (Shvetashvatara Upanishad 3/8)

"This person is within the sun, all golden in appearance; His eyes are (beautiful) like the red lotus blossoming in the rays of the sun." (Chhandogya Upanishad 1/6/6)

"Within the space inside the heart, this Person dwells; He abides in the heart. He is immortal, all golden." (Taittiriya Upanishad 1/6/1)

The words 'abides in the mind' (above) Upanishad mean "that he can be grasped only by the mind that is pure." "All the moments of time had their origin from this Person, who shines like lightning." (Taittiriya Narayana Upanishad 11/11)

"From this Person who shines like lightning" means from this Person whose color is like that of lightning.

[He has the complexion of radiant sun or pure gold in his cosmic form but he also lives within everyone's heart. By a pure mind (or heart), one can see him.]

[How does he appear in our hearts?]

'नीलतोयदमध्यस्था विद्युल्लेखेव भास्वरा; (तै० ना० उ० ११/११); मध्यस्थनीलतोयदा विद्युल्लेखेव; सेयं दहरपुण्डरीकमध्यस्थाकाशवर्तिनी वह्निशिखा स्वान्तर्निहितनीलतोयदाभ-परमात्मस्वरूपा स्वान्तर्निहितनीलतोयदा विद्युदिवाभातीत्यर्थः ।

"He shines like a streak of lightning which has the blue cloud amidst it." (Taittiriya Narayana Upanishad 13-2) It means the Supreme Being is luminous like a streak of lightning, which encloses the blue cloud between it.

The same Supreme Being shines like the flame of fire in the middle space of the lotus-like heart". It means: This flame of fire, which is in the space of the lotus (of the heart) has, in the middle of it, the form of the Supreme Being shining like a blue cloud and resembles, therefore, lightning, which has within it a blue cloud.

[Within our hearts, he shines in a blue form like a cloud amidst lightning all around it. It is the reverse of what we see in nature during lightning.]

[Sometimes seekers meditate on his other qualities like truth, all-pervasiveness, lightness like the sky, soul of all, etc.]

'मनोमयः प्राणशरीरो भारूपः । सत्यकामः सत्यसंकल्पः । आकाशात्मा सर्वकामा सर्वकामः सर्वगन्धः सर्वरसः सर्वमिदमभ्यात्तोऽवाक्यानादरः ।' (छा० उ० ३/१४/२), 'माहारजनं वासः' (बृ० उ० ४/३/६) इत्याद्याः ।

"He can be grasped only by the mind that is pure; He has all beings in the world for His body. He has a radiant form. His desire is always fulfilled; His will is irresistible. His form is as subtle as the sky; He is the sole doer of all that takes place; He has all objects of pure enjoyment; He has all (transcendental) fragrances and flavors. He has all these auspicious qualities since He is perfect in Himself. He is indifferent to everything and does not speak of anything". (Chhandogya Upanishad 3/14/2) "His color is like a cloth dyed with turmeric." (Brihat Aranyaka Upanishad 4/3/6), and so forth.

[These seekers also experience a similar form as the previous ones.]

[Now, Ramanuja describes his wives and his transcendental form, which liberated souls see.]

'अस्येशाना जगतो विष्णुपत्नी ।' (तै॰ सं॰ ४/४/१२/१४), 'ह्रीश्च ते लक्ष्मीश्च पत्न्यौ ।' (तै॰ आ॰ ३/१३/६), 'तद्विष्णो: परमं पदं सदा पश्यन्ति सूरय: ।' (सु॰ उ॰ ६), 'क्षयन्तमस्य रजस: पराके ।' (तै॰ सं॰ २/२/१२/१८), 'यदेकमव्यक्तमनन्तरूपं विश्वं पुराणं तमस: परस्तात् ।' (तै॰ ना॰ १/५), 'यो वेद निहितं गुहायां परमे व्योमन् ।' (तै॰ उ॰ १/१), 'योऽस्याध्यक्ष: परमे व्योमन् ।' (तै॰ ना॰ १/२), 'तदेव तदु भव्यमा इदं तदक्षरे परमे व्योमन्' (तै॰ ना॰ १/२) इत्यादिश्रुतिशतनिश्चितोऽयमर्थ: ॥

"The Spouse of Vishnu is the queen of the world". (Taittiriya Sanhita 4/4/12/14) "The goddess of the earth and the goddess Lakshmi are His wives". (Taittiriya Aranyaka 3/13/6) "The eternally enlightened seers (Suris) are always gazing at the supreme abode of Vishnu". (Subala Upanishad 6) "He lives beyond this universe of matter (rajas); (Taittiriya Sanhita 2/2/12/18) His celestial form is endless. His unmanifested form is infinite, the totality of this universe, ancient, omnipresent and beyond the region of darkness". (Taittiriya Narayana Upanishad 1/5) "He, who meditates on this Supreme Being, residing within the cave of the heart, attains his Supreme abode". (Taittiriya Upanishad 1/1) "He, who is the Lord of this, is in the highest heaven". (Taittiriya Narayana Upanishad 1/2) "He indeed is all this; all that is the past, that will be in the future, and that is present. It is that Supreme Being, in the Supreme space, that never changes". (Taittiriya Narayana Upanishad 1/2) It is from these and hundreds of such Upanishadic passages that all this is ascertained.

[His abode is beyond the constraint of time or mundane nature. It is composed of pure Sattva. He resides there with his wives and other liberated souls in his infinite magnificence.]

[Now, Ramanuja discusses the 'eternal associates of Supreme Being' or Suris.]

'तद्विष्णोः परमं पदम्' (सु० उ० ६) इति विष्णोः परस्य ब्रह्मणः परं पदं सदा पश्यन्ति सूरय इति वचनात्सर्वकालदर्शनवन्तः परिपूर्णज्ञानाः केचन सन्तीति विज्ञायते । ये सूरयस्ते सदा पश्यन्तीति वचनव्यक्तिः, ये सदा पश्यन्ति ते सूरय इति वा ।

In "That supreme abode of Vishnu etc., (Subala Upanishad 6)" it is stated that the enlightened seers are always looking at Him. From the words "always looking", it is learned that there are certain beings with perfect wisdom whose vision is eternal. The words may be interpreted to mean either "Those, who are eternally enlightened seers, see always" or "Those, who always see, are eternally enlightened seers ".

[The similar description is present in some other Upanishads as well.]

[The opposition objects to two types of interpretation of a single statement.]

उभयपक्षेऽप्यनेकविधानं न संभवतीति चेत् । न । अप्राप्तत्वात्सर्वस्य सर्वविशिष्टं परमस्थानं विधीयते । यथोक्तं – 'तद्गुणास्ते विधीयेरन्नविभागाद्विधानार्थे न चेदन्येन शिष्टाः' (जै० सू० १/४/९) इति । यथा 'यदाग्नेयोऽष्टाकपाल' (तै० सं० २/६/३/४) इत्यादिकर्मविधौ कर्मणो

गुणानां चाप्राप्तत्वेन सर्वगुणविशिष्टं कर्म विधीयते तथात्रापि सूरिभिः सदा दृश्यत्वेन विष्णोः परमस्थानमप्राप्तं प्रतिपादयतीति न कश्चिद्विरोधः ।

Objection - In both interpretations, one sentence makes two different assertions. It is not right for a single sentence to declare more than one thing.

Reply – No, there is no problem here. Since these assertions are not made anywhere else in the Upanishads, we interpret this passage as declaring the existence of a transcendent realm (space). The sage Jaimini says in his Purva Mimamsa: "If the ancillary aspects of a rite are not taught elsewhere, but mentioned along with the performance of the rite at one place, they should be considered as prescribed everywhere because they are inseparable from the rite itself." (Jaimini Sutra 1/4/9) For example, in instructions enjoining the rite like "The offering made to fire-god shall be in eight open cups," (Taittiriya Sanhita 2/6/3/4) Both rite and the ancillary features of the rite (like the eight cups) and the fire-god, which is not established elsewhere, should be considered as prescribed at all other places in fire-worship. So, here also, there is nothing inappropriate in saying that the Supreme Abode of the Supreme Being is declared to exist with eternally enlightened seers gazing at it always. Since it is not established elsewhere or otherwise, there is no contradiction in the above interpretation.

[There are three things we can infer from the sentence - the suris (enlightened souls) who are eternal; their vision, and the Supreme Abode which has them both or, in other words, the Supreme Abode qualified by the suris and their gaze is here declared to exist, as it has not been established elsewhere or by other evidence.]

[What is the normal procedure to interpret Vedic injunctions if we find some differences in their description in different texts?]

करणमन्त्राः क्रियमाणानुवादिनः स्तोत्रशस्त्ररूपा जपादिषु विनियुक्ताश्च प्रकरणपथिताश्चाप्रकर-
णपथिताश्च स्वार्थं सर्वं यथावस्थितमेवाप्राप्तमविरुद्धं ब्राह्मणवद्बोधयन्तीति हि वैदिकाः । प्रगीत
-मन्त्रसाध्यगुणिनिष्ठगुणाभिधानं स्तोत्रम् । अप्रगीतमन्त्रसाध्यगुणगुणिनिष्ठगुणाभिधानं शस्त्रम् ।
नियुक्तार्थप्रकाशनां च देवतादिष्वप्राप्ताविरुद्धगुणविशेषप्रतिपादनं विनियोगानुगुणमेव ।

Vedic scholars maintain that the mantras (hymns) related to
accessories of a ritual (e.g. offering in fire) simply translate the
action to be performed. Whereas the hymns recited with or without
chanting, hymns used for sacred repetition, etc. serve their purpose
according to the context. These hymns are either taken from the
relevant portion of the Vedas or are taken from elsewhere. They all
have their utility in what they affirm, like characteristics of the
Supreme Being, provided it is not already said elsewhere, without
being in conflict with each other. Two types of hymns are recited
in praise of a deity, a Stotra and a Shastra. A Stotra (eulogy) tells of
the attributes of a god and is intended to be chanted or sung. A
Shastra, on the other hand, speaks of the attributes of a god and is
to be uttered without being sung. All of these hymns have their
utility in describing the attributes of particular deities, which are
already known as well as unknown. The unknown attributes are
such that they have not been established otherwise are not
opposed to other known attributes, and are, therefore, meaningful
in their application to the rite.

[If various descriptions related to an injunction supplement each
other, there is no harm in taking the missing part from one
description into another. That's how all descriptions become
meaningful.]

[Now, Ramanuja justifies his interpretations using the above
procedure.]

नेयं श्रुतिर्मुक्तजनविषया । तेषां सदादर्शनानुपपत्तेः । नापि मुक्तप्रवाहविषया । सदा पश्यन्तीत्ये-
कैककर्तृकविषयतया प्रतीतेः श्रुतिभङ्गप्रसङ्गात् । मन्त्रार्थवादगता ह्यर्थाः कार्यपरत्वेऽपि
सिद्धान्तीत्युक्तम् । किं पुनः सिद्धवस्तुन्येव तात्पर्ये व्युत्पत्तिसिद्ध इति सर्वमुपपन्नम् ।

This passage in the Upanishad, viz., "The eternally enlightened seers always gaze at this supreme abode of Vishnu" is not concerned with souls that have obtained release, for the word "always" (which means eternally) would then be out of place. Nor can it be said that the eternally enlightened seers refer to the beginningless stream of released souls in which case "always" might be justified because some of them might always be gazing at the Supreme Being. "Gaze" always signifies that each of them is the doer of the action of gazing. So, this interpretation would be against the spirit of the Upanishad when the doer of the action changes. Even in regard to passages that refer to an action, we have already shown that hymns and laudatory explanations convey valid and useful ideas. Then, why should we take another meaning of the sentence, when the established entity is clearly reflected from the interpretation of the words? Therefore, our interpretations of the sentence regarding eternally enlightened seers are appropriate.

[Therefore, the mentioned statement of Subala Upanishad is evidence for the existence of Supreme Abode qualified by the suris and their gaze, as it has not been established elsewhere or by other evidence.]

[Some might say that there is no difference between the Supreme Being and his abode.]

ननु चात्र – 'तद्विष्णोः परमं पदम्' (सु॰ उ॰ ६) इति परस्वरूपमेव परमपदशब्देनाभिधीयते ।
'समस्तहेयरहितं विष्ण्वाख्यं परं पदम्' (वि॰ पु॰ १/२/५) इत्यादिष्वव्यतिरेकदर्शनात् । नैवम् ।
'क्षयन्तमस्य रजतः पराके' (तै॰ सं॰ २/२/१२/१८), 'तदक्षरे परमे व्योमन्' (तै॰ ना॰ १/२),
'यो अस्याध्यक्षः परमे व्योमन्' (तै॰ ना॰ १/२), 'यो वेद निहितं गुहायां परमे व्योमन्' (तै॰ उ॰

१/१) इत्यादिषु परमस्थानस्यैव दर्शनम् । तद्विष्णोः परमं पदमिति व्यतिरेकनिर्देशाच्च ।
विष्ण्वाख्यं परमं पदमिति विशेषणादन्यदपि परमं पदं विद्यत इति च तेनैव ज्ञायते । तदिदं
परस्थानं सूरिभिः सदादृश्यत्वेन प्रतिपाद्यते ॥

The (following) objection may be made here: "The word 'Supreme
Abode' in the phrase 'The Supreme Abode of Vishnu' really means
the essential nature of the Supreme Being. In passages like
"Supreme Abode, which has the name, Vishnu, is absolutely free
from all that is faulty". (Vishnu Purana 1/2/5) Supreme Abode and
Vishnu are spoken of as being identical. (So how could the
Upanishad in question prove the existence of the Supreme Abode of
Vishnu, distinct from Him?).

We answer: "It is not so. The Supreme Abode is distinctly declared
to exist in passages like the following: "He dwells beyond this world
of rajas or matter." (Taittiriya Sanhita 2/2/12/18) Rajas here, stands
for Sattvam and Tamas as well, all three being qualities of matter.
"He lives in the Supreme space (sky) which is imperishable."
(Taittiriya Narayana Upanishad 1/2) "He, who presides over all,
dwells in the Supreme Space." (Taittiriya Narayana Upanishad 1/2)
"He who knows Him that dwells in the Supreme Space within the
cave." (Taittiriya Upanishad 1/1)

The very description of the Supreme Abode as Vishnu's abode
points that the realm is different from Him. Further, the statement
'The highest abode of Vishnu' shows that there are several other
abodes of Vishnu, not one in substance with Vishnu. It is only that
Supreme Abode, other than the Supreme Abode with the name
Vishnu, which is said to exist and to be gazed at always by the
eternally enlightened seers.

[Since the Upanishads describe the Supreme Being and his abode
distinctly, we should not consider them the same. Moreover, we see
the presence of several abodes of Supreme Being.]

[Ramanuja explains that the Supreme Abode is used in multiple ways e.g. a divine abode, the greatest abode which is always seen by the enlightened seers, and the Supreme Being itself.]

एतदुक्तं भवति - क्वचित्परस्थानं परमपदशब्देन प्रतिपाद्यते, क्वचित्प्रकृतिवियुक्तात्मस्वरूपं, क्वचिद्भगवत्स्वरूपम् । 'तद्विष्णोः परमं पदं सदा पश्यन्ति सूरय' (सु० उ० ६) इति परस्थानम् । 'सर्गस्थित्यन्तकालेषु त्रिविधैव प्रवर्तते । गुणप्रवृत्त्या परमं पदं तस्यागुणं महत् ॥' (वि० पु० १/२२/४१) इत्यत्र प्रकृतिवियुक्तात्मस्वरूपम् । 'समस्तहेयरहितं विष्ण्वाख्यं परमं पदम् ।' (वि० पु० १/२२/५३) इत्यत्र भगवत्स्वरूपम् । त्रीण्यप्येतानि परमप्राप्तत्वेन परमपदशब्देन प्रतिपाद्यन्ते ।

It comes to mean this: In some places, the word Supreme Abode is used to denote the divine Abode; it is sometimes employed to denote the individual self freed from nature, and also used to denote the Supreme Being. The passage: "In that Suprmee Abode of Vishnu, the eternally enlightened seers are always gazing at it" (Subala Upanishad 6), refers to the divine abode.

In the passage "The great divine Abode, which is not associated with qualities (sattva, rajas, and tamas) during creation, continuance, and dissolution and is seen to be of three kinds" (Vishnu Purana 1/22/41), the word Supreme Abode means the soul freed from matter. In the passage "The Supreme Abode named Vishnu is without anything objectionable or faulty" (Vishnu Purana 1/22/53), the word means Vishnu. All these three meanings are conveyed by the word Supreme Abode, as each of them is the supreme object of attainment.

[Since all types of abodes are worthy of attainment, there is a description of all of them.]

[Why are all types of abodes worthy of attainment, not the Supreme Being alone?]

कथं त्रयाणां परमप्राप्यत्वमिति चेत् । भगवत्स्वरूपं परमप्राप्यत्वादेव परमं पदम् । इतरयोरपि
भगवत्प्राप्तिगर्भत्वादेव परमपदत्वम् । सर्वकर्मबन्धविनिर्मुक्तात्मस्वरूपावाप्तिर्भगवत्प्राप्ति-
गर्भा । 'त इमे सत्याः कामा अनृतापिधाना' (छा० उ० ८/३/१) इति भगवतो गुणगणस्य
तिरोधायकत्वेनानृतशब्देन स्वकर्मणः प्रतिपादनम् ॥

If it is asked how all these three could be supreme objects of
attainment, we answer as follows: The Supreme Being is obviously
the supreme end or goal to be attained. The other two are also
supreme objects of attainment, as they lead to or are the causes of
the attainment of the Supreme Being. The attainment of that
condition of the soul, which is free from all the bondage of nature
takes place along with the attainment of the Supreme Being, as
stated in the following Upanishad - "Those auspicious qualities that
are desired in liberation are obscured by untruth." (Chhandogya
Upanishad 8/3/1) The word untruth here means our actions, which
obscures the true qualities of the Supreme Being from us.

[Attainment of the Supreme Being is the highest attainment for an
individual soul. However, an individual soul, who, after getting
liberated from all his actions, attains any of these abodes, ultimately
attains Supreme Being.]

[The opposition might ask why we interpret untruth as actions
here.]

अनृतरूपतिरोधानं क्षेत्रज्ञकर्मेति कथमवगम्यत इति चेत् ।'अविद्या कर्मसंज्ञान्या तृतीया
शक्तिरिष्यते । यथा क्षेत्रज्ञशक्तिः सा वेष्टिता नृप सर्वगा ॥ संसारतापानखिलानवाप्नोत्यति-
संततान् । तया तिरोहितत्वाच्च' (वि० पु० ६/७/६१-६३) इत्यादिवचनात् । परस्थानप्राप्तिरपि
भगवत्प्राप्तिगर्भैवेति सुव्यक्तम् ।

If you ask, "How do we know that it is the actions of an individual
bound soul or untruth which obscure the reality from us?" We cite
the following verse to support our interpretation: "Ignorance, which

also has action as its name, is a third power of the Supreme Being. O king, this power envelops the soul in bondage. It is present in everyone by obscuring the consciousness of their soul. Owing to this obscuration, the soul experiences all sorts of suffering due to attainment of this world". (Vishnu Purana 6/7/61-63)

Even the attainment of the abode of the Supreme Being leads one to the attainment of the Supreme Being is also clearly stated.

[Using Vishnu Purana, we know actions hide the real nature of an individual soul. Chhandogya Upanishad says that untruth hides reality from us. To reconcile the two statements, we interpret untruth as actions.]

[The supreme abode of Lord Vishnu is beyond the three attributes of nature. This is described in various texts.]

'क्षयन्तमस्य रजसः पराके' (तै॰ सं॰ २/२/१२/१८) इति रजशब्देन त्रिगुणात्मिका प्रकृतिरु-
च्यते केवलस्य रजसोऽनवस्थानात् । इमां त्रिगुणात्मिकां प्रकृतिमतिक्रम्य स्थिते स्थाने क्षयन्तम्
वसन्तमित्यर्थः । अनेन त्रिगुणात्मकात्क्षेत्रज्ञस्य भोग्यभूताद्वस्तुनः परस्ताद्विष्णोर्वासस्थानमिति
गम्यते । 'वेदाहमेतं पुरुषं महान्तमादित्यवर्णं तमसः परस्तात्' (तै॰ आ॰ ३/१३/२) इत्यत्रापि
तमशब्देन सैव प्रकृतिरुच्यते । केवलस्य तमसोऽनवस्थानादेव । रजसः पराके क्षयन्तमित्यने-
नैकवाक्यत्वात्तमसः परस्ताद्वसन्तं महान्तमादित्यवर्णं पुरुषमहं वेदेत्ययमर्थोऽवगम्यते ।

In the Upanishad "He who dwells beyond this world of rajas" (Taittiriya Sanhita 2/2/12/18), rajas signify nature, which is endowed with three qualities sattva, rajas, and tamas, because mere rajas cannot stand by itself. So the passage means, "He dwells in a region, which lies beyond matter possessed of the three qualities". From this, we infer that Vishnu's abode lies beyond this nature. This world is constituted of sattva, rajas, and tamas, and is a place of enjoyment for bound souls. So also in the Upanishad: "I know this Supreme Person having the radiance of the sun and dwelling beyond ignorance (tamas),"(Taittiriya Aranyaka 3/13/2) the word 'tamas' signifies nature, as mere tamas cannot exist by itself. This passage means the same and speaks of Vishnu living beyond Rajas. It means "I know the Supreme Person radiant like the sun and dwelling beyond tamas or nature."

[Since three attributes of nature do not exist independently of each other, the abode of Vishnu is beyond all of them, not merely rajas.]

[Now, Ramanuja describes some more properties of the divine abode.]

'सत्यं ज्ञानमनन्तं ब्रह्म । यो वेद निहितं गुहायां परमे व्योमन् ।' (तै० उ० २/१); 'तदक्षरे परमे व्योमन्' (तै० ना० १/२) इति तत्स्थानमविकाररूपं परमव्योमशब्दाभिधेयमिति च गम्यते । 'अक्षरे परमे व्योमन्' (तै० ना० १/२) इत्यस्य स्थानस्याक्षरत्वश्रवणात्क्षररूपादित्यमण्डलादयो न परमव्योमशब्दाभिधेयाः ।

Further, it is said - "Supreme Being is truth, knowledge and infinite, and he who knows Him, and who dwells in the Supreme space within the cave" (Taittiriya Upanishad 2/1) and likewise, "In the imperishable Supreme space" (Taittiriya Narayana Upanishad 1/2). From these two Upanishad texts, it is learned that this abode is changeless and is called "the Supreme space". Since the quality of imperishability is attributed to the Supreme space in the Upanishad quoted above, this term cannot apply to the solar system, etc., which is perishable.

[Here, he derives that the supreme abode of Lord Vishnu is imperishable.]

[Who lives in this divine abode along with Lord Vishnu?]

'यत्र पूर्वे साध्याः सन्ति देवाः' (तै० आ० ३/१२/१८), 'यत्र ऋषयः प्रथमजा ये पुराणाः' (तै० सं० ४/७/१३/२) इत्यादिषु च त एव सूरय इत्यवगम्यते । 'तद्विप्रासो विपन्यवो जागृवांसः

समिन्धते विष्णोर्यत्परं पदम्' (सु० उ० ६) इत्यत्रापि विप्रासो मेधाविन:, विपन्यव: स्तुतिशीला:, जागृवांस: अस्खलितज्ञानास्त एवास्खलितज्ञानास्तद्विष्णो: परमं पदं सदा स्तुवन्त: समिन्धत इत्यर्थ: ॥

From passages like "Where there is a class of gods called "sadhya" (Taittiriya Aranyaka 3/12/18) and "Where there are ancient seers from the earliest times" (Taittiriya Sanhita 4/7/13/2), we learn that these refer to the eternally enlightened seers. The same idea is conveyed by the Upanishad. "Vishnu's supreme abode, where there are beings with divine wisdom singing (the praise of the Lord), ever vigilant in their vision." (Subala Upanishad 6) It means these radiant seers possess unfailing wisdom, and through it, they always sing praises of the supreme abode of Vishnu and thus flourish.

[The supreme abode is inhabited by the eternally enlightened sages, devoted to Lord Vishnu.]

[Where do these eternally enlightened sages live during the creation? It is said that in the beginning, Supreme Being alone was present.]

एतेषां परिजनस्थानादीनां 'सदेव सोम्येदमग्र आसीत्' (छा० उ० ६/२/१) इत्यत्र ज्ञानबलै-श्वर्यादिकल्याणगुणगणवत्परब्रह्म स्वरूपान्तर्भूतत्वात्सदेवैकमेवाद्वितीयमिति ब्रह्मान्तर्भावोऽव-गम्यते । एषामपि कल्याणगुणैकदेशत्वादेव 'सदेव सोम्येदमग्र आसीत्' इत्यत्रेदमिति शब्दस्य कर्मवश्यभोक्तृवर्गमिश्रतद्भोग्यभूतप्रपञ्चविषयत्वाच्च 'सदा पश्यन्ति सूरय:' (सु० उ० ६) इति सदादर्शित्वेन च तेषां कर्मवश्यानन्तर्भावात् ।

Since the Upanishad says, "This, my dear, existed at the beginning only as reality, alone and without a second" (Chhandogya Upanishad 6/2/1), it has to be understood that these followers, the abode, etc. are included in the essential nature of the Supreme Being, just like the multitude of his auspicious qualities like knowledge, strength, lordship, etc. The words "only as reality", "alone", and "without a second" show that they have to be included as being within the Supreme Being because they form part of His transcendental, non-material attributes. The word 'this' in "This, my dear, existed at the beginning as reality refers to this universe constituted of embodied souls, which are bound by action and the objects experienced by them. The assertion "The eternally enlightened seers always gaze at it" (Subala Upanishad 6) shows that they are not subject to action because their vision is eternal.

[These eternally enlightened seers or associates are an intrinsic part of the Supreme Being like his other auspicious attributes, which are always present in him. Therefore, these seers always retain their states of bliss, in which they always experience Lord Vishnu.]

[Not only do these eternally enlightened seers always maintain their position but also the materials, equipment, etc., which they use in the divine abode.]

'अपहतपाप्मा' इत्यादि 'अपिपासः' इत्यन्तेन सलीलोपकरणभूतत्रिगुणप्रकृतिप्राकृततत्संसृष्ट-पुरुषगतं हेयस्वभावं सर्वं प्रतिषिध्य सत्यकाम इत्यनेन स्वभोग्यभोगोपकरणजातस्य सर्वस्य सत्यता प्रतिपादिता । सत्याः कामा यस्यासौ सत्यकामः । काम्यन्त इति कामाः । तेन परेण ब्रह्मणा स्वभोग्यतदुपकरणादयः स्वाभिमता ये काम्यन्ते ते सत्याः नित्या इत्यर्थः । अन्यस्य लीलोपकरणस्यापि वस्तुनः प्रमाणसंबन्धयोग्यत्वे सत्यपि विकारास्पदत्वेनास्थिरत्वाद्तद्विपरीतं स्थिरत्वमेषां सत्यपदेनोच्यते ।

The Upanishad, which begins with "He is free from sin" and ends with "He has no thirst' declares that the Supreme Being is without any of those evil features seen in nature with its three qualities, its products, and in the individual souls who are inflicted with nature; these three form the materials of His cosmic play. Then, the same sentence declares by the word truthful desire that the objects and instruments of His enjoyment are true (i.e. eternal). He, whose objects of desire are true (i.e.) eternal, is of truthful desire. Therefore, whatever objects and instruments of enjoyment, the Supreme Being desires as suitable, are true (i.e.) eternal. The objects of His cosmic play, though real, are different from the objects and instruments of His enjoyment. Though they are grasped by the evidence, they are subject to modification, and are, therefore, unstable and changing. On the other hand, the objects and instruments of His enjoyment in the Supreme abode are eternal, unchanging, and stable, so they are referred to as true.

[Though this world in which we humans live, is changing and destructible, there is no change or instability of any type in the divine abode.]

[How do the objects of divine abode retain their permanence?]

सत्यसंकल्प इत्येतेषु भोग्यतदुपकरणादिषु नित्येषु निरतिशयेष्वनन्तेषु सत्स्वप्यपूर्वाणामपरि-मितानामर्थानामपि संकल्पमात्रेण सिद्धिं वदति । एषां च भोगोपकरणानां लीलोपकरणानां चेतनानामचेतनानां स्थिराणामस्थिराणां च तत्संकल्पायत्तस्वरूपस्थितिप्रवृत्तिभेदादि सर्वं वाति सत्यसंकल्प इति ॥

Supreme Being is also declared in that Upanishad to be of truthful resolve. It means that although He has countless, eternal, and wonderful objects and instruments of enjoyment, He could, by His mere will, create innumerable objects unseen before. Truthful resolve declares that the nature, existence, activity, and differences of all things, namely the materials of His cosmic play, the objects and instruments of His enjoyment, the sentient and the non-sentient, those that are not subject to change as well as those that are subject to change all these depend upon His mere will."

[The resolve of Supreme Being is truthful; if he wishes something to be permanent, it will remain that way. The free souls remain in these eternal worlds and the bound souls in the changing worlds.]

[The same sentiment is echoed in other sacred scriptures like Valmiki Ramayana.]

इतिहासपुराणयोर्वेदोपबृंहणयोश्चायमर्थ उच्यते – 'तौ ते मेधाविनौ दृष्ट्वा वेदेषु परिनिष्ठितौ ।
वेदोपबृंहणार्थाय तावग्राहयत प्रभुः ॥' (वा० रा० १/४/६) इति वेदोपबृंहणतया प्रारब्धे
श्रीमद्रामायणे, 'व्यक्तमेष महायोगी परमात्मा सनातनः । अनादिमध्यनिधनो महतः परमो महान्
॥ तमसः परमो धाता शङ्खचक्रगदाधरः । श्रीवत्सवक्षा नित्यश्रीरजय्यः शाश्वतो ध्रुवः ॥' (वा०
रा० ६/११४-११५), 'शारा नानाविधाश्चापि धनुरायतविग्रहम् । अन्वगच्छन्त काकुत्स्थं सर्वे
पुरुषविग्रहाः ॥' (वा० रा० ७/१०९/७), 'विवेश वैष्णवं तेजः सशरीरः सहानुगः ॥' (वा० रा०
७/११०/१२)

The same truth is conveyed by history texts (Itihasas) and Puranas which elaborate and elucidate the Vedas: Ramayana was composed solely to elucidate the Vedas, as may be seen from the following verse: "The great sage, Valmiki, found that these two boys, Kusha and Lava, were intelligent and well-versed in the Vedas and taught them the Ramayana to illustrate and explain the Vedas." (Ramayana 1/4/6)

In the Ramayana, which was started to explain the Vedas, we find the following: "Rama is surely the great Yogin, the eternal Supreme Self; He has no beginning, no middle, and no end; He is greater than the great; He dwells in the transcendental, non-material world beyond the darkness. He is the protector of the world armed with conch, discus, and mace. There is a Srivatsa mark on His chest; His spouse goddess Lakshmi is always inseparable from him. He is invincible, eternal, and immutable". (Ramayana 6/114-115) And, elsewhere, we find in the Ramayana the following: "All his arrows of various kinds and his long bow took human forms and followed Rama". (Ramayana Balakanda: 4-6 Yuddhakanda: 144-14) "He, with the same body, entered into his splendor of Vishnu, with all his followers". (Ramayana 7/110/12)

[Ramayana describes Lord Rama as Lord Vishnu, his wife Sita as goddess Lakshmi, and his weapons as eternal. These and other auspicious attributes are inseparable from him.]

[Vishnu Purana also describes the inseparable attributes of Lord Vishnu, like wife, abode, associates, etc. similarly.]

श्रीमद्वैष्णवपुराणे – 'समस्ताः शक्तयश्चैता नृप यत्र प्रतिष्ठिताः । तद्विश्वैरूप्यं रूपमन्त्यद्धुरेर्महत्
॥' (वि० पु० ६/७/७०), 'मूर्तं ब्रह्म महाभाग सर्वब्रह्ममयो हरिः ॥ (वि० पु० १/२२/६३),
'नित्यैवैषा जगन्माता विष्णोः श्रीरनपायिनी । यथा सर्वगतो विष्णुस्तथैवेयं द्विजोत्तम ॥' (वि०
पु० १/८/१७), 'देवत्वे देवदेहेयं मनुष्यत्वे च मानुषी । विष्णोर्देहानुरूपां वै करोत्येषात्मनस्तनुम्
॥' (वि० पु० १/१०/१४५), एकान्तिनः सदा ब्रह्मध्यायिनो योगिनो हि ये । तेषां तत्परं स्थानं
यद्वै पश्यन्ति सूरयः ॥' (वि० पु० १/६/३८), 'कलामुहूर्तादिमयश्च कालो न यद्विभूतेः
परिणामहेतुः ॥' (वि० पु० ४/१/३८)

In the Vishnu Purana, we find the following: "O king, Hari's majestic form is different from all else and is beyond all measure. In his divine form all the great powers are established." (Vishnu Purana 6/7/70)

"All, that is visible, is a form of Hari. All individual souls are pervaded by Him." (Vishnu Purana 1/22/63)

"The eternal mother of the world, Lakshmi, is inseparable from Him" Just as Vishnu pervades everywhere, Lakshmi, too, O best of Brahmans, pervades all. If Vishnu assumes the form of a god, she, too, assumes a like form. If He assumes the form of a human being, she, too, assumes a human form; she makes her form to always conform to that of Vishnu". (Vishnu Purana 1/8/17)

"The Yogis, ever in contemplation of Supreme Being, exclusive of all other things, attain His Supreme Abode, which the eternally enlightened seers are always gazing at". (Vishnu Purana 1/10/145)

"Divisions of time like (second, minute, etc.) and muhurta (one and a half hours) do not produce any change in His region (abode) of glory". (Vishnu Purana 4/1/38)

[This description gives evidence regarding his incarnation, his auspicious attributes, his wife, his supreme abode, and the eternality of all of these.]

[Mahabharat also describes the abode of Lord Vishnu to be beyond time.]

महाभारते च – 'दिव्यं स्थानमजरं चाप्रमेयं दुर्विज्ञेयं, चागमैर्गम्यमाद्यम् । गच्छ प्रभो रक्ष चास्मान् प्रपन्नान् कल्पे कल्पे जायमानः स्वमूर्त्या ॥' (म० भा० मौ० ५/३२), 'कालः स पचते तत्र न कालस्तत्र वै प्रभुः ।' (म० भा० शा० १९८/९) इति ॥

Mahabharata also says, "The Supreme Abode (Vaikuntah) is a celestial region, imperishable and incomprehensibly magnificent; it cannot be seen by our senses or intelligence; it can be understood only from the scriptures; it exists from the beginning. Go there, O Lord, and protect us in every epoch, we seek refuge in you, by incarnating in your divine forms". (Mahabharata Mausal Parva 5/32)

"Time, itself, is subject to change there. It has no control in that region". (Mahabharata Shanti Parva 198/9)

[Thus, we see a similarity of description in various texts regarding Lord Vishnu, his wife, abode, and eternally enlightened seers.]

[Now, Ramanuja describes the divine form of Lord Vishnu.]

परस्य ब्रह्मणो रूपवत्त्वं सूत्रकारश्च वदति – 'अन्तस्तद्धर्मोपदेशात्' (ब्र० सू० १/१/२१) इति । योऽसावादित्यमण्डलान्तर्वर्ती तप्तकार्तस्वरगिरिवरप्रभः सहस्रांशुशतसहस्रकिरणो गम्भीराम्भः- समुद्भूतसुमृष्टनालविकरविकसितपुण्डरीकदलामलायतेक्षणः सुभ्रूललाटः सुनासः सुस्मिताधर- विद्रुमः सुरुचिरकोमलगण्डः कम्बुग्रीवः समुन्नतांसविलम्बिचारुरूपदिव्यकर्णिकिसलयः पीन-

वृत्तायतभुजश्चारुतरातम्रकरतलानुरक्ताङ्गुलीभिरलंकृतस्तनुमध्यो विशालवक्षःस्थलः समविभ-
क्त सर्वाङ्गोऽनिर्देश्यदिव्यरूपसंहननः स्निग्धवर्णः प्रबुद्धपुण्डरीकचारुचरणयुगलः स्वानुरूप-
पीताम्बरधोऽमलकिरीटकुण्डलहारकौस्तुभकेयूरकटकनूपुरोदरबन्धनाद्यपरिमिताश्चर्यानन्तदिव्य
भूषणः शङ्खचक्रगदासिशार्ङ्गश्रीवत्सवनमालालङ्कृतोऽनवधिकातिशयसौन्दर्याहृताशेषमनो-
दृष्टिवृत्तिर्लावण्यामृतपूरिताशेषचराचरभूतजातोऽत्यद्भुताचिन्त्यनित्ययौवनः   पुष्पहाससुकुमारः
पुण्यगन्धवासितानन्तदिगन्तरालस्त्रैलोक्याक्रमणप्रवृत्तगम्भीरभावः   करुणानुरागमधुरलोचनाव-
लोकिताश्रितवर्गः पुरुषवरो दरीदृश्यते । स च निखिलजगदुदयविभवलयलीलो निरस्तसमस्त-
हेयः समस्तकल्याणगुणगणनिधिः स्वेतरसमस्तवस्तुविलक्षणः परमात्मा परं ब्रह्म नारायण
इत्यवगम्यते ।

The Vyasa, too, says about the divine form of the Supreme Being in
Brahma Sutra 1/1/21: "He, who is seen within the sun and within the
eye, is Supreme Being, because (in this Upanishad) attributes
peculiar to Him are taught".

This Sutra indicates that the Supreme Being has a form. Its meaning
is as follows: He, who is seen within the orb of the sun, is the
Supreme Being, Narayana. He shines like a mountain of molten gold;
He has the splendor of a hundred thousand suns; He has long and
clear eyes like the petals of a lotus opened by the rays of the sun,
and standing on a firm stalk in deep water; He has beautiful
eyebrows, a beautiful forehead, and a beautiful nose; His lips are
like coral and lit up with a smile. His cheeks are tender and lovely;
His neck is like the conch; His exquisitely divine ear-lobes are
almost touching his well-formed shoulders; His arms are robust,
round, and long. The palms of His hands are charming and rosy with
beautiful fingers of the same hue; He has a slender waist and a
broad chest. All parts of His body are well-proportioned; the divine
harmony of His body features defies all description; His complexion
is attractive; His two feet are as lovely as fully blossomed lotuses;
He is dressed in yellow raiment (robe) suiting His greatness; He
wears countless and wonderful ornaments of a celestial nature,
such as a brilliant crown, earrings, necklaces, the gem Kaustubha,
armlets, bracelets, anklets, and waistband; He is adorned with the

conch, the discus (chakra); the mace (gada), the sword, the bow (shranga), the Srivatsa mark, and the garland of wildflowers. By His unsurpassed beauty, He captivates all minds and eyes; He fills all things moving and non-moving, with the nectar of His loveliness; His youthfulness is eternal and is wonderful and inconceivable; His smile is as charming as a flower; by His holy fragrance, He fills all the quarters of this endless universe; by his grandeur, He overwhelms the three worlds; He blesses those that seek His protection with His sweet glance full of compassion and love.

He has, for play, the creation, maintenance, and dissolution of the entire world; He is free from all blemishes; He is the treasurehouse of all auspicious qualities and is absolutely different from all other things. He is the Supreme Lord.

[Thus, we see the description of his auspicious form based on various scriptures. His devotees meditate on this form to attain his closeness in his divine abode.]

[His auspicious attributes, which are unique to him and on which devotees meditate, are described in various texts.]

'तद्धर्मोपदेशात्' (ब्र० सू० १/१/२१), 'स एष सर्वेषां लोकानामीष्टे सर्वेषां कामानाम् स एष सर्वेभ्यः पापभ्य उदितः' (छा० उ० १/६/७) इत्यादिदर्शनात् । तस्यैते गुणाः – 'सर्वस्य वशी सर्वस्येशानः' (बृ० उ० ६/४/२२), 'अपहतपाप्मा विजर' (छा० उ० ८/१/५) इत्यादि 'सत्यसंकल्प' (छा० उ० ८/१/५) इत्यन्तम्, 'विश्वतः परमं नित्यं विश्वं नारायणं हरिम् । पतिं विश्वस्यात्मेश्वरम्' (तै० ना० १/२-३) इत्यादिवाक्यप्रतिपादिताः ॥

The words, "Because attributes peculiar to Him are taught" (Brahma Sutra 1/1/21), in the Sutra, referred to above, find their explanation in the following Upanishads: "He rules over all the worlds and fulfills all desires and He rises above all evil (actions)." (Chhandogya Upanishad 1/6/7) His attributes and qualities are brought out in the following Upanishads: "He has all things under His control. He is the

Lord of everything" (Brihat Aranyaka Upanishad 6/4/22); and the text commencing with "He is free from the taint of sin and ageless, etc." (Chhandogya Upanishad 8/1/5) and concluding with "His will fulfills itself without fail." (Chhandogya Upanishad 8/1/5) Similarly, the Upanishads say, "He is superior to all (sentient beings) in the Universe and is eternal. He is the soul of all. He is Narayana and is also called Hari". "He is the Supreme Lord of the Universe and the individual selves" (Taittiriya Narayana Upanishad 1/2-3).

[Whenever we find the mention of such unique attributes we should conclude that it is the Supreme Being, we are talking about. Since there is no one like him or superior to him, these attributes like creator, controller, etc. uniquely describe him.]

[Vakyakara Brahmanandi describes his Supreme form as auspicious in meditation for his devotees. Through an unmoving resolve, a devotee can experience it.]

वाक्यकारैश्चैतत्सर्वं सुस्पष्टमाह – 'हिरण्मयः पुरुषो दृश्यते' इति प्राज्ञः सर्वान्तरः स्याल्लोक-कामेशोपदेशात्तथोदयात्पाप्मनामित्यादिना । तस्य च रूपस्यानित्यतादि वाक्यकारेणैव प्रतिषिद्धम् 'स्यात्तद्रूपं कृतकमनुग्रहार्थं तच्चेतनानामैश्वर्यात्' इत्युपासितुरनुग्रहार्थः परमपुरुषस्य रूपसंग्रह इति पूर्वपक्षं कृत्वा, 'रूपं वातीन्द्रियमन्तःकरणप्रत्यक्षं तन्निर्देशात्' इति । यथा ज्ञानादयः परस्य ब्रह्मणः स्वरूपतया निर्देशात्स्वरूपभूतगुणास्तथेदमपि रूपं श्रुत्या स्वरूपतया निर्देशात्स्वरूपभूतमित्यर्थः ।

The Vakyakara has also conveyed all this meaning clearly as follows: "The passage in the Upanishad says, "A person radiant like gold is seen in the sphere of the sun." The person referred to in it is the Wise One, the Inner Self of all; for the Upanishad teaches that He is the Lord of the world and the dispenser of all that is desired. He is also described as being free from the taint of all sin". The Vakyakara also declares that this form of the Lord should not be considered as not being eternal: "It may be asked whether this form is one assumed by the Lord, for the time being, to bless His devotees. The Lord may be thought of as taking a form for showing His grace to His devotees." Having stated this prima facie view, he refutes it by saying, "This form (of the Lord) cannot be perceived by the senses. It can be apprehended only by the mind that is pure, for that is how it is described (in the Upanishad)". Knowledge and other qualities that define the intrinsic nature of the Supreme Being are His essential attributes and are, therefore, eternal. Similarly, this form is also spoken of in the Upanishad as defining the essential nature of the Supreme Being, which is also eternal.

[By constant meditation on his form, a devotee becomes free from his sins, and, thereafter, he can experience his divine form by a pure mind.]

[The great commentator Dramida also tells the same.]

भाष्यकारेणैतद्व्याख्यातम् – 'अञ्जसैव विश्वसृजो रूपं तत्तु न चक्षुषा ग्राह्यं मनसा त्वकलुषेण साधनान्तरवता गृह्यते', 'न चक्षुषा गृह्यते नापि वाचा' (मु० उ० ३/१/८), 'मनसा तु विशुद्धेन' इति श्रुतेः, न हि अरूपाया देवताया रूपमुपदिश्यते, यथाभूतवादि हि शास्त्रम्; 'महारजनं वासः' (बृ० उ० ४/३/६), 'वेदाहमेतं पुरुषं महान्तमादित्यवर्णं तमसः परस्तात्' (पु० सू० २०) इति प्रकरणान्तरनिर्देशाच्च साक्षिणं इत्यादिना । हिरण्यमय इति रूपसामान्याच्चन्द्रमुखवत्, न मयडत्र विकारमादाय प्रयुज्यते, अनारभ्यत्वादात्मन इति ।

Dramidacharya, the commentator, has explained it as follows: "This (form) of the Lord, who creates the world in an instant, is not merely an illusory appearance; it cannot be seen with the eye of the flesh; it is apprehended only by the pure mind with the help of other aids; for the Upanishad says, "It is not apprehended by the eye, not by speech, and can be apprehended only by the pure mind". (Mundaka Upanishad 3/1/8) A deity without form would not be taught by the Upanishad as having a form; the scriptures teach the truth about things just as they are. The Upanishads say: "His raiment (robe) is colored with saffron (and turmeric)" (Brihat Aranyaka Upanishad 4/3/6). "He shines radiantly like the sun in a region beyond darkness". (Purush Sukta 20; Shvetashvatara Upanishad 3/8) The statements made by the Upanishads in other contexts are also evidence. "Having the color of the gold" means resemblance in radiance and not "made of gold", as in the (phrase) "a face like a moon". So far the words of the Vakyakara; it has been commented upon as follows: "The suffix mayat (in 'hiranyamaya', hiranya means gold) does not signify 'made of gold' because the soul is not a thing made of anything".

[The supreme form of Lord Narayana is shining like thousands of suns together; its splendor is incomparable to anything else; it is like itself. Since it is radiant like the sun, we say its shining resembles that of gold, and its color is like fresh turmeric and saffron. That is why the sages wear robes of this color.]

[One can ask how we conclude that this person, radiant like the sun, is the Supreme Being and not anyone else.]

यथा ज्ञानादिकल्याणगुणगणाननन्तर्यनिर्देशादपरिमितकल्याणगुणगणविशिष्टं परं ब्रह्मेत्यवगम्यत एवमादित्यवर्णं पुरुषमित्यादिनिर्देशात्स्वाभिमतस्वानुरूपकल्याणतमरूपः परब्रह्मभूतः पुरुषोत्तमो नारायण इति ज्ञायते । तथा 'अस्येशाना जगतो विष्णुपत्नी' (तै० सं० ४/४/१२/१४), 'ह्रीश्च ते लक्ष्मीश्च पत्न्यौ' (तै० आ० ३/१३/६), 'सदा पश्यन्ति सूरयः' ' (सु० उ० ६), 'तमसः परस्तात्' (तै० ना० १/२), 'क्षयन्तमस्य रजसः पराके' (तै० सं० २/२/१२/१८), इत्यादिना पत्नीपरिजनस्थानादीनां निर्देशादेव तथैव सन्तीत्यवगम्यते । यथाह भाष्यकार - यथाभूतवादि हि शास्त्रम्' इति ॥

We know from the Upanishads that the Supreme Being has countless auspicious qualities like knowledge, etc. so when they talk of a being with innumerable auspicious qualities, we understand that it is the Supreme Being that is being talked about. Similarly, when the Upanishad says: "He has a form radiant like the sun"; we understand that it is Narayana, who is the Supreme Being, being talked about because he has the most auspicious form as per His liking and it suits His nature.

Similarly, from such Upanishads "The Spouse of Vishnu is the queen of the world" (Taittiriya Sanhita 4/4/12/14), "The goddess of the earth and the goddess Lakshmi are His wives"(Taittiriya Aranyaka 3/13/6); "The eternally enlightened seers are always gazing etc.," (Subala Upanishad 6) "beyond darness" (Taittiriya Narayana Upanishad 1/2) "dwelling in a region beyond rajas," (Taittiriya Sanhita 2/2/12/18) we learn that He has consorts, attendants, a place of abode, etc. Thus says the Bhashyakara (Dramidacharya): "The scripture teaches things just as they really are".

[Everywhere in Upanishads, his supreme form is stated like the radiance of the thousands of suns. These Upanishads also describe the attributes, which are unique to him, in the same context. Therefore, it is evident that he is being referred to everywhere whenever such a description comes up.]

[Now, Ramanuja summarizes this section.]

एतदुक्तं भवति - यथा 'सत्यं ज्ञानमनन्तं ब्रह्म' (तै० उ० १/१) इति निर्देशात्परमात्मस्वरूपं समस्तहेयप्रत्यनीकानवधिकानन्तैकतानतयापरिच्छेद्यतया च सकलेतरविलक्षणं तथा 'यः सर्वज्ञः सर्ववित्' (मु० उ० १/१/१०), 'परास्य शक्तिर्विविधैव श्रूयते स्वाभाविकी ज्ञानबलक्रिया च' (श्वे० उ० ६/८), 'तमेव भान्तमनुभाति सर्वं तस्य भासा सर्वमिदं विभाति' (कठ उ० २/५/१५) इत्यादिनिर्देशान्निरतिशयासंख्येयाश्च गुणाः सकलेतरविलक्षणाः । तथा 'आदित्य-वर्णम्' इत्यादिनिर्देशाद्रूपपरिजनस्थानादयश्च सकलेतरविलक्षणाः स्वासाधारणा अनिर्देश्यस्व-रूपस्वभावा इति ॥

Whatever is said means this: From the statement "Supreme Being is Truth, Knowledge, and Infiniteness" (Taittiriya Upanishad 1/1), we learn that the Supreme Being is free from all trace of blemish and is the abode of infinite bliss and has no limitations whatsoever and is therefore different from all other things. Similarly, from the Upanishads, "He knows all things; He knows all the characteristics of everything" (Mundaka Upanishad 1/1/10); "The divine power of the Supreme Being is of various types. It consists of intrinsic knowledge, might, and action, these are natural to him." (Shvetashvatara Upanishad 6/8); "He alone shines there, illuminating everything by its light. By his light, everything else shines (as if this light belongs to them)." (Katha Upanishad 2/8/15) we understand that He has unsurpassed and innumerable qualities which are different from those of all others. Similarly, from Upanishads like "He has a form radiant like the sun", we understand that He has a form, attendants, an abode, and other things different from those of others, unique and found exclusively in Him and that their nature and character baffle description.

[Thus, we have described some of the most auspicious attributes of the Supreme Being, his divine form, his wife and associates, his abode, etc. These auspicious attributes are inherent in him without any trace of any imperfections.]

Irrefutability and Eternality of the Vedas

[Now, opposition questions the authority of the Vedas.]

वेदाः प्रमाणं चेद्विध्यर्थवादमन्त्रगतं सर्वमपूर्वमविरुद्धमर्थजातं यथावस्थितमेव बोधयन्ति ।
प्रामाण्यं च वेदानाम् 'औत्पत्तिकस्तु शब्दस्यार्थेन संबन्धः' (पू० मी० सू० १/१/७) इत्युक्तम् ।
यथाग्निजलादीनामौष्ण्यादिशक्तियोगः स्वाभाविकः, यथा च चक्षुरादीनामिन्द्रियाणां बुद्धिविशेष
-जननशक्तिः स्वाभाविकी तथा शब्दस्यापि बोधनशक्तिः स्वाभाविकी ।

If the Vedas are valid sources of knowledge, instructions (which enjoin an activity), hymns (which sing the praises of deities), and laudatory praise (which explain the performance of the rites and give reasons for the injunction), should all be considered as valid sources of knowledge, provided these ideas have not been already established elsewhere, and are not opposed to the other evidence. The authority of the Vedas is thus declared in the Jaimini Sutra: "The relation between the word and its meaning is something innate (natural) and eternal." (Jaimini Sutra 1/1/7) Fire is hot and water cold by their very nature, the senses like sight have, by their very nature, the power of giving rise to knowledge of a specific kind, likewise, the power of a word to give rise to a meaning is innate and natural.

[Ramanuja maintains that the relation between a word and its meaning is natural and eternal. Our eyes have the capability to see but they cannot see in the absence of light. When the association of eyes with light occurs, eyes reveal the objects. In the same way, when we know the association between words and their meanings, words naturally reveal their meanings.]

[He now explains how we understand the relation between a word and its meaning as natural and eternal.]

न च हस्तचेष्टादिवत्संकेतमूलं शब्दस्य बोधकत्वमिति वक्तुं शक्यम् । अनाद्यनुसंधानाविच्छेदे-
ऽपि संकेतयितृपुरुषाज्ञानात् । यानि संकेतमूलानि तानि सर्वाणि साक्षाद्वा परंपरया वा ज्ञायन्ते ।
न च देवदत्तादिशब्दवत्कल्पयितुं युक्तम् । तेषु च साक्षाद्वा परंपरया वा संकेतो ज्ञायते । गवादि-
शब्दानां त्वनाद्यनुसंधानाविच्छेदेऽपि संकेताज्ञानादेव बोधकत्वशक्तिः स्वाभाविकी । अतोऽग्न्या-
दीनां दाहकत्वादिशक्तिवदिन्द्रियाणां बोधकत्वशक्तिवच्च शब्दस्यापि बोधकत्वशक्तिराश्रयणीया
॥

It cannot be maintained that the power of a word to convey a meaning is based on convention (set up by humans), just like conventional gestures made with the hand. The relation between the word and its meaning has continued from time immemorial without any break. Further, no one knows who established such a convention between the word and its meaning. Wherever there is a convention, the author of the convention is (invariably) known directly or indirectly. It cannot be stated that the relation between the word and its meaning is conventional as in the word "Devadatta" used as the name of a person. In such words as "Devadatta", it is known to be a convention directly or indirectly. (We know who gave the person the name "Devadatta"). But, in the case of words like "cow", though the meaning has been conveyed by the word from beginningless time, no one knows by whom any such convention as in "Devadatta" was first established. Therefore, the power of such words as "cow" to convey their respective meanings should be considered innate or eternal (and not conventional). It is as natural as the power of fire to burn and the power of the senses to generate perception.

[The relation between words and their meanings always exists like the capability of the fire to burn. Their relationship is not based on human conventions or gestures to understand their relationship.]

[The opposition asks if their relation is natural why do we need to study their association.]

ननु चेनिन्द्रियवच्छब्दस्यापि बोधकत्वं स्वाभाविकं संबन्धग्रहणं बोधकत्वाय किमित्यपेक्षते,
लिङ्गादिवदिति उच्यते - यथा ज्ञातसंबन्धनियमं धूमाद्यग्न्यादिविज्ञानजनकं तथा ज्ञातसंबन्ध-
नियमः शब्दोऽप्यर्थविशेषबुद्धिजनकः । एवं तर्हि शब्दोऽप्यर्थविशेषस्य लिङ्गमित्यनुमानं स्यात्
नैवम् । शब्दार्थयोः संबन्धो बोध्यबोधकभाव एव धूमादीनां तु संबन्धान्तर इति तस्य संबन्धस्य
ज्ञानद्वारेण बुद्धिजनकत्वमिति विशेषः । एवं गृहीतसंबन्धस्य बोधकत्वदर्शनादादनाद्यनुसंधाना-
विच्छेदेऽपि संकेताज्ञानाद्बोधकत्वशक्तिरेवेति निश्चीयते ॥

It may be asked, "If the word has the power of conveying a meaning
naturally just like the senses in giving perceptual knowledge, why
should a knowledge of the connection (association) between the
word and its meaning be necessary for conveying its meaning?" The
answer is "This necessity of connection is similar to when one
makes an inference based on previous knowledge". Just as the
knowledge of the invariable association between smoke and fire is
necessary while making the inference, "Because there is smoke
here, there must be fire here", likewise the knowledge of the
invariable association between the word and its meaning is
necessary for the conveyance of the specific meaning.

If so, it may be asked, "Would it not be a case of inference when a
word conveys its meaning?" We answer as follows: "No. The words
are related to things as their direct signifiers. The association or
relationship between a word and its meaning is of one kind (direct)
and that between a reason (smoke) and the knowledge derived from
inference (presence of fire) is of another kind (indirect). The
resemblance is only in respect of knowledge arising out of
knowledge of the relationship. In inference, the relationship is that
between cause (fire) and effect (smoke). Here, in the case of words
and their meanings, the relationship is that between the idea
conveyed and that which conveys it. Since the power of conveying
meaning is seen whenever the knowledge of the relationship
(between the word and its meaning) is present and since, in spite of
continuity, from beginningless time, of this power, no one has
known of anyone who established any such convention, even in the

absence of any gestures, we conclude that, in the word itself, there is an innate or natural power.

[Thus, the words have the natural ability to reveal their meanings when one knows about their relationship.]

[As words and their meanings are naturally connected, are the group of words and their meanings naturally connected in the same manner?]

एवं बोधकानां पदसंघातानां संसर्गविशेषबोधकत्वेन वाक्यशब्दाभिधेयानामुच्चारणक्रमो यत्र पुरुषबुद्धिपूर्वकस्ते पौरुषेयाः शब्दा इत्युच्यन्ते । यत्र तु तदुच्चारणक्रमः पूर्वपूर्वोच्चरणक्रम- जनितसंस्कारपूर्वकः सर्वदापौरुषेयास्ते च वेदा इत्युच्यन्ते।

Similarly, when several words, each with a meaning of its own, are employed to form a sentence, they express or convey a meaning, when the mutual relationship between the different words comes to be known. When how the words are uttered in succession depends upon the intelligence of a person, these sentences are of human authorship. On the other hand, when the order in which the words are uttered depends upon immemorial tradition, they are without human authorship and are called "Vedas". This is what is meant by saying that the Vedas are not of human authorship and that they are eternal.

[The combination of words in a sentence can happen in two ways by carefully deciding their order or spontaneously. The Vedas are uttered spontaneously, as per tradition, without any human intervention in their order.]

[Since Vedas are not based on human intellect, they are simply eternal or always existing.]

एतदेव वेदानामपौरुषेयत्वं नित्यत्वं च यत्पूर्वोच्चारणक्रमजनितसंस्कारेण तमेव क्रमविशेषं स्मृत्वा तेनैव क्रमेणोच्चार्यमाणत्वम् । ते चानुपूर्वीविशेषेण संस्थिता अक्षरराशयो वेदा ऋग्यजुः-सामाथर्वभेदभिन्ना अनन्तशाखा वर्तन्ते । ते च विध्यर्थवादमन्त्ररूपा वेदाः परब्रह्म-भूतनारायणस्वरूपं तदाराधनप्रकाराधितात्फलविशेषं च बोधयन्ति । परमपुरुषवत्तत्स्वरूप-तदाराधनतत्फलज्ञापकवेदाख्यशब्दजातं नित्यमेव ।

The words in Vedic passages are uttered in a certain order, which is invariably followed by a remembrance of the traditional order existing from time immemorial. It constitutes their non-human authorship and eternality. These collections of words or syllables existing in a certain order of succession are Vedas and they are four: Rik, Yaju, Sama, and Atharva, and each has innumerable branches. These Vedas consisting of instructions, mantras (hymns for worship), and explanatory comments teach us the essential nature of Narayana, the Supreme Being, the way of worshipping Him, and the result of such worship. The collections of words called 'Vedas' remind us of the Supreme Person, His worship, and the result of that worship is as eternal as the Supreme Person Himself.

[Vedas reveal those things which the human mind cannot conceive. Therefore, they are revealed to us by the Supreme Being.]

[Since Vedas are hard to understand, the Supreme Being directs some great authorities or sages to reveal their true meaning for all of us.]

वेदानामनन्तत्वाद्दुरवगाहत्वाच्च परमपुरुषनियुक्ताः परमर्षयः कल्पे कल्पे निखिलजगदुपकारार्थं वेदार्थं स्मृत्वा विध्यर्थवादमन्त्रमूलानि धर्मशास्त्राणीतिहासपुराणानि च चक्रुः ।

Since the Vedas are boundless and hard to understand, some great sages, directed by the Supreme Person, recollect the meaning of the Vedas in every epoch and composed Dharma (religious) scriptures, Ithihasas (history), and Puranas based on the instructions, mantras and explanatory comments of the Vedas for the benefit of the whole world.

[According to the instruction of the Supreme Being, these sages write various explanatory texts like Ramayana, Mahabharata, Puranas, Smritis, etc. to explain the statements of the Vedas]

[Now, Ramanuja explains the distinction between Vedic words usage and their worldly usage.]

लौकिकाश्च शब्दा वेदराशेरुद्धृत्यैव तत्तदर्थविशेषनामतया पूर्ववत्प्रयुक्ताः पारंपर्येण प्रयुज्यन्ते ।
ननु च वैदिक एव सर्वे वाचकाः शब्दाश्चेच्छन्दस्यैवं भाषायामेवमिति लक्षणभेदः कथमुपपद्यते ।
उच्यते - तेषामेव शब्दानां तस्यामेवानुपूर्व्यां वर्तमानां तथैव प्रयोगः । अन्यत्र प्रयुज्यमानानामन्य-
थेति न कश्चिद्दोषः ॥

The words, employed in ordinary life, were also picked from the Vedas and have been employed in successive ages to denote their respective meanings in the Vedas. "If so", it may be asked, (i.e.) if all words with their meanings are taken from the Vedas, why should a distinction be made between them saying, "This is so in the Vedas" and "This is so and so in ordinary language?" The answer is, "The words used in the Vedic order of succession retain their original meaning, whereas the same words used elsewhere in a different way might have a different meaning. So, there is no flaw in this procedure.

[The Vedic usage remains intact; however, practical use of words can change.]

Conclusion

[Ramanuja now summarizes the essence of the text so that everyone can understand it.]

एवमितिहासपुराणधर्मशास्त्रोपबृंहितसाङ्गवेदवेद्यः परब्रह्मभूतो नारायणो निखिलहेयप्रत्य-नीकः सकलेतरविलक्षणोऽपरिच्छिन्नज्ञानानन्दैकस्वरूपः स्वाभाविकानवधिकातिशयासंख्येय-कल्याणगुणगणाकरः स्वसंकल्पानुविधायिस्वरूपस्थितिप्रवृत्तिभेदचिदचिद्वस्तुजातोऽपरिच्छेद्य-स्वरूपस्वभावानन्तमहाविभूतिर्नानाविधानन्तचेतनाचेतनात्मकप्रपञ्चलीलोपकरण   इति प्रतिपादितम् ।

Thus, the Vedas, along with their auxiliary treatises, elucidated and explained further in Itihasas, Puranas, and Dharma scriptures, impart knowledge about Supreme Being, Narayana. He is knowable only from these texts. He is opposed to all that is impure and is different from all else. His essential nature is infinite knowledge and bliss. He has, by His very nature, unsurpassed, wonderful, and innumerable auspicious qualities. All things, sentient and non-sentient, owe their origin, their continuance, and their varied activities to His will. He has a region of supreme glory, which is infinite in its nature and character. So also He has, for the objects and instruments of His cosmic play, this world, constituted of countless varied beings, sentient and non-sentient.

[Narayana is the Supreme Being with infinite auspicious attributes. Knowledge and bliss are his intrinsic attributes. All living and non-living entities have a body-soul relationship with him. He creates, sustains, and dissolves this world.]

[There are hundreds of Upanishadic statements which unanimously support this view.]

‘सर्वं खल्विदं ब्रह्म’ (छा० उ० ३/१४/१), ‘ऐतदात्म्यमिदं सर्वं’, ‘तत्त्वमसि श्वेतकेतो’ (छा० उ० ६/८/७), ‘एनमेके वदन्त्यग्निं मरुतोऽन्यो प्रजापतिम् । इन्द्रमेके परे प्राणमपरे ब्रह्म शाश्वतम् ॥’ (म० स्मृ० १२/१२३), ‘ज्योतींषि शुक्लानि च यानि लोके त्रयो लोका लोकपालास्त्रयी च । त्रयोऽग्नयश्चाहुतयश्च पञ्च सर्वे देव देवकीपुत्र एव ॥’ (वि० पु० ६/५/७२), ‘त्वं यज्ञस्त्वं वषट्कारस्त्वमोंकारः परंतपः ।’ (वा० रा० ६/१२०/२०), “ऋतुधामा वसुः पूर्वो वसूनां त्वं प्रजापतिः ॥’ (वा० रा० ६/१२०/७), ‘जगत्सर्वं शरीरं ते स्थैर्यं ते वसुधातलम् । अग्निः कोपः प्रसादस्ते सोमः श्रीवत्सलक्षणः ॥’ (वा० रा० ६/१२०/२६), ‘ज्योतींषि विष्णुर्भुवनानि विष्णुर्वनानि विष्णुर्गिरयो दिशश्च । नद्यः समुद्राश्च स एव सर्वं यदस्ति यन्नास्ति च विप्रवर्य ॥’ (वि० पु० २/१२/३८) इत्यादिसामानाधिकरण्यप्रयोगेषु सर्वैः शब्दैः सर्वशरीरतया सर्वप्रकारं ब्रह्मैवाभिधीयत इति चोक्तम् ।

In passages like the following: "All this is, indeed, Supreme Being" (Chhandogya Upanishad 3/14/1); "All this has Supreme Being as its soul". "You are that, O Shvetaketu" (Chhandogya Upanishad 6/8/7); "Some call Him fire-god, some call Him wind-god, others call Him Prajapati (Brahma), some again call Him Indra, others again call Him Prana (vital air), and, yet others call Him the eternal Supreme Being". (Manu Smriti 12/123) "Whatever shining lights there are in this world, the three worlds, the three lords of these three worlds, the three Vedas, the three fires, the five kinds of offerings made in the fire, all the gods - all these are only the son of Devaki (i. e.) Sri Krishna". (Vishnu Purana (6/5/72) "You are the sacrifice, you the sacred oblation (vashatkara), you are the holy syllable Om." (Ramayana 6/120/20) "You are the Vasu Ritudhama among the Vasus. Before that you are Prajapathi (Brahma)" (Ramayana 6/120/7), "The whole Universe is your body; your stability is the earth; Fire is your wrath and the Moon your grace". (Ramayana 6/120/26) "All the shining lights are Vishnu; all the worlds are Vishnu; the mountains, the four quarters, the rivers, and the oceans - all these are only Vishnu. He is O best of Brahmins, everything that exists as perceived by the senses and so also everything, not perceived by the senses." (Vishnu Purana 2/12/38) In all these sentences it is only the Supreme Being that is denoted by all the words because he is the common basis (soul) of all. It is possible to denote Him like this since everything else is His body and is a mode of His. This has been already stated.

[Just as we use the same words to refer to body and soul, we can use the same words to refer to the Supreme Being and other entities as everything is his body or a mode.]

[His will is infallible and he can create everything by his mere will.]

सत्यसंकल्पं परं ब्रह्म स्वयमेव बहुप्रकारं स्यामिति संकल्प्याचित्समष्टिरूपमहाभूतसूक्ष्मवस्तु भोक्तृवर्गसमूहं च स्विमन् प्रलीनं स्वयमेव विभज्य तस्माद्भूतसूक्ष्माद्वास्तुनो महाभूतानि सृष्ट्वा तेषु च भोक्तृवर्गात्मतया प्रवेश्य तैश्चिदधिष्ठितैर्महाभूतैरन्योन्यसंसृष्टैः कृत्स्नं जगद्विधाय स्वयमपि सर्वस्यात्मतया प्रविश्य परमात्मत्वेनावस्थितं सर्वशरीरं बहुप्रकारमवतिष्ठते ।

The Supreme Being, who is omnipotent, willed, of His own accord, to become many; In Him, were submerged the Primal fundamental elements in their subtle form, comprising the sum total of non-sentient nature. The multitudes of individual souls were also submerged in Him; He then created from the subtle fundamental elements the five primary elements (fire, air, water, earth, and sky) in their gross form by differentiating them. He entered the individual souls, who experience, as their souls. In his superintendence as the soul of individual souls, He created the whole world out of these five elements mixed up with one another; He then entered into all as the soul of everything and stands in multiple ways, with all things as His body, without giving up His nature as the Supreme Being.

[Since everything dissolves in him, it is through him that they sprout again. He holds everything together. Though insentient entities change, the Supreme Being does not change as they have a body and soul relationship.]

[He classifies all entities into distinct names and forms by entering into them.]

यदिदं महाभूतसूक्ष्मं वस्तु तदेव प्रकृतिशब्देनाभिधीयते । भोक्तृवर्गसमूह एव पुरुषशब्देन चोच्यते । तौ च प्रकृतिपुरुषौ परमात्मशरीरतया परमात्मप्रकारभूतौ । तत्प्रकारः परमात्मैव प्रकृतिपुरुषशब्दाभिधेयः । 'सोऽकामयत बहु स्यां प्रजायेयेति ... तत्सृष्ट्वा तदेवानुप्राविशत् तदनुप्रविश्य सच्च त्यच्चाभवन्निरुक्तं चानिरुक्तं च निलयनं चानिलयनं च विज्ञानं चाविज्ञानं च सत्यं चानृतं च सत्यमभवत्' (तै० उ० २/६) इति पूर्वोक्तं सर्वमनयैव श्रुत्या व्यक्तम् ॥

These Primal fundamental elements in their subtle form are called Nature. The collection of experiencing individual souls is called Purushas (sentient beings); Nature and collective individual souls are both the bodies of the Supreme Being and are, therefore, His modes. The Supreme Being, who has them as His modes, is denoted by words Nature and Purusha. Everything that has been said so far is stated clearly in the following Upanishad: "He willed (saying)" "I will become many". Having created it, He entered into it; having entered into it, He became reality (sat), the sentient being, (which remains the same always), and unreality (tyat), the non-sentient thing (which is ever subject to change). He became the sentient being that cannot be described (in terms of attributes) and the non-sentient thing that can be so described. He became the non-sentient thing, which is supported by the sentient being, and also the sentient being, which supports the non-sentient thing; He became the knowing sentient self and non-sentient matter. He became the sentient being, which is not subject to change and is therefore called "the truth" and the non-sentient thing subject to change and hence called the unreal. Despite His becoming unreal, He remains the truth." (Taittiriya Upanishad 2/6)

[Since nothing is different from him, all changes are also within him. Thus, he is beyond reality and unreality both.]

[After describing the fundamental characteristics of the Supreme Being, Ramanuja states how one can attain him.]

ब्रह्मप्राप्त्युपायश्च   शास्त्राधिगतततत्त्वज्ञानपूर्वकस्वकर्मानुगृहीतभक्तिनिष्ठासाध्यानवधिकातिशय-
प्रियविशदतमप्रत्यक्षतापन्नानुध्यानरूपपरभक्तिरेवेत्युक्तम् । भक्तिशब्दश्च प्रीतिविशेषे वर्तते ।
प्रीतिश्च ज्ञानविशेष एव । ननु च सुखं प्रीतिरित्यनर्थान्तरम् । सुखं च ज्ञानविशेषसाध्यं पदार्था-
न्तरमिति हि लौकिकाः । नैवम् । येन ज्ञानविशेषेण तत्साध्यमित्युच्यते स एव ज्ञानविशेषः
सुखम् ॥

The means of attaining the Supreme Being is stated to be only (supreme) devotion (surrender), which is of the nature of constant meditation so intense that it becomes like vivid perception. This supreme devotion results from following the path of devotion, after knowing the essence of scriptures. This gives rise to the performance of the prescribed duties and rites by one's caste and stage of life. The word devotion is used in the sense of a special form of love, and love is a special type of knowledge.

It may be stated by way of objection: "Pleasure and love are synonymous terms and worldly people say that pleasure is something different from knowledge and that it is the effect of knowledge and not knowledge itself." It is not so. The special kind of knowledge that results in pleasure is pleasure itself.

[Through supreme devotion or unbounded love, one can attain the Supreme Being. This supreme devotion results after one worships the Lord by righteously fulfilling his duties and offering their results to him. This devotion or love is not different from pleasure.]

[Ramanuja now explains how pleasure and knowledge are the same.]

एतदुक्तं भवति - विषयज्ञानानि सुखदुःखमध्यसाधारणानि । तानि च विषयाधीनविशेषाणि तथा भवन्ति । येन च विषयविशेषेण विशेषितं ज्ञानं सुखस्य जनकमित्यभिमतं तद्विषयं ज्ञानमेव सुखं, तदितरेकि पदार्थान्तरं नोपलभ्यते । तेनैव सुखित्वव्यवहारोपपत्तेश्च ।

It comes to mean this: The knowledge of objects may be of three types - pleasure, pain, and that which is neither pleasure nor pain. These acquire their special character as pleasure or pain or that which is neither pleasure nor pain from the nature of the objects. That knowledge of a particular object, which is said to produce pleasure, is itself a pleasure. There is nothing other than that knowledge to be called pleasure. From this knowledge of a certain kind of object, we can explain whatever is meant by the word 'pleasure' (and there is no need to postulate an additional entity called 'pleasure').

[When we see poison, weapons, etc., we experience grief (fear) because we confuse our body with our soul and fear our destruction by them, hence, dislike them. Otherwise, in the absence of our ignorance, knowledge is not different from pleasure.]

[What is the difference between knowledge of an ordinary object and the Supreme Being?]

एवंविधसुखस्वरूपज्ञानस्य विशेषकत्वं ब्रह्मव्यतिरिक्तस्य वस्तुनः सातिशयमस्थिरं च । ब्रह्मणस्त्वनवधिकातिशयं स्थिरं चेति । 'आनन्दो ब्रह्म' (तै० उ० ३/६/१) इत्युच्यते । विषयायत्तत्वाज्ज्ञानस्य सुखस्वरूपतया ब्रह्मैव सुखम् ।

This knowledge, which is of the nature of pleasure, is, in the case of objects other than the Supreme Being, limited and changing. In the case of the Supreme Being, this knowledge, which is of the nature of pleasure, is boundless and constant. Therefore, does the Upanishad say, "Supreme Being is bliss." (Taittiriya Upanishad 3/6/1) Knowledge is concerned with objects and depends upon them. Therefore, the Supreme Being, which is of the nature (object) of pleasure, its knowledge is called pleasure itself.

[Knowledge of a worldly object can only give momentary pleasure; it might not last long. Moreover, this pleasure is finite.]

[Since Supreme Being is the origin of all pleasures, all other pleasures are secondary to him.]

तदिदमाह – 'रसो वै सः रसं हे एवायं लब्ध्वानन्दी भवति' (तै० उ० २/७/१) इति ब्रह्मैव सुखमिति ब्रह्म लब्ध्वा सुखी भवतीत्यर्थः । परमपुरुषः स्वेनैव स्वयमनवधिकातिशयसुखः सन् परस्यापि सुखं भवति । सुखस्वरूपत्वाविशेषात् । ब्रह्म यस्य ज्ञानविषयो भवति स सुखी भवतीत्यर्थः ।

The Upanishad says, "He is indeed a delight, and the individual self, having attained Him, becomes blissful." (Taittiriya Upanishad 2/7/1) This means that since the Supreme Being is bliss, the soul that has attained the Supreme Being becomes blissful. Supreme Being is in Himself blissful and He becomes the cause of bliss in others as well. Since the Supreme Being is a special form of delight, the person who knows the Supreme Being becomes blissful.

[If an individual soul experiences the bliss of the Supreme Being, it becomes eternally blissful as he is bliss personified.]

[Then, what is the utmost duty of an individual soul?]

तदेवं परस्य ब्रह्मणोऽनवधिकातिशयासंख्येयकल्याणगुणगणाकरस्य निरवद्यस्यानन्तमहाविभूते-रनवधिकातिशयसौशील्यसौन्दर्यवात्सल्यजलधेः सर्वशेषित्वादात्मनः शेषत्वात्प्रतिबंधितयानु-संधीयमानमनवधिकातिशयप्रीतिविषयं सत्परं ब्रह्मैवैनमात्मानं प्रापयतीति ॥

The Supreme Being is the abode of boundless, unsurpassed, and innumerable, auspicious attributes; He is free from all blemishes;

He owns endless and supreme glory. He is the ocean of boundless and wonderful qualities like goodness, beauty, and love. He is the principal entity in everyone. The individual soul exists for the fulfillment of His purposes. If a seeker meditates upon Him as one for whom he exists, such that the Supreme Being becomes an object of boundless and supreme love to him, the Supreme Being himself will lead the seeker to Himself.

[One, with all his might, should serve the Supreme Being alone as he is the ocean of boundless love and pleasure. This would lead him to eternal bliss]

[The opposition might object to it and say how service to someone else can be ever blissful.]

ननु चात्यन्तशेषतैवात्मनोऽनवधिकातिशयसुखमित्युक्तं भवति । तदेतत्सर्वलोकविरुद्धम् । तथाहि सर्वेषामेव चेतनानां स्वातन्त्र्यमेव इष्टतमं दृश्यते, पारतन्त्र्यं दुःखतरम् । स्मृतिश्च – 'सर्वं परवशं दुःखं सर्वमात्मवशं सुखम् ।' (म० स्मृ० ४/१६०) तथाहि – 'सेवा श्ववृत्तिराख्याता तस्मात्तां परिवर्जयेत् ।'(म० स्मृ० ४/६) इति ।

It may be asked here by way of objection, "What has been said would mean that absolute dependence (upon the Lord) leads to boundless and unsurpassed pleasure or bliss. But this is entirely opposed to all worldly experience. To all beings, endowed with intelligence, independence is the most desirable, and dependence (upon others) is always painful. The memory-based text (smriti), too, says: "The state of dependence on others is everywhere painful; independence of others or self-sovereignty is always happiness. (Manu Smriti 4/160) It also says - Service has been described as a dog's life, and hence it should be given up". (Manu Smriti 4/6)

[Opposition cites references from Manu Smriti to support their claim.]

[Ramanuja explains why such a doubt has arisen in the doubters.]

तदिदमनधिगतदेहातिरिक्तात्मरूपाणां शरीरात्माभिमानविजृम्भितम् । तथा हि - शरीरं हि मनुष्यत्वादिजातिगुणाश्रयपिण्डभूतं स्वतन्त्रं प्रतीयते । तस्मिन्नेवाहमिति संसारिणां प्रतीतिः । आत्माभिमानो यादृशस्तदनुगुणैव पुरुषार्थप्रतीतिः । सिंहव्याघ्रवराहमनुष्ययक्षरक्षःपिशाचदेव-दानवस्त्रीपुंसव्यवस्थितात्माभिमानानां सुखानि व्यवस्थितानि । तानि च परस्परविरुद्धानि । तस्मादात्माभिमानानुगुणपुरुषार्थव्यवस्थया सर्वं समाहितम् ।

This objection can be raised only by those who think that the soul is identical to the body and who have not understood the essential nature of the soul as being different from the body. It is due to their mistaken attachment to the body as self. To explain: The word 'body' refers to a mass (of flesh) characterized by a species such as 'humans' and qualities that belong to 'humans'. A worldly person, who is bound in this world, considers the 'I' in his body. The objects that a person considers desirable are in accordance with his view of what the soul is. The objects desired by lions, tigers, boars, yakshas, demons, ghosts, gods, evil spirits, women, and men are such as depend on their respective conception of what their soul is. These various conceptions of desirable and undesirable objects are mutually contradictory. Therefore, the conception of desirable and undesirable is well established and depends on what an individual soul conceives it to be.

[Our soul and body are intrinsically very different; we cannot apply notions related to the body to our soul. For example, one soul can inhabit entirely different bodies without any intrinsic change in itself.]

[What is the intrinsic nature of the soul?]

आत्मस्वरूपं तु देवादिदेहविलक्षणं ज्ञानैकाकारम् । तच्च परशेषतैकस्वरूपम् । यथावस्थिता-त्माभिमाने तदनुगुणैव पुरुषार्थप्रतीतिः । 'आत्मा ज्ञानमयोऽमलः' (वि० पु० ६/७/२२) इति

स्मृतेर्ज्ञानैकाकारता प्रतिपन्ना । 'पतिं विश्वस्य' (तै० ना० ११/३) इत्यादि श्रुतिगुणैः परमात्म-
शेषतैकाकारता च प्रतीता । अतः सिंहव्याघ्रादिशरीरात्माभिमानवत्स्वातन्त्र्याभिमानोऽपि
कर्मकृतविपरीतात्मज्ञानरूपो वेदितव्यः ।

The essential nature of the soul is different from that of bodies such as those of gods and is of the form of knowledge only. And, this knowledge is characterized by entire dependence on the Supreme Self. The Smriti says, "The soul is of the nature of knowledge and is pure". (Vishnu Purana 6/7/22) This shows that the soul is wholly of the form of knowledge. There are hosts of Upanishads like "He (Supreme Being) is the Lord of the Universe" (Taittiriya Narayana Upanishad 11/3), which show that the soul exists only for the fulfillment of the Lord's purposes. Therefore, we should understand that this desire for independence is also incorrect, like identification of the soul with bodies like those of the lion, the tiger, etc, due to past actions and false knowledge.

[The intrinsic nature of an individual soul consists of knowledge; its only purpose is to serve the Supreme Being, the lord of all individual souls. If one thinks that he is an independent soul, he errs.]

[Serving the Supreme Being alone can provide an unlimited bliss to an individual soul.]

अतः कर्मकृतमेव परमपुरुषव्यतिरिक्तविषयाणां सुखत्वम् । अत एव तेषामल्पत्वमस्थिरत्वं च
परमपुरुषस्यैव स्वत एव सुखत्वम् । अतस्तदेव स्थिरमनवधिकातिशयं च, 'कं ब्रह्म खं ब्रह्म'
(छा० उ० ४/१०/३), 'आनन्दो ब्रह्म' (तै० उ० ३/६/१), 'सत्यं ज्ञानमनन्तं ब्रह्म' (तै० उ०
१/१) इति श्रुतेः ।

Therefore, the notion that things, other than the Supreme Being, are objects of pleasure is due only to past actions. That is why they are only pleasant to a very limited extent and for a very short time. Only the Supreme Being is, by His very nature, bliss. Therefore, the bliss attained from Him is permanent and boundless. The Upanishads say - "Supreme Being is a pleasure. Supreme Being is the (conscious) sky" (Chhandogya Upanishad 4/10/3); "Supreme Being is bliss" (Taittiriya Upanishad 3/6); "Supreme Being is (eternal) reality, knowledge, and infinite". (Taittiriya Upanishad 1/1)

[There is no other way to attain this unlimited pleasure but single-mindedly serve the Supreme Being.]

[The father of Vyasa, Parashara thinks the same.]

ब्रह्मव्यतिरिक्तस्य कृत्स्नस्य वस्तुनः स्वरूपेण सुखत्वाभावः कर्मकृतत्वेन चास्थिरत्वं भगवता पराशरेणोक्तम् – 'नरकस्वर्गसंज्ञे वै पापपुण्ये द्विजोत्तम । वस्त्वेकमेव दुःखाय सुखायेर्ष्यागमाय च । कोपाय च यतस्तस्माद्वस्तु वस्त्वात्मकं कुतः ॥' (वि० पु० २/६/४४-४५) सुखदुःखाद्येका-न्तरूपिणो वस्तुनो वस्तुत्वं कुतः । तदेकान्तता पुण्यपापकृतेत्यर्थः ।

Everything else except the Supreme Being is, by its essential nature, not pleasant. That the (limited) pleasure arising from objects is due to action and is transient is stated as follows by Lord Parashara: "O best of Brahmins, by Hell and Heaven only demerits and merits are meant. The same (thing) causes pain to one person, pleasure to another, jealousy to a third, and anger to yet another; how could then these pleasure or pain, derived from them, be called the essential nature of the objects?" (Vishnu Purana 2/6/44-45) This means: How can then one characterize the objects only based on pleasure and pain? If the objects appear exclusively as pleasure or as pain, it is due to a person's past actions, good or bad.

[Parashara says that pleasure and pain are not intrinsic properties of an object.]

[He explains why pleasure and pain are not intrinsic to an object.]

एवमनेकपुरुषापेक्षया कस्यचित्सुखमेव कस्यचिद्दुःखं भवतीत्यवस्थां प्रतिपाद्य, एकस्मिन्नपि पुरुषे न व्यवस्थितमित्याह – 'तदेव प्रीयते भूत्वा पुनर्सुःखाय जायते । तदेव कोपाय यतः प्रसादाय च जायते ॥ तस्माद्दुःखात्मकं नास्ति न च किंचित्सुखात्मकम् ।' (वि० पु० २/६/४५-४६) इति सुखदुःखात्मकत्वं सर्वस्य वस्तुनः कर्मकृतं न वस्तुस्वरूपकृतम् । अतः कर्मावसाने तदपैतीत्यर्थः ॥

Thus, having shown that among many persons, the same object causes pleasure to one man and pain to another, he (Parashara) next proceeds to say that, even in the same person, there is no certainty of an object continuing to give pleasure or pain. "The same object having previously caused pleasure, now, causes pain; later it may cause anger and later still, peace of mind. Therefore, no object is exclusively pleasant or exclusively painful." (Vishnu Purana 2/6/45-46) That is, an object is pleasant or painful by past action and not by its own essential nature; as soon as that action is worked out (exhausted), the pleasure or the pain due to that object ceases.

[If we assume the favourability as the intrinsic property of the object, then what is the problem? If we assume favourability to be present in the object itself then sandals, flowers, etc., which some person at some place or time likes then he cannot dislike them at some other place and time. Similarly, if one person likes them at some place and time then another person, present at the same place and time, will also have to like them.]

[Now, Ramanuja explains how exclusive dependence on the Supreme Being is the most pleasant objective for an individual soul. He also cites various references to support his claim.]

यत्तु सर्वं परवशं दुःखमित्युक्तं तत्परमपुरुषव्यतिरिक्तानां परस्परशेषशेषिभावाभावात्तद्व्यति-रिक्तं प्रति शेषता दुःखमेवेत्युक्तम् । सेवा श्रुवृत्तिराख्यातेत्यत्राप्यसेव्यसेवा श्रुवृत्तिरेवेत्युक्तम् । स ह्याश्रमैः सदोपास्यः समस्तैरेक एव त्विति सर्वैरात्मयाथात्म्यवेदिभिः सेव्यः पुरुषोत्तम एक एव ।

यथोक्तं भगवता – 'मां च योऽव्यभिचारेण भक्तियोगेन सेवते । स गुणान् समतीत्यैतान् ब्रह्मभूयाय कल्पते ॥' (गीता १४/२६) इति ।

The remark "dependence on anything or anyone is painful" simply means that dependence on anything or anyone, other than the Supreme Person is, of course, painful because there is no relationship between the principal entity and the subsidiary between anyone other than the Supreme Being and oneself. The saying "Service is a dog's life" is true only of the service of those, who are unworthy to be served. It is stated that He alone is to be worshipped by all, whatever their stage of life may be; (e.g.) by all who understand the true nature of the soul, the only person to be served, is the Supreme Being. As the Lord, Himself, says, "He, who serves me exclusively using undivided devotion, transcends the attributes of nature and attains liberation." (Gita 14/26)

[Since the individual soul is part of the Supreme Being, it is his intrinsic nature to serve him. Moreover, this service results in his liberation.]

[This rendering of service to the Supreme Being with love is not different from devotion. Ramanuja explains how this devotion leads to knowing of the Supreme Being.]

इयमेव भक्तिरूपा सेवा, 'ब्रह्मविदाप्नोति परम्' (तै॰ उ॰ २/१), 'तमेवं विद्वानमृत इह भवति' (तै॰ आ॰ ३/१२/१७), 'ब्रह्म वेद ब्रह्मैव भवति' (मु॰ उ॰ ३/२/९) इत्यादिषु वेदनशब्देनाभि-धीयत इत्युक्तम् । 'यमेवैष वृणुते तेन लभ्यः' (मु॰ उ॰ ३/२/३) इति विशेषणाद्यमेवैष वृणुत इति भवगता वरणीयत्वं प्रतीयते । वरणीयश्च प्रियतमः । यस्य भगवत्यनवधिकातिशया प्रीति-र्जायते स एव भगवतः प्रियतमः । तदुक्तं भगवता – 'प्रियो हि ज्ञानिनोऽत्यर्थमहं स च मम प्रियः ।' (गीता ७/१७) इति । तस्मात्परभक्तिरूपापन्नमेव वेदनं तत्त्वतो भगवत्प्राप्तिसाधनम् ॥

This devotion, which is a form of service, is expressed by the word 'know' (vedana) in such texts as: "He who knows Supreme Being attains the Supreme." (Taittiriya Upanishad 2/1) "Having known Him in this way, he becomes immortal." (Taittiriya Aranyaka 3/12/17); He, who knows that supreme reality, he himself becomes that reality. (Mundaka Upanishad 3/2/9) This has already been explained.

In the Upanishad text: "He, whom this (Supreme Being) chooses, by him alone, can He be attained," (Mundaka Upanishad 3/2/3) from the qualification of 'being chosen' it is evident that the person should deserve to be chosen. He, who deserves to be chosen, should be the dearest. Dearest to the Lord is he, who has boundless and unsurpassed love for Him. So Lord says: "I am, indeed, very dear to a person of knowledge (love), and he too is dear to me". (Gita 7/7)

Therefore, only that knowledge, which has reached the intensity of supreme devotion, is, in reality, the means of attaining the Supreme Being.

[Only those, who serve the Supreme Being with utmost devotion, deserve his grace. Through His grace, one knows him and his devotion for him becomes exclusive and intense. With this supreme love, he experiences the Supreme Being.]

[Vyasa has also concluded it in the section of Mahabharata that is related to liberation.]

यथोक्तं भगवता द्वैपायनेन मोक्षधर्मे सर्वोपनिषद्व्याख्यानरूपम् – "न संदृशे तिष्ठति रूपमस्य न चक्षुषा पश्यति कश्चनैनम् । भक्त्या च धृत्या च समाहितात्मा ज्ञानस्वरूपं परिपश्यतीतीह ॥" (म० भा० शा० २२९/६९) इति । धृत्या समाहितात्मा भक्त्या पुरुषोत्तमं पश्यति साक्षात्करोति प्राप्नोतीत्यर्थः । 'भक्त्या त्वनन्यया शक्यः' (गीता ११/५४) इत्यनेन ऐकार्थ्यात् । भक्तिश्च ज्ञानविशेष एवेति सर्वमुपपन्नम् ॥

The same teaching is conveyed by Lord Dvaipayana (Vyasa) in his Moksha Dharma (a section of Mahabharata Shanti Parva, which is related to liberation), which is a commentary on all the Upanishads: "His (Supreme Being's) form does not appear before our sight, and no one can see Him with his eyes. He, who has attained peace of mind by his firmness, sees the Supreme Being, who is of the nature of knowledge, by his devotion." (Mahabharata Shanti Parva 229/69) It means that he who has attained mental peace by his firmness of discipline will see and attain the Supreme Lord by his devotion. It means the same as the sentence, "By exclusive (undivided) devotion, He can be attained." (Gita 11/54) As devotion is only a special type of knowledge, all that is said here, is appropriate and logical.

[Vyasa has also accepted that only through firm devotion, one can attain the Supreme Being. Since knowledge is also said to be a means to experience him in the Upanishads, it is only possible if knowledge and devotion are not different. Hence, devotion is a special type of knowledge.]

[Ramanuja concludes this text by citing those who will like it most.]

सारासारविवेकज्ञा गरीयांसो विमत्सराः ।
प्रमाणतन्त्राः सन्तीति कृतो वेदार्थसङ्ग्रहः ॥

Those great persons, who can distinguish between what is essential and what is not, who have widely heard (and learned) the Vedas, and are completely free from envy, and guided only by the evidence, it is for them that this Vedartha Sangraha has been written.

[If a person studies this text with an open mind, keeping scriptural integrity in mind, he will benefit from it the most.]

Published Books

1. Seven Works of Shankaracharya
2. Five Works of Shankaracharya
3. Timeless Sanskrit Quotes
4. Wise Sanskrit Sayings
5. Atma Bodha By Shankaracharya
6. Tattva Bodha By Shankaracharya
7. Rama Gita
8. Gitartha Sangrah by Yamunacharya
9. Stotra Ratna by Yamunacharya
10. Four Works of Shankaracharya
11. Two Works of Shankaracharya
12. Aparokshanubhuti By Shankaracharya
13. Three Works of Shankaracharya
14. Isha Upanishad – With the Commentary of Shankara
15. Narad Bhakti Sutra
16. Shandilya Bhakti Sutra
17. Artha Panchkam of Lokacharya Pillai
18. Tattva Trayam of Lokacharya Pillai
19. Svatma Prakashika of Shankaracharya
20. Tattva Upadesha of Shankara
21. Jeevanmukta Gita of Dattatreya
22. Hansa Gita
23. Mandukya Karika of Gaudapada
24. Kena Upanishad – With Two Commentaries of Shankara
25. Yoga Sutra of Patanjali
26. Atma Anatma Viveka of Shankara
27. Advaita Anubhuti of Shankara
28. Brahma Sutra according to Shankara Advaita Vedanta
29. Vedanta Tattva Sara of Ramanuja

Manufactured by Amazon.ca
Acheson, AB